GW01227210

Marygrove
EX LIBRIS

895.09
B64

ROMAN DECLAMATION

IN THE

LATE REPUBLIC

AND

EARLY EMPIRE

BY

S. F. BONNER, M.A.

Senior Lecturer in Latin and Greek in the University
of Liverpool, formerly Scholar of Pembroke College,
Cambridge

UNIVERSITY OF CALIFORNIA PRESS
BERKELEY AND LOS ANGELES
1949

TO MY WIFE

PRINTED IN ENGLAND BY EATON PRESS LTD., AND
PUBLISHED IN GREAT BRITAIN BY UNIVERSITY PRESS OF LIVERPOOL.

PREFACE

MY interest in the practice of declamation at Rome was first aroused by a perusal, in the year 1939, of the works of the elder Seneca, who first attracted me as a literary critic and contemporary of Dionysius of Halicarnassus, the subject of an earlier study. Criticism, as is usual in classical antiquity, again went hand in hand with her step-dame, Rhetoric, but this time Rhetoric herself surrendered her keys, and led me to the august precincts of the Law. Throughout the war-years, Seneca accompanied my wanderings, a strange *commilito*, a veteran indeed, blessed by Memory, but nowadays paid scant respect. His introduction to those lively and entertaining gentlemen, the declaimers of the early Roman Empire, led to a gradual conviction that beneath the follies and extravagances of their oratorical exhibitions lay a far closer acquaintance with the Roman Law than had commonly been suspected. Since the war, a study of the history of declamation and the laws utilised in it has only served to deepen this conviction, and emboldened me to suggest that we may have here, amid some useless lumber, genuine and valuable relics, not merely of Roman advocacy, but even of the provisions of the Law itself.

My grateful thanks are due to those scholars who have read the book, in whole or in part, at various stages, namely the following: Dr. J. F. Mountford, Vice-Chancellor of the University of Liverpool, and formerly Professor of Latin, who spared the time from his many administrative duties to read it; Dr. David Daube, of Gonville and Caius College, Cambridge, who not only read and approved the legal chapters in the original draft, but has given most willing help, which I have tried to acknowledge in the footnotes, in subsequent correspondence and discussion; Professor J. F. Lockwood, Professor of Latin in University College, London, and Professor H. F. Jolowicz, Regius Professor of Civil Law in the University of Oxford, who jointly read the manuscript with great care, and did me the service of recommending it for publication, and to both of whom I am very much indebted for their valuable criticisms and suggestions; Professor F. W. Walbank, Professor of Latin in the University of Liverpool, who very kindly assisted me in proof-correction and made several helpful comments; Professor D. S. Robertson, Regius Professor of Greek in the University of Cambridge, and Mr. W. Geddes, Barrister-at-Law of Lincoln's Inn, and Lecturer in Roman Law in the University of Liverpool,

PREFACE

who both encouraged me to persevere with my task. The University Press of Liverpool has been most generous in its acceptance of the work and its agreement to defray the costs of publication—practical help, indeed, in these difficult days. The Secretary to the Press, Mr. R. A. Downie, has also given me much assistance in the reading of proofs and advice regarding the general set-up of the book.

It is well known to research-workers in classical subjects how difficult a matter it is to secure all the works which one feels it to be necessary to read, published as they are at such various times and places. Here I must record my appreciation of the work of the Librarian and Staff of the Harold Cohen Library of the University of Liverpool, and make special mention of Miss Eda Whelan, who has been untiring and very successful in her efforts to obtain books for me both from other Universities and from various sources at home and abroad; particularly through the valuable service of the National Central Library.

In conclusion, it should perhaps be made clear that the views expressed in this book are my own, unless otherwise acknowledged, and should not be regarded as necessarily committing any of the scholars whom I have named. I am, of course, fully conscious of the fact that I have not enjoyed the benefit of a legal training, which is so desirable in an investigation of this kind, but venture to think that I may be able to throw some light on a subject which classical and legal scholars have not yet combined to examine in full.

West Kirby, Cheshire,   S.F.B.
    October, 1948.

TABLE OF CONTENTS

PREFACE ... ... iii—iv.

CHAPTER I.
    The Origins and Early Development of Roman Declamation ... ... 1—26

CHAPTER II.
    Declamation from Cicero to the elder Seneca ... 27—50

CHAPTER III.
    The Procedure of the developed Declamation and its chief Rhetorical Characteristics ... ... 51—70

CHAPTER IV.
    Declamation and its Ancient Critics ... ... 71—83

CHAPTER V.
    The Laws in the Senecan Declamations ... ... 84—107

CHAPTER VI.
    The Laws in the Senecan Declamations (*continued*) 108—132

CHAPTER VII.
    Literary Criticism, Quotation, and Allusion in the Senecan Declamations ... ... 133—148

CHAPTER VIII.
    Some Indications of Declamatory Influence on the Literature of the Early Empire ... ... 149—167

BIBLIOGRAPHY ... ... 169—177

INDEX 178

INTRODUCTION

THE study of declamation at Rome had, in the period of the late Republic and early Empire, a twofold importance. In the first place, it was the exercise *par excellence* in which the education of the Roman boy culminated. It is clear to any student of the Roman educational system that preparation for public speaking was the chief preoccupation of teachers, parents, and pupils alike, and that education was accordingly mainly linguistic and literary in its earlier stages, and predominantly oratorical and legal in its more advanced form. Successful declamation was the crowning achievement to which the long study of grammar, essay-writing, paraphrase, character-delineation, commonplaces, panegyric and invective, and the other exercises which filled the Roman school curriculum, was designed to lead. It was the study on which many of the best Roman orators, including Cicero, based their early training, and it was regarded by that paragon of learning and commonsense, Quintilian, as an invaluable preparation, if well taught. Abused and often badly taught it certainly was, and the examples which have survived of declamatory exercises have not tended to raise it in the estimation of classical scholars, who think, like Juvenal, of the *crambe repetita* of their stock subjects, and, like Petronius and Tacitus, of the remoteness of those subjects from real life. When Roman parents flocked to hear their young offspring performing prodigies of declamation, and the scholar's place in class depended on his sententiousness and volubility, there was no doubt often plenty of material for the jibes of the satirist and the despair of the true educationist. But the Romans were above all a practical people; and declamation did not always bear the stigma with which it was subsequently branded.

Nor, indeed, was it by any means confined to the effusions of the adolescent in the schoolroom. By the time of Augustus it was a popular social activity among adults, an activity in which professors of rhetoric and gentlemen of leisure rivalled one another in contests of wit and wisdom, and were often patronised not merely by contemporary men of letters, such as Livy and Ovid but also by statesmen like Maecenas and Pollio, and even, upon occasion, by the Emperor Augustus himself. Declamation became a new fashion for the *intelligentsia* of Rome and other centres of learning, and, for good or ill, had a considerable influence in forming the style of Latin Literature under the Empire.

Clearly, then, the subject is one which deserves more attention than is commonly devoted to it. How did the practice gain acceptance at Rome? How and when did it develop, or degenerate? Where did the Romans find their subjects, and why were they often so bizarre ? What was the exact procedure of a 'declamatory' session ? Finally—the most vital question—was there really any value in it, or was it merely a waste of time for youths and an odd pastime for adults ? What, in particular, was the relation of declamation to Roman legal thought and practice, and were the laws they used in their exercises mainly fictitious, or can any of them be referred to genuine legislation ? To attempt to provide an answer to these questions, which must often have occurred to students of classical antiquity, is the main purpose of the present book. Much of this investigation will be based on the *Oratorum et Rhetorum Sententiae, Divisiones, Colores* of the elder Seneca, father of the philosopher, whose lifetime extended at least from 55 B.C. to 37 A.D. In his repeated visits from Corduba to Rome he acquired a unique knowledge of the declaimers, and it is to his well-stored and amazingly retentive memory that we owe most of our information on the subject of declamation in the most interesting period of the reigns of Augustus and Tiberius.

LIST OF ABBREVIATIONS

A.J.P.	*American Journal of Philology.*
A.K.	*Die Antike Kunstprosa*, by E. Norden, 2 vols., (Leipzig, 1898).
Bornecque, *Déclam.*	*Les Déclamations et les Déclamateurs*, by H. Bornecque (Lille, 1902).
Bornecque, vol. I, II.	*Sénèque le Rhéteur, Controverses et Suasoires*, edited by H. Bornecque, 2 vols. (Paris2, Garnier, 1932).
Buckland, *Text Book.*	*A Textbook of Roman Law* by W. W. Buckland, (Cambridge2, 1932).
Calp. Flacc.	*Calpurnii Flacci Declamationes* ed. Lehnert (Leipzig, Teubner, 1903).
Cod. Iust.	*Codex Iustinianeus* (in *Corpus Iuris Civilis*, ed. Krüger-Mommsen, 6th stereotyped edn., Berlin, 1893).
Cod. Theod.	*Codex Theodosianus*, ed. Mommsen, 2 vols. (Berlin, 1905).
Coll.	*Mosaicarum et Romanarum Legum Collatio* (in Girard's *Textes de Droit Romain*, Paris3, 1903).
Contr.	The elder Seneca's *Controversiae.*
C.J.	*Classical Journal.*
C.P.	*Classical Philology.*
C.R.	*Classical Review.*
Dar.-Sag.	*Dictionnaire des Antiquités grecques et romaines*, ed. C. Daremberg, and E. Saglio (Paris, 1881-1919).
Decl. maior.	*Declamationes Maiores*, ascribed to Quintilian, ed. G. Lehnert (Leipzig, Teubner, 1905).
Decl. min.	*Declamationes Minores*, ascribed to Quintilian, ed. C. Ritter (Leipzig, Teubner, 1884).
Dig.	*Digest* (in *Corpus Iuris Civilis*, ed. Krüger-Mommsen).
J.H.S.	*Journal of Hellenic Studies.*
J.R.S.	*Journal of Roman Studies.*
Just., *Inst.*	*The Institutes of Justinian* (in *Corpus Iuris Civilis*, ed. Krüger-Mommsen).
L.Q.R.	*Law Quarterly Review.*
Mommsen, *Straf.*	*Römisches Strafrecht* by T. Mommsen (Leipzig, 1899)
P.-W.	*Realencyclopädie der Altertumswissenschaft*, ed. Pauly-Wissowa-Kroll.
Paul, *Sent.*	*Iulii Pauli Sententiae* (in Girard, *Textes de Droit Romain*).
Phil. Woch.	*Philologische Wochenschrift.*
Rh. M.	*Rheinisches Museum für Philologie.*
Rhet. Graec. (Walz)	*Rhetores Graeci*, ed. C. Walz, 9 vols. (Tübingen, 1832-6).
R.L.M.	*Rhetores Latini Minores*, ed. C. Halm (Leipzig, 1863).
Spengel	*Rhetores Graeci*, ed. L. Spengel, 3 vols. (Leipzig, Teubner, 1853).
Suas.	The elder Seneca's *Suasoriae.*
T.A.Ph.A.	*Transactions of the American Philological Association.*
Volkmann, *Rhet.*	*Die Rhetorik der Griechen und Römer in systematischer Übersicht*, by R. Volkmann (Leipzig2, 1885).
Wien. Stud.	*Wiener Studien.*
Z.S.S.	*Zeitschrift der Savigny-Stiftung für Rechtsgeschichte, Romanistische Abteilung.*

CHAPTER I

THE ORIGINS AND EARLY DEVELOPMENT OF ROMAN DECLAMATION[1]

In the Preface to his first book of *Controversiae* (§ 12), the elder Seneca gives the following valuable information on the history of declamation at Rome :—

'Declamabat autem Cicero non quales nunc controversias dicimus, ne tales quidem, quales ante Ciceronem dicebantur, quas thesis vocabant. hoc enim genus maxime[2], quo nos exercemur, adeo novum est, ut nomen quoque eius novum sit. controversias nos dicimus ; Cicero causas vocabat. hoc vero alterum nomen Graecum quidem, sed in Latinum ita translatum, ut pro Latino sit, 'scholastica', controversia multo recentius est, sicut ipsa 'declamatio' apud nullum antiquum auctorem ante Ciceronem et Calvum inveniri potest, qui declamationem a dictione distinguit ; ait enim declamare iam se non mediocriter, dicere bene[3] ; alterum putat domesticae exercitationis esse, alterum verae actionis. modo nomen hoc prodiit ; nam et studium ipsum nuper celebrari coepit ; ideo facile est mihi ab incunabulis nosse rem post me natam.'

---

[1] See : H. Tivier, *De arte declamandi et de romanis declamatoribus qui priore post J.C. saeculo floruerunt* (Paris, 1868), pp. 47 ff. ; G. A. Hulsebos, *De educatione et institutione apud Romanos* (Utrecht, 1875), pp. 103-133 ; F. Marx, *Incerti auctoris ad Herennium libri iv* (Leipzig, 1894), *Prolegomena*, pp. 102 ff.; H. Nettleship, *Lectures and Essays*, 2nd Series (Oxford, 1895), pp. 111-114; T. S. Simonds, *Themes treated by the elder Seneca* (Baltimore, 1896); O. Rossbach, article *Declamatio* in *P.-W.* ; G. Boissier, 'Les Ecoles de Déclamation à Rome' (*Revue des deux mondes* xi [1902] = *Tacitus and other Roman Studies*, trans. W. G. Hutchison, [London, 1906], pp. 163-194); and article *Declamatio* in Dar.-Sag. ; H. Bornecque. *Les Déclamations et les Déclamateurs* (Lille, 1902), pp. 39-48 ; A. S. Wilkins, *Roman Education* (Cambridge, 1905), pp. 79-88 ; W. C. Summers, *Select Letters of Seneca* (London, 1910), Introduction, pp. xxix ff. ; and in *Proc. Class. Assoc.* x (1913), pp. 87-102 ; H. Kohl, *De scholasticarum declamationum argumentis ex historia petitis* (Paderborn, 1915), pp. 3-7 ; R. P. Robinson, edn. of Suetonius, *De gramm. et rhet.* (Paris, 1925), pp. 41-2 (an important note); A Gwynn, *Roman Education from Cicero to Quintilian* (Oxford, 1926), pp. 116 ff., 164 ff.; W. A. Edward, *The Suasoriae of Seneca the Elder* (Cambridge, 1928), Introduction, pp. xiv ff. On θέσεις, see S. Striller, *De Stoicorum Studiis Rhetoricis* (Breslau, 1886), pp. 22-4 ; G. Thiele, *Hermagoras* (Strassburg, 1893), pp. 27 ff.; H. von Arnim, *Leben und Werke des Dio von Prusa* (Berlin, 1898), pp. 93 ff., 107 ff ; E. G. Sihler, ' θετικώτερον ' (*A.J.P.* xxiii [1902], pp. 283 ff.); W. Kroll, *Rh. M.* lviii (1903) pp. 564 ff; H. Throm,' Die Thesis' (*Rhetorische Studien*, xvii [Paderborn, 1932])—a thorough investigation ; Jean Cousin, *Etudes sur Quintilien*, vol. i. (Paris, 1936), p. 116, n.4.

[2] materiae mss ; the text of Seneca quoted throughout is that of H. Bornecque, *Sénèque le Rhéteur, Controverses et Suasoires* (2nd edn., Paris, 1932), but important variations from the standard Teubner text (by Kiessling, Leipzig, 1872) are noted as they occur.

[3] ' declamare est domi non mediocriter dicere.' bene alterum . . . Kiessling. The emendation is due to Madvig.

From this it appears that Seneca recognised three main stages of development : (i) the pre-Ciceronian *thesis* (ii) the privately rehearsed declamations of Cicero and his contemporaries, known to them as *causae* (iii) the declamation proper, known as *controversia* and subsequently also as *scholastica*. Seneca has no occasion here to make special mention of *suasoriae*, to which he subsequently devoted a separate book[1]; and his account is not free from difficulties, in view of the evidence of other writers, such as the author of the treatise *Ad Herennium* and Cicero himself ; but it will provide the groundwork for an investigation.

(*i*) *Philosophical 'theses' and their relation to 'controversiae' and 'suasoriae'*

What, then, were these earliest exercises, related to declamation, known as ' theses ' ? The earliest definition which we have is that of Aristotle (*Topica*, I, 11) : θέσις ἐστὶν ὑπόληψις παράδοξος τῶν γνωρίμων τινὸς κατὰ φιλοσοφίαν τινά, i.e. an assertion (or negation) of some exceptional philosophical tenet. The examples which he gives take the form of definite statements of view, e.g. ' that everything is in a state of flux,' ' that all existence is One.' The paradoxical element survives in the essays of Cicero entitled *Paradoxa Stoicorum*, e.g. ' that every foolish man is mad ' (iv), or ' that the wise man alone is rich ' (vi). These essays are, in fact, philosophical theses rhetorically developed, and it is noteworthy that in his preface to them (§ 5) Cicero says : ' degustabis genus exercitationum earum quibus uti consuevi, cum ea quae dicuntur in scholis θετικῶς ad nostrum hoc oratorium transfero dicendi genus.'

Such examples are strictly in accord with the natural meaning of the term—a proposition, or set theme. But Aristotle himself adds that in his day almost all dialectical problems were called θέσεις, and the examples given by subsequent writers generally take the form of a question. So Cicero's most common rendering of the term is *quaestio* (*De Inv.* I, 6, 8; *De Orat.* I, 31, 138; II, 19, 78; *Orat.* 14, 46; 36, 125) or *infinita quaestio*, (*De Orat.* II, 15, 65-66; 31, 134), though particularly in his later works, he uses *propositum* (*Top.* 21, 79 ; *Part. Or.* 18, 61) or *consultatio* (*De Orat.* III, 29, 111, *Part. Or.*, 1, 4; 19, 67 ; *Ad Att.* IX, 4, 3). His terminology was somewhat unsettled, as frequently happened—so in *De Orat.* III, 27, 109, he says 'haec autem altera quaestio infinita et quasi proposita consultatio nominatur.' When he uses the term θέσις itself (*Orat.* 14, 46 ; 36, 125 ; *Top.* 21, 79 ; *Ad Att.* IX, 4 ; cf. *Ad Q.F.* III, 3, 4) he

---

[1] *Contr.* II, 4, 8 ' suo loco reddam, cum ad suasorias venero ' ; Schanz-Hosius, *Geschichte der römischen Literatur*, II (Munich, 1935), § 335.

does so in the Greek form, and it is not until the elder Seneca that the Latinised *thesis* appears[1].

From the time of Hermagoras onwards (c. 150 B.C.), the term was commonly used in the rhetorical schools; and the definitions (which probably derive from him) agree that it means 'the consideration of a subject without reference to specific circumstances', i.e. in an abstract fashion, without immediate reference to a given person, place or time[2]. It is in the *Rhetorica* of Cicero, the *Institutio Oratoria* of Quintilian, and the later Greek and Roman rhetoricians, that specific examples of subjects of *theses* are found. They represent the major problems of the world and its meaning, of human life and conduct, which the Greeks debated through the ages, from the cities of Asia Minor to the groves of the Academy, from the Garden and the Porch to the villas of Italy and the colonnades of Rome. Here are some of them, classified under general headings[3]:—

The Universe and its Problems: What is the shape of the earth? (Cic., *De Inv.* I, 6, 8, from Hermagoras—cf. *De Orat.* II, 15, 66). What is the size of the sun? (Cic., *De Inv. ib.*, *De Orat. ib.*)[4] Is the world governed by Providence? (Quint., III, 5, 6; V, 7, 35; VII, 2, 2; XII, 2, 21; cf. Theon, *Progymn.* c. 12 [II, 126, Spengel]). Can we trust the evidence of sense-perception? (Cic., *De Inv.* loc. cit., *Part. Or.* 18, 62).

Law and Government: Did law originate naturally or by a definite agreement among men? (Cic., *Top.* 21, 82). What is the difference between a king and a tyrant? (Cic., *Top.* 22, 85) Is Might Right? (*ib.* 22, 83). Is Right the interest of the majority? (*De Orat.* III, 29, 115).

Man and his social duties: How should parents be cherished? (Cic., *Part. Or.* 19, 67—cf. *De Orat.* II, 16, 67 'de pietate'). Should a man marry? (Quint., II, 4, 25; III, 5, 8; Hermog.,

---

[1] See Sandys, and Kroll, on *Orat.* 14, 46; Kroll thinks that Cicero may have latinised the term, but I doubt this. On the terminology, see also Peterson on Quint., X, 5, 11, Gwynn, *op. cit.*, pp. 164-5, Throm, *op. cit.*, p. 105, n. 1.

[2] Cic., *De Inv.* I, 6, 8 (criticism of Hermagoras); *De Orat.* I, 31, 138; *Orat.* 14, 46 ('haec igitur quaestio a propriis personis et temporibus ad universi generis rationem traducta appellatur θέσις'); Quint., III, 5, 5, ff.; Theon, *Progymn.* c. 12 (II, 120, 13, Spengel) 'θέσις ἐστὶν ἐπίσκεψις λογικὴ ἀμφισβήτησιν ἐπιδεχομένη ἄνευ προσώπων ὡρισμένων καὶ πάσης περιστάσεως'; Hermog., *Progymn.* c. 11 (p. 24, Rabe); Aphthonius, *Progymn.* c. 13 (II, 49, Spengel); Nicolaus, *Progymn.* c. 13 (III, 493, Spengel). See further, Throm, pp. 104 ff.

[3] A different, and rather artificial, classification, into *practical* and *theoretical*, was current in antiquity; cf. Cic., *De Orat.* III, 29, 111-2, *Part. Or.* 18, 62, *Top.*, 21, 81-2; cf. Quint., III, 5, 6; Theon, *Progymn.* c. 12 (II, 121, 6, Spengel) etc.; Throm, pp. 80 ff. I have purposely avoided this classification, with its minute sub-divisions, in order to give a general picture.

[4] cf. Hermogenes, *Progymn.* c. 11 (p. 25, Rabe) εἰ σφαιροειδὴς ὁ οὐρανός, εἰ πολλοὶ κόσμοι, εἰ ὁ ἥλιος πῦρ;

Progymn. c. 11 (p. 24, Rabe).[1] Should he bring up children? (Cic., *Top.* 22, 86, Theon *Progymn.* c.12 (II, 120, Spengel)). Is it honourable to die for one's country? (Cic., *Top.* 22, 84, cf. *De Orat.* III, 29, 116). How should captives be treated? (Cic., *De Orat.* III, 28, 109). How should friendship be cultivated? (Cic., *Part. Or.* 18, 62). Should one face peril and unpopularity for a friend? (*ib.* 19, 66). Should one prefer friends even to relatives? (*ib.*). What is the difference between friendship and flattery? (Cic., *Top.* 22, 85). How should one live in poverty? (Cic., *Part. Or.* 18, 63). Should the wise man engage in politics? (Cic., *Top.* 21, 82, *De Orat.* III, 29, 112 ; cf. Quint., III, 5, 6, Theon, II, 123, Sp.)
Man and his moral duties : Should one desire wealth and eschew poverty? (*Top.* 22, 84). Should one prefer fame to riches? (*ib.* cf. *De Orat.* III, 29, 116). Should a good man ever tell lies? (*De Orat.* III, 29, 113). Should one avenge an injury? (*Top.* 22, 84, cf. *De Orat.* III, 29, 116).
Questions of Abstract Thought : Is Virtue an end in itself? (Quint., III, 5, 12). How is Virtue to be attained—by nature or by training? (*Part. Or.* 18, 64, *Top.* 21, 82). Should Virtue be sought for its own sake or for the advantage it brings? (*De Orat.* III, 29, 112). Can Virtue in a man ever become Vice? (*ib.*114). Is there such a thing as Honour, or Justice? (*Top.* 21, 82). Is the just life worth while? (*Part. Or.* 18, 62). Is there such a thing as wisdom? What is it? (*De Orat.* III, 29, 113). Can there ever be a perfectly wise man? (*Part. Or.* 18, 64).
Questions of Everyday Life : Is town life or country life preferable? (Quint., II, 4, 24). Is legal or military fame the greater? (*ib.* cf. Cic., *Pro Mur.* §§ 22 ff.). Should one sail the seas? (Aphthonius, *Progymn.* c. 13; Augustinus, *De Rhet.* 5 [Libanius], *Progymn.* XIII). Should one engage in philosophy? (Aug., *l.c.*); or rhetoric? (Hermog., *Progymn.* p. 25, Rabe). How should one achieve fame? (*Part. Or.* 18, 63). How may one achieve eloquence? (*Top.*, 21, 82). Is distinguished speech the prerogative of the orator alone? (*De Orat.* III, 29, 115). How should one avoid Envy? (*Part. Or.* 18, 63). Are philosophers more influenced by the praise of the wise or by popular approval? (*De Orat.* III, 29, 117). And, finally, a fitting *thesis* to close a list so typical of the inquiring minds of the Greeks : ' *Why* do the experts differ ?' (*De Orat.* III, 29, 114).

Many of these subjects must have been current in philosophical circles for centuries, and can hardly be credited to any single school. In some of them, such as the question : ' Is Might Right ?', and abstract topics such as those on Virtue, we may hear the voice of Socrates disputing with contemporary sophists. Even Protagoras,

---

[1] Sketched, as a θέσις, by Libanius, *Progymn.* XIII (= vol. VIII, pp. 550 ff, Foerster).

indeed, is said to have composed θέσεις[1]. Theses on friendship particularly recall the 8th and 9th books of the *Ethics* of Aristotle (who also wrote φιλικαί θέσεις)[2], which were followed by the lost περί φιλίας of Theophrastus, and these questions find close parallels in the *Laelius* of Cicero[3]. Both Aristotle and Theophrastus, in fact, wrote several books of 'theses,'[4] and made particular use of them for combined philosophical and rhetorical training, in debates both *pro* and *contra*[5]. In the problems of physical science we may recognise the strivings after knowledge of the Ionian physicists, the scientists of Alexandria, and the Stoic and Epicurean schools. Questions such as the size of the sun, particularly, though not exclusively, suggest Epicurean dogma[6]; as does that on the validity of sense-perception[7]. Discussions on the importance of participation in political life, on the question whether the world is governed by Providence or not, on the natural or artificial origin of Law, clearly suggest irreconcilable divergencies between the Stoic and Epicurean schools[8]. The recurrent thesis on whether marriage is desirable or not may date back as far as Theophrastus[9], and here again Stoics and Epicureans took different views. Finally, it is clear that the Academy must have been Cicero's source for some of these subjects, for while in the *De Oratore*[10] he refers to both Peripatetic and Academic ' politici philosophi,' at the end of the *Partitiones Oratoriae*[11] he makes special mention of the latter school.

In his earliest rhetorical work, the *De Inventione*[12], of c.84 B.C., Cicero informs us that Hermagoras was the first to divide the subject-matter of the orator into *quaestiones* (θέσεις), which did not concern any specific individual, and *causae* (ὑποθέσεις), in which definite persons were introduced. The examples of *quaestiones* which Cicero quotes, namely, 'ecquid sit bonum praeter honestatem?', ' verine sint sensus ?', ' quae sit mundi forma ?', ' quae sit solis magnitudo ', are, as he says, exclusively philosophical, and he

1 Diog. Laert. IX, 53 ; cf. Cic., *Brutus*, 12, 46 (the closely allied *loci communes*) ; Throm, pp. 166-171, Cousin, *l.c.*
2 cf. Kroll on Cic., *Orator*. 14, 46.
3 e.g. c. 25, on friendship and flattery.
4 Theon, *Progymn*. c. 2 (II, 69, 3, Spengel) cf. Throm, pp. 171-179.
5 Cic., *loc. cit.* ; cf. Quint., XII, 2, 25 (' nam thesis dicere exercitationis gratia fere est ab illis institutum ') and the notes of R. G. Austin's edition (Oxford, 1948) *ad loc.*
6 cf. Lucretius, V, 564 ff.; contrast Cic., *N.D.* II, 36, 92, and see Mayor *ad loc.*
7 cf. C. Bailey's edn. of Lucretius (Oxford. 1947), *Prolegomena*, pp. 52 ff.
8 cf. Cic., *De Orat*. III, 17, 64. Sen. *Dial*. VIII, 3, 2 (politics); Quint., V, 7, 35 (providence); Horace, *Sat*. I, 3, 111 ff.; Diog. Laert. VII. 128; Stobaeus, *Ecl*. II, 7 [II, p. 94, Wachsmuth] (law).
9 Hieron. *adv. Jovinianum*, quoted by Throm, p. 174.
10 III, 28, 109.
11 40, 139. See also Quint., XII, 2, 25 and Throm, pp. 179 ff. Further indications of sources in Thiele, *op. cit.*, pp. 30 ff., and Kroll, *Rh. M.* LVIII, 566 ff. pp. 94-5.
12 1, 6, 8; cf. *De Orat*. II, 15, 66; Quint., II, 21, 21, III, 5, 14; See von Arnim, *op. cit.*, 9-10.

criticises them as unduly extending the range of knowledge required of the orator—a point of view which he subsequently modified[1]. The examples selected are perhaps extreme ones; but why, in an *Art of Rhetoric*, should Hermagoras have given a place to philosophy ? The answer may be twofold ; first, that the wider and deeper consideration of the problems of the universe, life, and conduct, could not fail to have a beneficial effect on the orator's mind, and to give him a culture and breadth of outlook which would be quite as valuable in public speaking as the study of invention, arrangement, and style. Secondly, experience of oratorical pleading itself, whether in actual practice or in school exercises, must have revealed that frequently behind the specific case, with its limited relation to person, time, and place, lay a wider issue of equity, the decision upon which called for the balance, the sense of justice, the moral values inculcated by a philosophical training[2]. To enable the pleader to grasp the essential problem inherent in a given case was the purpose of the rhetorical doctrine of στάσεις so intimately connected with the name of Hermagoras[3] and although many cases would hinge on questions of fact or of legal interpretation, others would only be decided by transcending the immediate circumstances and grasping the fundamental issue which lay beyond them in the domain of moral philosophy.

The philosophical thesis, therefore, is immanent in certain types of legal debate. We may now take the forward view and proceed to give examples where its influence appears even in the intricate and highly-developed *controversiae* of the elder Seneca. These exercises frequently involve questions of disinheritance ; to decide how far, if at all, the parent is justified in each case, it becomes necessary to answer the question : ' Should a son obey his father in all matters, or are there circumstances in which disobedience is justified, and if so, how are they to be defined ?' (cf. *Contr.* II, 1, 20 'an in omnia patri parendum sit'). This Seneca describes as ' vetus et explosa quaestio ' ; it had evidently been a common problem in the rhetorical schools, and it is fully argued in 'Quint.', *Decl. min.* 257[4]. If we now turn to Aristotle, *Nic. Eth.* IX, 2, 1, we find him posing this precise question : πότερα δεῖ πάντα τῷ πατρὶ ἀπονέμειν καὶ πείθεσθαι ; it has therefore probably come into the range of rhetorical studies from philosophy[5]. Then

[1] cf. *De Orat.* III, 27, 107-8; 30, 120; Quint., III, 5, 15.
[2] cf. Cic., *Orat.* 14, 45; *Top.* 21, 79-80. cf. Jaeneke (work cited p. 15 below) pp. 107-110.
[3] Cic., *ib.* ; Quint., III, 6, 21, 56.
[4] pp. 49-50 (Ritter).
[5] cf. Gellius II, 7, 1 'Quaeri solitum est in philosophorum disceptationibus an semper inque omnibus iussis patri parendum sit'; Musonius XVI, εἰ πάντα πειστέον τοῖς γονεῦσιν. I am indebted for the latter reference to my friend Dr. R. E. Witt.

again, questions involving conflict of duty to parents arise, as in *Contr.* VII, 4, 3, where it should be noticed that Seneca says that Latro treated 'tamquam thesim' the following problem: 'Should a son go away to ransom his father, captured by pirates, or rather stay at home to support his blind mother ?' Aristotle again supplies a close parallel, which is particularly interesting as an early example of the pirate-ransom theme which is common in the declamations. In *Nic. Eth.* IX, 2, 4, he says :—' Suppose one has been ransomed from brigands ; ought one to ransom one's ransomer, whoever he may be, . . . or ought one to ransom one's own father ? for it might be thought to be a man's duty to ransom his father even before himself.' It has been well observed[1] that these cases of Aristotle 'are all *bona fide* ones, though the form in which some of them are presented reminds one of the Debating Society.' Closely allied to these subjects is that which concerns the sanctity and binding nature of the oath. In *Contr.* I, 6, a son who has been captured by pirates writes to ask his father to ransom him and is refused ; he is then constrained to give his oath to marry the pirate's daughter, as the price of his freedom ; after fulfilling his oath, he is disinherited by his father for not divorcing the woman and marrying a lady of his father's choice. The debate hinges on the questions : 'Is an oath given under duress, to be regarded as inviolable[2] ?' and 'Is a man guilty of moral error for an action he takes under duress against the terms of his oath ?' Both are problems of moral philosophy, and the former is discussed by Cicero in *De Officiis*, Book III, and certainly dates back to his Stoic sources ; so in §107, he argues that the breaking of an oath given to pirates is allowable, since pirates are not lawful enemies, but the common foes of all mankind[3]. A further exercise involving the obligations incurred by an oath is *Contr.* II, 2. Then again, exercises sometimes (*Contr.* II, 5 and IX, 1) involve questions of ingratitude ; the legal validity of 'actio ingrati' will be fully discussed later[4] but the kind of question on which the debate centres is : 'Is everyone who does not return a favour liable to be accused of ingratitude ?' What, in fact, constitutes 'beneficium'? In view of the attention paid to 'beneficia' by Aristotle[5], and the Stoics, whom Cicero followed, and the doctrines which the younger Seneca so fully expounds in his *De Beneficiis*, it can hardly be doubted that here again is an example of the influence of the philosophical thesis on the declamations. Finally, it is noteworthy

[1] J. A. Stewart, *Notes on the Nicomachean Ethics* (Oxford, 1892), vol. II pp. 345-6.
[2] In Roman Law the answer was in the negative.
[3] cf. Bornecque, vol. I, note 69.
[4] cf. below, p. 87.
[5] *Nic. Eth.*, VIII, 13 ; IX, 1.

that in *Contr.* I, 3, 8, Cestius contrives to make one of his basic questions that regarding the interest of the gods in the affairs of men —' an dii immortales rerum humanarum curam agant '; this Albucius expanded into one of those *problemata philosophumena* to which he gave special rather than incidental attention, and it is closely allied to the θέσις mentioned above, from Quintilian and Theon, ' an providentia mundus regatur ?'. Albucius was unduly fond of introducing philosophical speculation into his speeches[1], but, as will be shown below[2], a variety of commonplaces of philosophical origin were used by all the declaimers.

But not only was the philosophical θέσις implicit in some declamations and introduced as a show-piece in others ; it was also used as a basis for the invention of subjects, particularly *suasoriae*. Quintilian (II, 4, 25; III, 5, 5 ff.) shows how this occurred and thereby affords a valuable glimpse into the development which took place when *controversiae* and *suasoriae* began to supersede the old θέσεις. He gives us practical examples of the way in which a θέσις of purely speculative content could become a *suasoria* by being referred to some historical personage or event, and thus given a specific relation, that is, made into what Hermagoras called a ὑπόθεσις.

We have, says Quintilian, a θέσις—' An uxor ducenda,' on which divergent views may be held ; if that subject is applied to an individual, we may put the question in the form of a deliberation, ' Deliberat *Cato* an uxor ducenda,' and by advising Cato to marry or not to marry we develop a *suasoria*. Cato (of Utica) seems to have been a favourite subject for *suasoriae*, and we find not only Quintilian[3] referring to a debate ' An Cato recte Marciam Hortensio tradiderit,' but also Martianus Capella[4] mentioning the subject : ' Deliberat Cato an se debeat, ne victorem aspiciat Caesarem, trucidare.' Clearly beneath these two lie the problems of justification of divorce and suicide. Similarly, there was, according to Cicero and Quintilian, a θέσις ' an accedendum ad rempublicam,' which suggests, as we have seen, the debates between Stoics and Epicureans on participation in political life. Surely, then, the following passage from the younger Seneca[5] gives the type of arguments used when this θέσις had proceeded

---

[1] *Contr.* I, 7, 17 ; VII, *Praef.* 1.
[2] pp. 60 ff.
[3] III, 5, 11 ; cf. x, 5, 13. Lucan, II, 338 ff. is practically a verse *suasoria* from Marcia's point of view.
[4] *R.L.M.* p. 456, 1, 30 (Halm). So Persius, (III 44-7) tells how he shirked, as a boy, the oft-repeated declamation, before father and friends, of the high-flown speech of dying Cato.
[5] *Epp.* XIV, 13 ff. ; *Dial.* VIII (*De otio*) is an expanded treatment of the same general theme.

a stage further, and centred itself around the personality of Cato at the time of the Civil War :—' *Potest aliquis disputare an illo tempore capessenda fuerit sapienti respublica.* "Quid tibi vis, Marce Cato ? Iam non agitur de libertate ; olim pessum data est. Quaeritur, utrum Caesar an Pompeius possideat rempublicam : quid tibi cum ista contentione ? Nullae partes tuae sunt ; dominus eligitur. Quid tua, uter vincat ? Potest melior vincere, non potest non peior esse qui vicerit".'· These sentences, with their point, their pungency, and their rhetorical questions, remind one strongly of the declamations preserved by the elder Seneca, and we may not be far wrong in recognising here traces of a *suasoria*—' Deliberat Cato, an bello civili capessenda sit republica ' —formed as a concrete case to illustrate and give practice in handling the general question.

Similarly, the ' thesis ' ' an navigandum ?'[1] may have suggested the formation of the *suasoria* ' Deliberat Alexander, an Oceanum naviget ;'[2] for the effusion of Fabianus (who was a philosopher quite as much as a rhetorician) in this first exercise of Seneca's collection, could have served almost equally well as a general disquisition on the perils of the sea, so loosely is it attached to the person of Alexander himself. But, although this close relationship between ' thesis ' and *suasoria* is sometimes demonstrable, it would be a mistake to suppose that all, or even most, *suasoriae* must have originated in this way. Any famous character, Demosthenes, Hannibal, Scipio, Sulla, Pompey, Caesar, could be taken as subject[3], and the more critical the dilemma, the better the chance of a good debate. Caesar, for instance, debates whether to invade Germany (Quint., III, 8, 19), Pompey whither to flee after Pharsalus (*ib.*, 33). Normally, then, subjects of *suasoriae* were drawn directly from Greek and Roman History (or mythology), but the development from a general question appears to have been one of the ways in which the fertile imagination of the rhetoricians worked in their invention of new themes.

We may now ask : ' Could a θέσις be used to form a *controversia* ?' Less commonly, perhaps, as the *controversia* generally presupposes a more intricate concatenation of circumstances, such as might present itself in a lawsuit, whereas the *suasoria* is of a more general and straightforward nature. We have already given examples of the presence of a θέσις even in a *controversia*. Cicero (*Top.* 22, 86) gives as a general question ' suscipiendine sint liberi ?' ; when, therefore, there appears in

[1] See above, p. 4.
[2] *Suas.* I; cf. *Contr.* VII, 7, 19; Quint. III, 8, 16. Curtius IX, 4, 18 clearly contains reminiscences of this famous debate.
[3] Kohl, *op. cit.*, has collected several hundreds of historical declamations and placed them in chronological order. See his pp. 90 ff. for Roman themes.

Suas. II, 21 a reference to a *controversia* ' de ea, quae apud matronas disserebat *liberos non esse tollendos* et ob hoc accusatur reipublicae laesae,' one is inclined to suspect that the situation may have been evolved for the purpose of giving that general subject a more specific reference[1].

So far, then, Seneca has given us a useful historical perspective in referring first to θέσεις in the history of Roman declamation. But he is less accurate in his implication that Cicero did not declaim them, for in a letter to Atticus (IX, 4; cf. Quint., x, 5, 11) Cicero gives a list of subjects which he himself declaimed in private and which he calls θέσεις. They are almost exclusively concerned with the subject of tyrants and tyranny—' Should one continue to live in a country under a tyrant ?' ' Should one work for the tyrant's downfall, even though it may jeopardise the State, or merely prevent his overthrower's elevation ?' ' Should one attempt to help one's country, when subject to a tyrant, by opportune speech rather than by force of arms ?'. There are eight such subjects, which Cicero says he declaimed in Greek and Latin, both for and against, in order to take his mind off his present troubles. The letter, indeed, was written in a dark hour[2] (March 12th, 49 B.C.) and Cicero is clearly hinting at the coming domination of Caesar; to the student of development, it is particularly interesting, for it shows the kind of θέσεις that were still debated at the end of the Republic, and their subject, concerning tyrants, is one which becomes most popular in the declamations of the Empire.

In the scheme of rhetorical training in the schools, θέσεις appear to have been studied in the early stages, and are mentioned by Suetonius along with ἀνασκευαί and κατασκευαί, which were preliminary exercises involving the refutation or confirmation of legendary stories[3]. It is clear that they were also closely allied to the *loci communes*[4], the chief difference being that whereas the *locus* was a diatribe on set lines on a given subject, the *thesis* was more in the nature of a debatable question which invited argument from opposite points of view[5]. Suetonius[6] tells

---
[1] The speeches of Augustus on the importance of family life as given by Dio Cassius LVI, 2-9 may be regarded as mainly a rhetorical θέσις on the subject.
[2] Pompey was closely beset by Caesar at Brundisium, and, a few days after this date, left Italy never to return (cf. Lucan's fine lines, III, 1-7).
[3] *De Rhet.* c. 1; cf. Libanius, *Progymn.* v (VIII, 123 ff., Foerster). cf. Quint., II, 4, 18, x, 5, 12 ' his confinis est destructio et confirmatio sententiarum. These are fully dealt with by Hermogenes, Aphthonius, and Theon (II, 8; II, 27; II, 93, Spengel). See further, Hulsebos, *op. cit.* pp. 110 ff., and Jullien, *Les Professeurs de Littérature dans l'ancienne Rome* (Paris, 1885) pp. 294 ff.
[4] Quint., II, 1. 9.
[5] cf. Quint., II, 4, 22-25 ; Theon, *Progymn.* c. 12 (II, 120, Spengel) διαφέρει δὲ τοῦ τόπου, ὅτι ὁ μέν ἐστιν ὁμολογουμένου πράγματος αὔξησις, ἡ δὲ θέσις ἀμφισβητουμένου.
[6] *De Rhet.* c. 1, ' donec sensim haec exoluerunt et ad controversiam ventum est.'

us that *theses* gradually became obsolete and gave place to the *controversiae*, but from their reappearance in Quintilian, Hermogenes, and the progymnasmatists[1] it is evident that they still formed part of the regular curriculum in the rhetorical schools well on into the Empire.

(ii) *Greek rhetorical studies as a background to 'suasoriae' and 'controversiae'*

There is, then, undoubtedly a relationship between the philosophical thesis and the declamation proper, particularly the *suasoria*. But it would be wrong to suppose that the intricate declamations of the Empire or even those of the Sullan era, had a merely—or even mainly—philosophical origin. It is often a far cry from such abstract speculations to the situations in which the heroes and tyrants, the forlorn maidens and disinherited sons of the fully developed declamation find themselves. The *suasoriae* and *controversiae* practised by the Romans are rhetorical exercises designed to develop skill in deliberative and forensic oratory respectively, and as such have a long history in the rhetorical schools of the Greeks.

The *suasoria*, an exercise in persuading or dissuading a person or an assembly to or from a given course of action, is a Roman development of the λόγος προτρεπτικός and the λόγος ἀποτρεπτικός of which Aristotle makes constant mention in his discussion of deliberative oratory in the first book of his *Rhetoric*[2]. By the time of the writer of the *Rhetorica ad Alexandrum*[3] (probably Anaximenes[4], a contemporary of Alexander the Great) the rules for such speeches were already formulated in considerable detail[5]—the speaker must urge the justice or injustice, legality or illegality, expediency or inexpediency, attractiveness or unattractiveness, ease or difficulty, of the proposed action. From this elaborate system, and the expression 'τὸ μὲν οὖν δίκαιον οὕτω μελετῶν πολλάκις λήψῃ' (I, 177, Sp.) it may be deduced that speeches of the nature of *suasoriae*, based probably on situations which would constantly recur in the Greek city state, such as debates on war and peace,

---

1 Such as Aphthonius and Theon (II, 49 ff. and 120 ff., Spengel). An interesting illustration of the amazing longevity of θέσεις is their re-appearance in the curricula of the schools in XVIth century England. Cf. T. W. Baldwin's substantial work, *William Shakespere's Small Latine and Lesse Greeke* (University of Illinois Press, Urbana, 1944) vol. II *passim*, and esp. pp. 288 ff. on the use of Aphthonius.
2 I, 3, 3-6, and I, 4. Mythological subjects go right back to the early sophists.
3 cc. 1-2 and c. 34; cf. Volkmann, *Rhet.* pp. 300 ff.
4 cf. P. Wendland, *Anaximenes von Lampsakos* (Berlin, 1905).
5 Further development in Quint., III, 8, on which see Cousin, *op. cit.*, I, pp. 196-203. See also J. Klek, *Symbuleutici qui dicitur sermonis historia critica* (Paderborn, 1919), pp. 157-162, on the *suasoria*. Hofrichter's work, cited in Bibliography below, is known to me only from *Phil. Woch.* 1936, 1223 ff.

national defence, and public expenditure (subjects mentioned by Aristotle), were practised in the Greek rhetorical schools in the last decade of the 4th century B.C.

The *controversia*, a purely forensic exercise, may have had an equally long ancestry, for Philostratus, in his *Lives of the Sophists*[1], says that themes involving types such as the poor man and the rich, the prince and the tyrant, were handled by Aeschines, who founded a school at Rhodes after his exile from Athens in 330 B.C.; and that Aeschines was therefore regarded as the ultimate founder of the 'second sophistic.' These speeches, however, may only have been straightforward type-declamations such as 'against a rich man' or 'against a tyrant' and would perhaps hardly be intricate exercises at that date, possibly little more than *loci communes*[2]. Philostratus also mentions 'themes suggested by history' which would probably be deliberative speeches concerned largely with the recent disputes between Aeschines and Demosthenes over the policy of Greece towards Philip of Macedon. Quintilian[3] tells us that it was commonly stated in his day that 'themes in imitation of law-court cases and of public debates' were invented as early as the time of Demetrius of Phalerum, but that there was no definite evidence available.[4] Demetrius, a pupil of Theophrastus, governed Athens from 317-307 B.C., and died in 283 B.C., so the dating of Quintilian agrees (for *suasoriae* at any rate) with the indications which are found in the *Rhetorica ad Alexandrum*. But this work, although it devotes considerable attention to forensic oratory and the stock arguments of prosecutor and defendant, produces no example of a fictitious theme like a *controversia*. Such themes, in fact, only begin to be common in Greek in the works of Hermogenes (c. 170 A.D.) and Apsines (c. 235 A.D.). But it is probable that examples of exercises of this type were included in the lost *Art of Rhetoric* of Hermagoras in the second century B.C.

Hermagoras, whose introduction of θέσεις into rhetoric has already been noticed, paid great attention to forensic oratory, and elaborated a system of basic types of case, which he called στάσεις[5] and which the Romans generally translated *status*; the στάσις was the 'stand' taken as a result of the conflicting allegations

---

[1] Book I, p. 481. The vague ὑπετυπώσατο is noteworthy.
[2] cf. Quint., II, 4, 22-23; Libanius, VIII, 195 ff. (Foerster). Seneca, indeed, says of Aeschines' day 'tunc enim non declamandi studium erat,' but Bornecque brackets this as interpolated. See, however, *Declam.*, pp. 40-41.
[3] II, 4, 41.
[4] Even earlier, Antiphon's *Tetralogies* show general affinities.
[5] The name was used before Hermagoras; cf. Quint., III, 6, 3; the doctrine may have been partly earlier (cf. Quint., III, 6, 31) but is especially associated with him.

of prosecutor and defendant, the 'set-up' of the case[1]. If the defendant denied the charge outright, the question became one of conjecture—did he commit the crime or not? (στοχασμός, *status* or *constitutio coniecturalis*). If he admitted the act but declared that it was not the same as that with which he was charged, the question became one of definition (ὅρος, *status definitivus*, *constitutio definitiva*). If he admitted the act, but declared that he was justified in committing it, the question became one of quality (ποιότης, *status generalis*, or *constitutio iuridicialis*). Finally, if he admitted the act, but declared that it could not be dealt with by the court before which he was summoned, the question became one of *competence* (μετάληψις, later μετάστασις, *status translativus*); this last στάσις was typical of Hermagoras and his followers, and was not universally accepted[2]. This system is known to us mainly from the *De Inventione* of Cicero[3], who made considerable use of it, from hints in the detailed discussion of Quintilian[4], and from the work of Hermogenes περὶ τῶν στάσεων, and the *Ars Rhetorica* of St. Augustine, which were probably based upon it; a similar system appears in the *Ad Herennium*[5] and is fully expounded in Cicero's *Partitiones Oratoriae*[6].

The application of the *status*—doctrine may be more clearly apprehended by the following practical examples from Roman oratory. A good example of the *status coniecturalis* is Cicero's speech *Pro Sexto Roscio Amerino*[7]. The conflict of arguments producing the *status*, and the technical names for the rhetorical divisions were as follows: (a) You killed your father. (*intentio*, κατάφασις) (b) I did not kill him. (*depulsio*, ἀπόφασις) (c) General question: Did he or did he not commit parricide? (*quaestio*, ζήτημα). (d) No motive can be assigned to me for so terrible a crime, but Chrysogonus and the kinsmen of the deceased had both motive and opportunity. (*ratio*, τὸ συνέχον) (e) But you were relegated by your father, and he thought of disinheriting you, so clearly a state of ill-feeling existed. (*rationis infirmatio*, τὸ αἴτιον). Special question for the jury: Which persons had the better motive and opportunity for committing the crime—the defendant

---

[1] The στάσις doctrine did in fact embrace other branches of oratory too, but was mainly forensic; cf. Cic., *Top.* 25, 93-4 with *Part. Or.* 28, 98 ff., where the doctrine is treated in detail in the forensic section.
[2] cf. Quint., III, 6, 53, 56, 60.
[3] I, 8, 10 ff.; II, 4, 14, ff. Hermagoras is specifically mentioned in I, 9, 12 and I, 11, 16; cf. Quint., III, 11, 18, 'nam in Rhetoricis... Hermagoran est secutus.'
[4] III, 6; cf. III, 11, 1-20.
[5] I, 11, 18 ff.
[6] 29, 101 ff.
[7] The hint is given by Quint., VII, 2, 2, and 23. The Greek terms for (d) and (e) are uncertain; Cicero's evidence is inconsistent (cf. Quint., III, 11, 18); I follow Volkmann, *Rhet.* p. 94, and Jaeneke, pp. 111-2.

or his prosecutors ? (*iudicatio*, τὸ κρινόμενον). Throughout this *status* the enquiry is one of fact, not definition or justification.

An example of the *status definitivus* is the trial of Norbanus for treason in 94 B.C., because, as tribune, he had used violent measures to procure the banishment of Caepio, the commander responsible for the defeat at Arausio in 105 B.C.[1] The arguments were :—
(a) You committed treason in acting thus. (*intentio*) (b) I did not commit treason. (*depulsio*) (c) Did he or did he not commit treason ? (*quaestio*) (d) As tribune and representative of the people, I did what the people approved. (*ratio*) (e) But by inciting sedition against a former commander, you diminished the majesty of the Roman people. (*rationis infirmatio*). (f) Special question for the jury : Is a tribune who uses force to carry out the people's wish diminishing the majesty of the Roman people or not ? (*iudicatio*). Here the emphasis is throughout on the precise definition of *maiestas*.

An example of the *status generalis* or *iuridicialis* was the declamatory speech which Brutus composed in defence of Milo[2]. He admitted that Milo deliberately killed Clodius, but claimed that the act was fully justified because it was in the public interest. Cicero himself felt that such a defence was risky, and although he based his speech as a whole on the argument of justification, he took the safer line of declaring that Milo was acting in self-defence. To prove this, he had to prove that Clodius plotted the ambush, so that in essence his case was a *status coniecturalis*[3], and the *iudicatio* was ' uter utri insidias fecerit ?' (§ 23). Such a mixture of *status*, as Quintilian (III, 6, 94) says, naturally occurs in complex cases.

The *status translativus* rarely occurred in practice as a basis for an entire case[4], because they were no legal grounds for asserting lack of competence once the case had reached the court, but elements of the *status* might occur within the defence itself.

This represents the main *status*-doctrine, or *status rationales*. But in Hermagoras' system there were also subsidiary *status* called στάσεις νομικαί (*status* or *quaestiones legales*), which in some subsequent systems became subordinated to the *status generalis*[5]. They were as follows :—(a) Cases involving a conflict between the letter and the spirit of the law (*ex scripto et sententia*, κατὰ ῥητὸν καὶ διάνοιαν) (b) Cases involving ambiguity (*ambiguitas*, ἀμφιβολία) (c) Cases involving conflict of statutes, or of provisions of the same

---

[1] cf. Cic., *De Orat.* II, 25, 107, *Part. Or.* 30, 105 ; Quint., VII, 3, 35.
[2] Asconius, *in Milonianam* § 30, Quint., III, 6, 93, cf. Reid's *Pro Milone* (Cambridge, 1894), App. B.
[3] cf. Quint., III, 6, 12; III, 11, 15 ' iudicatio coniecturalis, an Clodius insidias fecerit '; VII, 1, 34 ff.; Volkmann, *Rhet.*, pp. 79-80.
[4] *Ad Herennium* I, 12, 22; Cic., *De Inv.* II, 19, 57 ff.
[5] cf. Volkmann, *Rhet.*, pp. 88-92.

statute (*contrariae leges*, ἀντινομία) (d) Cases involving an omission in the law, which must be supplied by deduction and analogy (*collectio*, συλλογισμός). This doctrine also existed in germ in Aristotle and the *Rhetorica ad Alexandrum*, and is fully expounded in Cicero's *De Inventione*[1]; its inclusion here is important because of the question of its relation to Roman jurisprudence, which will arise later.

Several varieties of the *status*-system were current in antiquity, but the extremely important point for the present purpose is that the *illustrations* of the various types of στάσις given in the rhetorical handbooks are remarkably like simple and straightforward declamatory exercises. For instance, Quintilian[2] tells us that one of the commonest examples of the *status generalis* type current in nearly all handbooks (i.e. probably including Hermagoras) was the killing by Orestes of his mother Clytaemnestra, and his self-justification on the ground that she had murdered his father Agamemnon. Clearly, one speaker would prosecute Orestes, and another would defend him, and the speeches which they would make would in effect be declamations. Similarly, there is constant reference in Hermogenes[3] to the case of a man who is accused of murder because he is found standing over a dead body ; in the *Ad Herennium*[4] it is applied to Ulysses, found standing over the body of Ajax, who had in fact committed suicide. The case is one of the *status coniecturalis* type, and would be argued by both prosecution and defence. Finally, a case of the *status definitivus* type ; a man has stolen private moneys from a shrine, and is accused of sacrilege, but another accuser says he is a thief and must therefore pay back double the amount—the question is what is sacrilege and what is theft ?[5] There are many such exercises in Hermogenes, generally briefly sketched *en passant*, but not all can be proved to date back to such early writers as Hermagoras ; but the three examples selected all appear in Cicero's *De Inventione*, and two antedate even Hermagoras. Hermagoras is, indeed, but a shadowy figure, a dim signpost in the desert that divides the *Rhetoric* of Aristotle and of Anaximenes from the earliest Roman rhetorical treatises[6]. But the indications are that there existed in the heart of the Greek

---

[1] II, 40, 116 ff.
[2] III, 11, 4 ; cf. Cic., *De Inv.* 1, 13, 18 ff.; Libanius, *Decl.* VI (vol. V, pp. 370 ff. Foerster). Diog Laert. VI, 15 (Subject to a speech of Antisthenes).
[3] π. στάσ., p. 49, l. 16; p. 54, l. 5, etc. (Rabe).
[4] I, 11, 18 ; cf. Cic., *De inv.* I, 8, 11, Quint., IV, 2, 13-14.
[5] Hermog. π. στάσ., p. 62, l. 2 (Rabe). cf. Cic., *De Inv.* I, 8, 11, Quint., IV, 2, 8, 68; VII, 3, 9 ; Arist., *Rhet.* 1, 7, §5.
[6] His doctrines have been reconstructed as far as possible by Thiele, *op. cit.*, and G. Jaeneke, *De statuum doctrina ab Hermogene tradita*, (Diss., Leipzig, 1904), pp. 79-117; cf. Radermacher in *P.-W.*, s.v. Hermagoras, no. 5; on στάσεις see also Volkmann, *Rhet.* pp. 38 ff., and J. Cousin, *op. cit.*, I, pp. 176-190.

rhetorical handbooks of the 2nd century B.C., these germs of the fully-blown *controversia*.

The historical significance of this relationship between declamatory exercises and the *status*-doctrine is further seen in the seventh book of Quintilian, where scholastic themes closely parallel to the Senecan declamations are inextricably intermingled with genuine cases from the Roman courts, and both are used to illustrate the rhetorical doctrine. So there is at least a *prima facie* case already for supposing that the declamations were related to legal practice; exactly how close that relationship was will be seen later, but at any rate we now have the Greek background, a background essential for a full understanding of the Roman declamations. Three main Greek strands went to the weaving of the Roman exercise—the philosophical thesis, the protreptic and apotreptic speech, and the example illustrating the *status*-theory[1].

(iii) *Declamation at Rome up to the time of Sulla.*

So far, following and supplementing the elder Seneca, we have traced the earliest indications available to us of declamatory subjects; Greek rhetoricians and Greek schools were mainly responsible for propagating these exercises throughout the third and second centuries B.C. But from the middle of the second century B.C., when the Scipionic Circle represented the Hellenising movement, the Romans began to be influenced more and more by this, as by every other, form of Greek culture. At first there was considerable opposition among the more conservative Romans, and the elder Cato, the foremost orator and legal scholar of his time, in sturdily defining the orator as ' vir bonus dicendi peritus,' laid quite as much stress on moral worth as on rhetorical skill[2]. In 161 B.C. Greek rhetoricians and philosophers alike were expelled from Rome[3], and the old Roman attitude of distrust of the theories of Greek rhetoric persists in Cicero's *De Oratore*[4], and even survives in the declamations of the elder Seneca[5]. But the more progressive Romans were quick to see that much was to be learnt from the long oratorical experience of the Greeks and the study of the Greek rhetorical systems was soon taken as a matter of course[6]. In the

---

[1] Such illustrations would be developed as advocates' speeches in an imaginary trial. Butler (Loeb Library Quintilian, vol. II, p. 523) is right in saying that there was 'nothing in the schools of rhetoric which corresponded with the mock-trials employed today for the training of law students,' but that some cases were very near it is perhaps to be deduced from the expression ' propter quam *iudicium constitutum est*' in Quint., III, 11, 5. So Quint., IV 2, 7, after mentioning the school-case of Horatius and his sister, speaks of *iudex*.
[2] cf. J. F. D'Alton, *Roman Literary Theory and Criticism* (London, 1931) pp. 29 ff., and R. G. Austin on Quint., XII, 1, 1.
[3] Gellius, xv, 11; Suet., *De Rhet.*, c. 1.
[4] II, 19, 77 ff. (Antonius).
[5] *Contr.* I, 7, 12.
[6] Cic., *De Orat.* I, 31, 137 ff. (Crassus).

fragments of the orators of the second century B.C. rhetorical *schemata* begin to be noticeable[1] ; the Stoics took up the study of rhetoric with thoroughgoing, if somewhat misguided, enthusiasm ; the school of Hermagoras gained a following[2] ; and by 100 B.C. the rhetorical school of Rhodes in particular was attracting the young Romans of well-to-do parents in their preparation for a public career. Cicero himself, although he could have joined the newly-formed Roman rhetorical schools, travelled abroad from 79-77 B.C., and studied rhetoric at both Athens and Rhodes, at the former under Demetrius and at the latter under Molon, whose lectures he had heard in Rome some years before[3].

The introduction of Greek rhetoric at Rome must have given a great stimulus to the study of all forms of oratory ; but the earlier Roman orators themselves had not neglected those preliminary studies which are so essential for success[4]. So, in his *Brutus*[5], Cicero says of Caius Papirius Carbo, contemporary of Caius Gracchus : ' Addebat (*sc.* L. Gellius) industrium etiam et diligentem, et in exercitationibus commentationibusque multum operae solitum esse ponere.' We know from the *De Oratore*[6] that these preparatory exercises consisted in rendering and delivering in the speaker's own words a passage of Ennius or speeches of Caius Gracchus. This, then, was a form of private declamation, before the term ' declamare ' was invented ; and it is interesting to note that Cicero twice[7] uses the word ' commentari ' in close conjunction with *declamare* or *declamitare*. Similarly, he says of Marcellus[8], ' sese cotidianis commentationibus acerrime exercuit,' and of his own son-in-law, C. Piso[9], ' nullum tempus illi umquam vacabat aut a forensi dictione aut a commentatione domestica.' The young Crassus, who successfully prosecuted Carbo at the age of 21 in 119 B.C., had already extended the practice of his adversary to speeches of the great Greek orators, which he delivered in Latin guise[10].

It is now time to turn to the earliest school of rhetoric opened by a Roman, that of L. Plotius Gallus, who taught in Cicero's

[1] Marx, *op. cit.*, *Prolegomena*, pp. 134 ff. : even Cato's speeches showed evidence of Greek rhetorical influence (Cic., *Brut.* 17, 69); the earliest Roman reference to rhetoric appears to be in Ennius (p. 217 of Vahlen's stereotyped edn., Leipzig, Teubner, 1928).
[2] cf. Cic., *Brut.* 76, 263 ; 78, 271.
[3] Cic., *Ep. ad Titinium*, ap. Suet., *De Rhet.* c. 2; *Brut.* 89, 307; 90, 312; 91, 313-6.
[4] cf. Boissier, *op. cit.* (Eng. trans), pp. 165-6.
[5] 27, 105.
[6] I, 34, 154. (Crassus).
[7] *Brut.* 90, 310 ' commentabar declamitans—sic enim nunc loquuntur' ; *Pro S. Rosc. Am.* 29, 82, quoted below, p. 28 ; cf. *Brut.* 89, 305.
[8] *Brut.* 71, 249.
[9] *ib.* 78, 272.
[10] *De Orat.* I, 34, 155.

boyhood in the first decade of the 1st century B.C.[1] His school became very popular, but it seems likely that he incurred official disfavour[2], for by a censorian edict of 92 B.C. the schools of the 'Latini rhetores,' (which must have included his, in that Quintilian II, 4, 42 says he was teaching 'extremis L. Crassi temporibus', i.e. before 91 B.C.) were closed[3]. It seems highly probable that Plotius Gallus utilised fictitious declamatory themes closely modelled on actual law-court cases[4], for not only does Quintilian imply this, but Crassus, in the *De Oratore*[5], is made to give his approval to the contemporary custom of positing 'causa aliqua . . . consimili earum, quae in forum deferuntur . . . quam maxime ad veritatem accommodate.' He adds that the practice was abused by those who paid more attention to speed of delivery than to the subject, but makes it clear that the exercises, which he calls 'exercitationes' or 'dictiones' (sometimes extempore—'subitae'), but not yet 'declamationes,' were designed as a practical aid to training for the Roman courts. This was indeed a great step forward in the history of declamation at Rome.

In his essay on the Roman rhetoricians[6], Suetonius shows how ineffectual the ban on rhetoric soon became, and it is significant that he alludes particularly to the popularity of declamation, which was practised by such prominent figures as Cicero, Pompey, Mark Antony, Augustus and Nero. After observing that the numerous professors (some of whose names he later gives) had various methods of teaching, including the development of famous maxims known as χρεῖαι, the expansion of narratives or contraction of them into *précis* form, translation from the Greek, exercises in panegyric and vituperation, θέσεις, and ἀνασκευαί and κατασκευαί, he proceeds to give us most valuable evidence regarding the types of subject used in the schools at the earliest period. The *veteres controversiae*, collections of which were extant in his day, were, he says, drawn 'aut ex historiis . . . , sicut sane nonnullae usque adhuc, aut ex veritate ac re, si qua forte recens accidisset.' *Historiis* here is usually taken to mean 'history,' but there is clearly an antithesis intended between this word and 'veritate ac re,' and it would seem more likely that Suetonius meant 'collections of stories,' as opposed

---

[1] See Cic., *De Orat.* III, 24, 93 ; Sen Rhet., *Contr.* II, *Praef.* 5 ; Tac., *Dial.* c. 35 ; Quint., II, 4, 42 ; Suet., *De Rhet.*, c. 2 ; cf. Cucheval, *Histoire de l'Eloquence romaine* (Paris, 1893) vol. I, pp. 224 ff.
[2] A. Gwynn, *op. cit.*, pp. 59-69, ascribes this to political reasons, but I think that the use of the term 'impudentia' in Cic., *De Orat.* III, 24, 93 and Tac., *Dial.* c. 35 and the fact that the edict was *censorian* point to a moral objection.
[3] Suet., *De Rhet.* c. 1 ; Gellius XV, 11.
[4] See also the remarks of J. Aistermann, *De M. Valerio Probo Berytio capita quattuor* (Bonn, 1910), pp. 24-7.
[5] I, 33, 149 ff.
[6] c. 1. See the notes in R. P. Robinson's edition (Paris, 1925), 37-42.

to actual events of recent occurrence. This is borne out by his examples, for the first has quite an 'Arabian Nights' setting[1]: 'In the summer certain city youths went to Ostia, and going down to the shore approached the fishermen who were dragging in their nets, and fixed a price with them for the catch; they paid the money, and waited a long time until the nets were hauled in. When they were finally drawn up, there were no fish in them, but there was a casket of gold, sewn up. The purchasers thereupon claimed the catch as their own, and the fishermen as theirs.' This exercise would have given rise to argument on the precise meaning of the word 'catch' (bolus) and might be compared with the exercises of the *constitutio legitima ex definitione* type which appear in the *Ad Herennium*[2]. Despite its romantic flavour, therefore, the exercise would not be devoid of legal value, but would be classed as an *invented* case (ficta) rather than a strictly *forensic* case (iudicialis), according to the distinction which Suetonius immediately proceeds to give.

The second example of Suetonius is much more true to life, and is clearly *iudicialis*. 'A slave-dealer, bringing ashore a gang of slaves at Brundisium, adorned a handsome and valuable slave with the embroidered toga and the *bulla* of a free-born youth, being afraid of the customs-officers; he easily got away with the the deception. On arrival at Rome, the truth was discovered, and a claim was put in on the slave's behalf for his freedom, on the ground that he was free by his master's desire.' This exercise may well be taken 'ex veritate ac re'; for it recurs in the lesser declamations attributed to Quintilian (340) and the controlling law ' Qui voluntate domini in libertate fuerit, liber sit ' (which recurs in 342), has been shown to be genuinely relatable to cases in which the slave was granted the *tuitio* of the *praetor*[3]. Both examples differ from the later *causae* and *controversiae* in the fact that they are given specific local settings (Ostia, Brundisium), whereas the Senecan exercises are given no such definite background. The exact terminology which was used to describe these early exercises is not certain owing to a corruption in the text of Suetonius, which is printed by its latest editor in the form ' olim autem eas appellationes, Graeci συντάσεις vocabant '; but variant readings such as *synthesis* and *syntaxis* exist. If the term ' appellationes ' is genuine (and the emendation 'appellatione Graeca'

---

[1] A. A. Day, *Origins of Latin Love Elegy* (Oxford, 1938), p. 63, compares the dispute in Plautus, *Rudens* 938 ff. (Act IV, Sc. iii).
[2] I, 12, 21. cf. below, p. 25.
[3] Wlassak, ' Die prätorischen Freilassungen ' *Z.S.S.* XXVI (1905) pp. 374-8; F. Lanfranchi, *Il diritto nei retori romani* (Milan, 1938), pp. 184 ff.; Buckland, *The Roman Law of Slavery* (Cambridge, 1908) pp. 444-6. (Gaius, *Inst.* III, 56; *Frag. Dosith.* 5, 6).

has long been in the field) it may refer either to these local settings, or perhaps be connected with 'appellare' 'to prosecute,' i.e. 'court-cases.' Whichever is the truth, it seems certain that συντάσεις must be emended to συστάσεις, for, as we have seen, the examples of *controversiae* given by the author of *Ad Herennium*, by Cicero, *De Inventione*, and by Quintilian (Book VII), occur as illustrative material for the various types of legal issue, viz. *constitutiones causae*; and the Greek rhetorical term for *constitutiones* is clearly συστάσεις, though the simple στάσεις was more commonly used, whereas συντάσεις has little or no authority[1]. It is clear, then, that from their earliest occurrence in Latin, these exercises not only formed part of the rhetorical doctrine of classification of legal issues such as has been expounded above[2], but were actually made the subjects of live debate. At this point, we may turn to the terminology and subjects of declamation in the earliest extant Latin treatise on rhetoric, which dates from 86-82 B.C.

The treatise *Ad Herennium* is the earliest work in Latin in which the term *declamatio* appears[3], but it is immediately noteworthy that its use is confined to one section (III, 11 and 12, 20), where the author is discussing the subject of delivery (*pronuntiatio*). Speaking of voice-training, he says that the exercise of declamation is especially conducive to flexibility and adaptability of voice—'mollitudinem vocis, hoc est, ut eam torquere in dicendo nostro commodo possimus, maxime faciet exercitatio declamationis,' and also to firmness of tone ('de ea parte firmitudinis quae conservatur ratione declamationis'). That is, it will give the orator practice in speaking either in a conversational fashion (*sermo*), or a more combative and argumentative style (*contentio*), or an amplified tone designed to arouse anger or sympathy (*amplificatio*) (III, 13, 23). So Quintilian (XI, 3, 25) recommends the learning by heart of passages which will require loud, or argumentative, or colloquial, or modulated intonation ('clamorem et disputationem et sermonem

[1] This point is fully argued in my article 'Rhetorica' in *C.R.* LXI (1947) pp. 84-6, where it is observed that the confusion of σύντασις, σύνταξις, and σύστασις occurs in the text-tradition of Thucydides VII, 71.
[2] pp. 12 ff.
[3] Allied terms (*declamito, declamatorius*) appear in the *De Oratore*, but it is doubtful whether the dramatic date (91 B.C.) should be pressed to afford evidence of terminology, though the general ideas may well often belong to the period of the discussion itself. The question of the Greek equivalent to *declamatio* and *declamare* is a difficult one ; the term the Greeks generally use is the vague μελέτη; cf. Throm, *òp. cit.* p. 111. In *C.R.* XXXVI (1922) pp. 116-117, F. H. Colson argues that *declamare* = κατηχεῖν, but ἀναφωνεῖν and ἀναφώνησις appear more likely, and the use in Greek of these terms, and the simple φωνασκεῖν, φωνασκία, φωνασκός in reference to declamation, agrees with the kind of explanation which the *Ad Herennium* passage suggests —i.e. that the term originally referred to voice-training. See also Boissier, *op. cit.*, p. 169, and Peterson on Quint., x, 1, 71.

et flexus '), and it seems probable, therefore, that the rehearsal, either by the master for imitation or by the pupil for criticism, of sections of speeches for this strictly limited purpose of *pronuntiatio* was what *declamatio* originally meant. The great exponents of *pronuntiatio*, of course, were the best actors of the stage ; and the Roman student of rhetoric, who frequently had (as we shall see) to impersonate historical or mythological personages in his exercises, and to simulate their emotions, needed to be something of an actor.[1] Quintilian, indeed, recommends the student to learn from the actor and to declaim passages from comedy (I, 11, 12-14) and observes (III, 8, 51) that the declaimers needed almost as many types of intonation as the comic actors[2]. When therefore, we find that the term ' declamitant ' is applied to the rehearsals of tragic actors by Antonius in Cic., *De Orat.*, I, 59, 251, we are inclined to believe that the early use of the term *declamatio* at Rome, may have had a close connection with the stage. It is remarkable that the exercise of training the voice by gradually raising and then lowering it through all the tones, which Antonius there ascribes to the actors, and Crassus subsequently (III, 61, 227) seems to approve, is mentioned by the elder Seneca as a common practice among declaimers (I, *Praef.* 16)[3]. And it is from the old tragedies of Pacuvius and Accius that Crassus gives examples of different kinds of *pronuntiatio*[4]. The term *declamatio* had originally nothing derogatory about it ; indeed, had not Demosthenes himself said that delivery was *the* primary necessity in oratory[5], and had not Gaius Gracchus distinguished himself by it ?[6] But the practice obviously lay open to abuse ; powerful and clear intonation sometimes gave place to mere clamour and rant, and some declaimers, mistaking volubility for eloquence, set out to ' beat the clock '[7]. It is precisely for this fault that some declaimers are criticised by Crassus in the *De Oratore*, (I, 33, 149) as spoiling a naturally good exercise ; and Messala in the *Dialogus* (c. 31 *init.*) complains that declaimers merely develop a fluent tongue, and miss all the value of a serious moral training. Others, particularly those of the Asiatic style, which characterised so many later declaimers, sought to imitate the *recitative* of the stage and produced a kind of monotonous

---

[1] cf. Quint., XI, 1, 38 ff. Sen. Rhet., *Contr.* III *Praef.* 3 says of the *pronuntiatio* of Cassius Severus that it would have made an actor's reputation.
[2] cf. the story of Cicero's competitions with Roscius in Macrobius, *Sat.* III, 14, 12. The actors' voice-training is fully described by A. Krumbacher, *Die Stimmbildung der Redner in Alterthum bis auf die Zeit Quintilians* (Rhetorische Studien, X, Paderborn, 1920), pp. 81 ff.
[3] cf. also Sen., *Epp.* XV, 7, Quint., XI, 3, 22.
[4] *De Orat.* III, 58, 217 ff.
[5] Cic., *De Orat.* III, 56, 213 ; *Brut.* 38, 142 ; *Orat.* 17, 56 ; Quint., XI, 3, 6.
[6] Cic., *De Orat.* III, 56, 214.
[7] *De Orat.* II, 20, 86 ; III, 34, 138 (' ad clepsydram latrare ') ; *Quint.*, II, 12

sing-song[1] which subsequently became one of the most marked features of bad oratory, and earned the severe criticism of Quintilian[2] and Dio Chrysostom[3].

But this degeneration had hardly set in during the Sullan Age, and, although rhetorical studies were in full swing, the term *declamatio* as yet implied no adverse criticism, and referred only to a course of elocution, or a private rehearsal, not a full scale speech delivered in a competitive spirit and replete with sententious comments.

The term *controversia*, also, appears to have had a more restricted meaning in the Sullan Age ; it meant the point at issue, the dispute itself involved in an' exercise, generally, but not exclusively, of the forensic type, but does not seem to have been extended as yet to mean the exercise itself, which was normally ὑπόθεσις in Greek, and *causa* in Latin. It is the kernel rather than the whole (cf. *Ad Herenn.* I, 2, 2; 1, 3, 4; I, 10, 17; I, 11, 18, 19, 20 *et saep.*) The same meaning occurs repeatedly in Cicero's *De Inventione*, written very little later than the *Ad Herennium* (cf. I, 8, 10 and 11; 9, 12 *et saep.*). Every forensic *controversia* would be of a certain fixed type (*constitutio*) and so we frequently find these two words in close association. According to the new reading in Suetonius, the Greeks extended σύστασις to apply to the whole exercise ; the Romans did not exactly do this, and call their exercises *constitutiones*, but they did something extremely similar in developing the scope of the term *controversia*. The term *suasoria* is not used ; a deliberative speech is *deliberatio*, and, although Cicero is a step nearer to it when he uses *suasio*,[4] we do not meet *suasoria* until we reach the elder Seneca.

The technical phraseology, then, was not set in the mould familiar to us, in the years 86-82 B.C. ; on the other hand, the reader of the *Ad Herennium* is constantly confronted with examples of subjects of exercises on fictitious themes which bear considerable resemblance to those of the early Empire. This is particularly true of deliberative exercises ; for example, debates on Hannibal's dilemmas, which later aroused the ridicule of Juvenal[5], were evidently popular in the Sullan Age, e.g. 'Hannibal deliberates whether, on being summoned to return from Italy to Carthage, he should remain in Italy, or return home, or proceed to Egypt and seize

---

[1] Cic., *De Orat.* I, 23, 105 ('ex scholis cantilenam'); *Orat.* 18, 57 ; Sen., *Suas.* II, 10; Sen., *Epp.* 114, 1; Philost., *Vit. Soph.* pp. 513, 589. See Norden, *A.K.* I, 294-5; D'Alton, *op. cit.* p. 213, and Gudeman on Tac., *Dial.* c. 26, 4.
[2] XI, 1, 56 ; 3, 57 ff ; cf. XII, 8, 3.
[3] *Oration* 32, 68.
[4] *De Orat.* II, 81, 333; *Orat.* 11, 37; *Part. Or.* 4, 11 and 13; 24, 85.
[5] *Sat.* VII, 162-4 ; X, 166-7.

Alexandria' (III, 2, 2). The *deliberatio* of the men of Casilinum, when surrounded by the Carthaginians (III, 5, 8) is not very different from Seneca's *suasoria* of the 300 Spartans who debate whether or not to stay at Thermopylae (*Suas.* II). In each case the exercise involves military forces in a desperate situation. Another theme relating to the period of the 2nd Punic War is that concerning the Senate's deliberation whether or not to redeem its captives (III, 2, 2), a theme which is also mentioned by Cicero[1]. The end of the wars with Carthage provides another subject (*ib.*) : ' Should Carthage be destroyed or permitted to survive ?'—a debate which would give ample opportunity for utilising the famous ' delenda est Carthago' of the elder Cato, and which reappears not only in Cicero but also in the later Latin rhetoricians—another indication of the remarkable persistence of some of these themes[2]. Other debates based on Roman history are : ' The Senate debates whether or not to exempt Scipio (Africanus minor) from the laws so that he may become consul before the legal age ' (III, 2, 2), and, most recent of all ; ' The Senate debates whether or not to grant the allies citizenship in the Italian war ' (*ib.*).

It is remarkable how thoroughly Roman are these themes ; the custom of inventing themes from recent history remained in the elder Seneca's day, for two of his collection of *suasoriae* concern the murder of Cicero. But Seneca's subjects also include examples from Greek History (*Suas.* I, II, IV) and Greek Tragedy (*Suas.* III). It is probable that such subjects also existed at the time of the *Ad Herennium*, but that the author of the treatise, being a thorough-going, practical Roman, avoided them[3]. The treatment of these subjects was clearly on stereotyped lines (cf. III, 5, 8-9), but may not have had the superficial brilliance, the piquancy and point which we meet with in the early Empire. As far as subjects of deliberative exercises are concerned, it seems difficult to refuse to admit, with Marx, that collections like that of the elder Seneca may have existed even as early as the age of Sulla.

Among the many subjects of forensic exercises quoted or alluded to by the author of the *Ad Herennium*, one or two are from Greek Tragedy[4], centred around such figures as Ajax or Orestes, e.g. ' Ajax, after realising what he had done in his madness, fell on his sword ; Ulysses came upon the scene, saw his body, and drew forth the blood-stained weapon ; Teucer appeared, saw his brother murdered, and his brother's enemy holding a blood-

---
1 *De Orat.* III, 28, 109; cf. Marx, edn. of *Ad Herennium, Prolegomena*, p. 103.
2 *De Inv.* I, 8, 11 ; I, 12, 17 ; Sulp. Vict., *R.L.M.* p. 346, 35, (as a *controversia*) ; cf. Kohl, *op. cit.* p. 96. This debate, of course, is quite historical.
3 cf. Marx, *op. cit.*, p. 104.
4 cf. above, p. 15.

stained sword ; he accuses him of murder' (I, 11, 18)—a good subject for discussion of the value of circumstantial evidence. Questions of moral justification as well as legal right appear in the exercise 'Agamemnon was admittedly killed by Clytaemnestra, and Clytaemnestra by Orestes ; did Orestes act legally, and had he the moral right to act thus ?' (I, 10, 17). Here, in the expression ' iure fecerit et licueritne facere ' we see the division of the argument into *ius* and *aequitas* which is so common in the Senecan declamations[1]. No subjects from Greek Tragedy occur in the Senecan collection of *controversiae*, but other subjects in the *Ad Herennium* bear a close relationship to those of the Empire. In the first place, a law is posited (or a number of laws) to which the incident discussed bears a close reference, e.g. ' Suppose the law orders those who abandon ship in a storm to forfeit their possessions, which, together with the ship, are to revert to those who remained on board.' An incident is now invented, in which all the crew abandon ship and take to a dinghy, except one sick man, who is too ill to move ; by chance, the ship survives to reach harbour, and the sick man takes possession ; whereupon the original owner claims it (I, 11, 19, cf. Cic., *De Inv.* II, 51, 153-4). Here the law itself may have been Rhodian[2], and the exercise is a study in the conflict between the spirit and the letter (*ex scripto et sententia*). A further example involves a direct conflict of two laws (*ex contrariis legibus*) : ' The law forbids a man who has been condemned for embezzlement to speak in the assembly [3]; another law[4] orders an augur who wishes to replace a dead colleague to name his successor in the assembly ; an augur condemned for embezzlement does so, and is ordered to pay a fine ' (I, 11, 20). Other examples[5] quoted are based on the exact interpretation of an ambiguous phrase in a will (*ex ambiguo* I, 12, 20, cf. Cic., *De Inv.* II, 40, 116), or an insufficient definition of the law of *maiestas* (*ex definitione*, I, 12, 21), or upon the necessity for deciding whether a case is one of *furtum* or *peculatus* (*ex translatione* I, 12, 22), or for deciding how a number of laws interact in a case (*ex ratiocinatione* I, 13, 23). The last-named is quite a complicated exercise, at the head of which four laws are quoted ; even in the elder Seneca three is the maximum number of laws governing an exercise, and

---

[1] See below pp. 46 ff., 57.
[2] *Dig.* XIV, 2, ' De Lege Rhodia de Iactu ' ; cf. E. G. Sihler, *A.J.P.* XXIII (1902), p. 287 ; it recurs in Hermogenes, π.στάσ. p. 85, l. 2, (Rabe) ' ὁ ἐπιμείνας χειμαζομένῃ νηῒ δεσπότης ἔστω τῆς νεώς '; but there is no exact legal parallel.
[3] cf. the subsequent provisions of the *Lex Iulia Municipalis* col. 110 ff. (Girard, *Textes de Droit romain*, p. 85) and the similar declamatory laws in Sen. rhet., quoted below, p. 105.
[4] Marx, *op. cit.*, p. 108, refers this to a *Lex Domitia*, abrogated by Sulla.
[5] See Marx, *op. cit.*, pp. 104-110, for a full collection and detailed examination.

one or two is normal, though Quintilian (III, 6, 96) has an example with six. The extremely important point is that at least three of the laws in this case (*Ad Herennium* I, 13, 23) are genuine enactments of the XII Tables[1] ; this cannot be too strongly emphasised.

These exercises mostly occur in the section of the treatise devoted to the type of case known as *constitutio legitima* in which it is not a question whether an illegal act was actually committed or not (*constitutio coniecturalis*, e.g. the Ajax-Ulysses case), or even whether it was justifiable or not (*constitutio iuridicialis*, e.g. the Orestes case), but whether it is punishable according to the express wording of the law or laws ; and it is noteworthy that exercises in the Senecan collection frequently involve this principle. We may now attempt to decide, exactly how, if at all, these exercises of the *Ad Herennium* differ from those of the Augustan Age.

It has been asserted by Marx[2] that there was no difference, but the evidence hardly warrants this deduction. There is no exercise in the *Ad Herennium* based on tyranny, piracy, rape, or adultery ; on the other hand, we do find exercises involving treason (*laesae maiestatis*, I, 15, 25, cf. Sen. rhet., *Contr.* VII, 7, IX, 2), insanity (*dementiae*, I, 13, 23, cf. *Contr.* VI, 7, X, 3, and II, 3, 4, 6, VII, 6), parricide (I, 13, 23, cf. *Contr.* III, 2 ; V, 4 ; VII, 3, 5), and insult and injury (*iniuriarum* I, 14, 24 ; II, 13, 19, cf. *Contr.* IV, 1 ; V, 6 ; X, 1, and 6). The exercises in the *Ad Herennium*, both deliberative and judicial, are in the main strictly practical and designed as a training for the senate or the law-courts. With the exception of the examples from tragedy, the situations they envisage are not fanciful or remote from the likelihood of actual occurrence. This may partly be due to the author himself, for Suetonius' example of a fictitious subject, given above[3], has to be borne in mind ; but it is clear that the rhetoricians did not yet give the almost unlimited rein to the imagination that became permissible under the Empire. We do not yet meet the ' magicians and step-mothers more cruel than those of tragedy,' of which Quintilian[4] complains. The practice of ' declamation ' was, in all probability, confined to the rhetorical school, or to the privacy of the house, and it had by no means become a social pursuit. Its very terminology was new ; and neither

---

[1] cf. Bruns, *Fontes Iuris Romani Antiqui* (6th edn. by Mommsen and Gradenwitz, Leipzig, 1893), pp. 22-3. Mommsen, *Römisches Strafrecht* (Leipzig, 1899), p. 643 n. 6, denies that the second of the four laws belongs to the XII Tables.

[2] p. 103. His comparison of the form of words in *Ad Herenn.* I, 3, 5 (' pro viro forti contra parricidam ') with some of the longer declamations of pseudo-Quintilian (e.g. II = ' pro caeco contra novercam ') is good, but the evidence is not sufficiently conclusive as a whole. cf. W. C. Summers, Introdn. to his edn. of *Select Letters of Seneca*, (London 1910), p. xxxiii, n. 3.

[3] p. 19.

[4] II, 10, 5, cf. below, p. 80.

declamatio nor *controversia* had yet taken on the meanings they subsequently acquired.

These considerations suggest that the elder Seneca is expressing himself very generally when he refers to declamation as 'rem post me natam'; his statement needs qualification, and he probably referred more to the circumstances than the subjects of declamation. It is possible that he did not know of the *Ad Herennium*[1], which appears to have been little read (unless we accept the view that its author is the Cornificius mentioned in Quintilian), though its doctrines must have been widely current. His statement that *declamatio* does not occur in any author prior to Cicero and Calvus is, strictly, incorrect, though the *Ad Herennium* might almost be classed as belonging to the age of Cicero[2]. To that age, and the youthful utterances of the master-orator on the theory of his art, we may now turn.

---

[1] This point is undecided; cf. Gudeman's query on Tac. *Dial.* 31, 1 (= p. 425 of his 2nd edn., Leipzig, Teubner, 1914): 'oder hielt Seneca diese Schrift für ciceronisch, denn gekannt wird er sie wohl haben?'
twas in fact ascribed to Cicero from St. Jerome to Laurentius Valla.

Chapter II

DECLAMATION FROM CICERO TO THE ELDER SENECA

(i) Cicero and Declamation

Although the terms *declamare* and *declamatio* do not occur in Cicero's *De Inventione*, there are close resemblances between his subjects of rhetorical exercises and those of the *Ad Herennium*. The deliberative exercise on the fate of Carthage is paralleled by I, 8, 11 and I, 12, 17 (cf. I, 39, 72), where two further examples from Roman History appear, namely a debate ' Should we declare war on Corinth ?' and another ' Should an army be sent against Philip of Macedon or retained in Italy to augment the forces opposing Hannibal ?' In II, 57, 171 the debate of the surrounded men of Casilinum, alluded to in *Ad Herennium* III 5, 8, reappears, and the arguments applicable are considered at some length. Similarly, exercises of the forensic type are also common in the *De Inventione*. In I, 13, 18, a long excerpt is given from the case of Orestes, on trial for the murder of his mother ; in I, 49, 92 we meet the Ajax-Ulysses case again ; in II, 51, 153-4 we have a longer version of the exercise concerning the sick man who did not abandon ship ; in II, 40, 116 the case of the ambiguous phrase in a will reappears, together with other exercises based on ambiguous phraseology, one of which (II, 40, 118) appears in Hermogenes (π.στάσ. c. 12) and is probably Greek, and the other (II, 42, 122) based on an actual court-case mentioned twice in the *De Oratore* (I, 39, 180 and esp. II, 32, 140-141). In II, 50, 148 the case of parricide is the same, except for the omission of one law, as that in *Ad Herennium* I, 13, 23. Finally the case of Popillius, accused of *maiestas*, given in *Ad Herennium* I, 15, 25, is considered in *De Inv.* II, 24, 72-3.

The treatise also contains a number of exercises which do not appear in the *Ad Herennium* ; as for instance, that concerning a murder at an inn, selected as an example of the *constitutio coniecturalis* (II, 4, 14)—drawn, in all probability, from real life; that of Flaminius, accused of *maiestas* (II, 17, 52), based on the agrarian reforms of that turbulent tribune in 233 B.C., and that concerning Horatius' murder of his sister (II, 26, 78). In II, 49, 144 we first encounter the person of the tyrant, who becomes so characteristic of later exercises. First, two laws are quoted : (i) ' Whoever kills a tyrant may claim the rewards of Olympian victors, and demand anything he pleases from the magistrate, who must grant it '—the familiar ' Tyrannicidae praemium ' law of the elder Seneca (*Contr.* IV, 7) and later compilers of declamations[1]; and

---

[1] 'Quint', *Decl. min.* 282, 288, 345, Calp. Flacc., *Decl.* 13, 22, Fortunatianus, p. 96 28 (Halm), Syrianus IV, p. 216 (Walz);. cf. below, p. 104.

(ii) 'After a tyrant has been slain the magistrates shall put to death his five nearest relatives.' The following situation is then propounded, to give an exercise in the conflict of statutes : ' Alexander, tyrant of Pherae in Thessaly, was killed by his wife Thebe one night as he slept beside her. She demanded that she be given her son by the tyrant as a reward.' Clearly this is a Greek invention, of little use except in academic controversy. It has been observed[1] that Cicero refers on three occasions in this treatise to Rhodes (I, 30, 47 ; II, 29, 87 ; 32, 98) and this may be an indication that the exercises with a Greek setting may have originated in that centre of study, and may possibly have reached him through Molon of Rhodes, whom he heard in 88 B.C.[2]

At this point it may be convenient to classify the types of subject so far encountered. They may be broadly grouped as either (i) Based on events of Roman History, or occasionally cases of Roman Law, (ii) Fictitious cases, involving legal problems ; where specifically Roman, they are generally of practical utility and possible in real life ; where obviously Greek they are more remote from likelihood, (iii) Mythological subjects from Greek Tragedy, or occasionally subjects based on collections of stories. As a whole it may be said that the themes are not wildly improbable, nor are they highly intricate; Greek influence is, naturally, rather more in evidence in the *De Inventione* than in the *Ad Herennium*, but the parallels of sound Roman subjects are more striking than the divergencies.

The earliest reference to the term *declamare* in Cicero occurs in the speech *Pro S. Roscio Amerino*, of 80 B.C., where (29, 82) he rebuts the charges of peculation brought by Erucius in the words : 'quae mihi iste (Erucius) visus est ex alia oratione *declamare*, quam in alium reum commentaretur.' It is possible[3] that the word here merely means 'to shout aloud,' but in view of the context, which implies stock rhetorical argument, and the statement of the 'Auctor ad Herennium' that *declamatio* was an exercise, it seems more likely that even here a more technical meaning may underlie it and that it should be translated 'to practise aloud.'[4] There seems to be less evidence for technical allusion, however, in *In Verrem* IV, 66, 149 (70 B.C.)[5], or *Pro Murena* 21, 44 (63 B.C.)[6], though in 66 B.C. Cicero still frequented the school of the grammarian and rhetorician M. Antonius Gnipho, who

[1] By Bornecque, *Déclam.* p. 42.
[2] *Brutus* 89, 307.
[3] cf. *Thes. Ling. Lat.* s.v. *Declamo*.
[4] cf. Landgraf's edition (Berlin,2 1914) *ad. loc.*, where this view is taken, and see above (p. 17) for the association of 'commentari' with declamation.
[5] 'Ille autem insanus, qui pro isto vehementissime contra me declamasset ...'
[6] 'non declamatio potius quam persalutatio' (*sc.* mihi placet). Madvig's argument in favour of the reading 'denuntiatio' (*Adversaria critica*, II, p. 208) is not accepted by Heitland in his edn. (Cambridge, 1876).

gave declamatory displays[1] ; this the orator probably did for amusement and relaxation[2]—the first indication of this attitude to declamation. The *De Oratore*, of 55 B.C., makes Cicero's position clear regarding what was by that date an increasingly popular form of rhetorical training ; the whole argument of the work is directed to establishing the superiority of a wider cultural education for the orator over the rigid formulism of contemporary handbooks. In I, 16, 73 Crassus, who later (I, 33, 149) admits the value of practising with cases parallel to those of real life, says, ' facile declaratur utrum is, qui dicat, tantummodo in *hoc declamatorio* sit *opere* iactatus (' this declamatory business ') an ad dicendum omnibus ingenuis artibus instructus accesserit.' References in the *De Oratore*, of course, need to be used with care, as the dramatic date of that dialogue is 91 B.C., and it is sometimes difficult to decide whether Cicero himself is speaking (e.g. in the guise of Crassus), or whether his words are intended to refer strictly to that period. In this instance, the use of the expression ' hoc declamatorio opere ' seems to be Cicero's own, for in a letter to his brother Quintus (*Ad Q.F.* III, 3, 4) of 54 B.C., he writes, regarding Quintus' son : ' sed nostrum instituendi genus esse paulo eruditius et θετικώτερον non ignoras. quare neque ego impediri Ciceronis iter atque disciplinam volo, et ipse puer magis *illo declamatorio genere* duci ac delectari videtur '[3] In these contexts ' opus declamatorium ' and ' genus declamatorium ' clearly cannot mean merely a voice-exercise ; evidently the declamatory elements had become so characteristic of the whole rhetorical training that the term *declamare* had now extended to become a general term for the whole of that training. Similarly, in *De Orat.*, III, 28, 109, *controversia* is for the first time extended to be a full equivalent of *causa*. So in the *Pro Plancio*[4], of the same year, we notice the first appearance of the noun *declamator*, which seems to suggest that the declaimer was now becoming a notorious figure. The contrast in this passage between the declaimer and the professional lawyer shows that the divorce between practical oratory and scholastic rehearsal must already have been beginning at this period, and it may well be at about this time that Calvus, who was born in 82 B.C., and died in 47 B.C., made the remark quoted by the elder Seneca (*Contr.* I, *Praef.* 12), distinguishing declamation from real oratory[5]. By the

[1] Suet., *de gramm.* c. 7, 2.
[2] Macrobius, III, 12, 8 ' cuius scholam Cicero post laborem fori frequentabat.'
[3] cf. E. G. Sihler, *op. cit.*, pp. 283-294 (an excellent discussion of θετικώτερον).
[4] 34, 83 ' non vobis videtur cum aliquo *declamatore* . . . disputare.' The term *declamator* is read by some editors in *De Orat.* III, 34, 138; the text is uncertain, but cf. *Orat.* 14, 47. Also in *Pro Plancio* (19, 47), we find ' vulgari et pervagata declamatione contendere.'
[5] ' declamare se non mediocriter, dicere bene ' (Madvig's correction, printed by Bornecque).

time of the *Orator*[1] (46 B.C.), Cicero uses the word *declamator* as a term of contempt.

Although Cicero was fully aware of the limitations of declamatory practice, he himself declaimed in his youth and middle age in both Greek and Latin, up to the time of his praetorship (66 B.C.), as Suetonius tells us in his *De Rhetoribus*[2]; though he probably did not call his early exercises *declamationes*, for he says (*Brutus*, 90, 310) ' commentabar declamitans—*sic enim nunc loquuntur*.' The elder Seneca's statement that Cicero declaimed *causas* (that is, the kind of exercises which appear in the *Ad Herennium* and *De Inventione*) receives confirmation from his words in *Tusc. Disp.* I, 4, 7 ' ut enim antea declamitabam causas, quod nemo me diutius fecit.' A further example of the type of *causa* current in the schools in Cicero's youth is given by Antonius in *De Orat.* II, 24, 100, as follows : ' The law forbids a foreigner to climb the city-wall ; a foreigner does so, repels the enemy, and is then prosecuted.' This is classed as an ' easy ' case, and insufficiently technical to be of much practical value, but was still in use in Quintilian's day (IV, 4, 4; VII, 6, 6-7), and had some legal basis.[3]

Cicero seems generally to have preferred the wider and more philosophical subject-matter of the θέσεις to the limited scope afforded by the rhetorical *causa* ; but an interesting passage in the elder Seneca[4], which is difficult to reconcile with his statement in the Preface to Book I of the *Controversiae*, shows that Cicero must have declaimed an exercise which was in subject extremely close to the fourth *controversia* of Seneca's first book. This probably refers to Cicero's later years when, as Suetonius says, he declaimed particularly in Latin ; and although Cicero may have called it a *causa* rather than a *controversia*, it is important in that it shows that towards the end of the Republic subjects which remained popular under the Empire were already in use.

In his later years, Cicero seems to have been particularly attracted to declaiming on philosophical themes, for in *Tusc. Disp.* I, 4, 7 (cf. II, 11, 26) he refers to his recent private exhibitions among friends at Tusculum as his *senilis declamatio*, and calls the exercises *scholae* (' disquisitions '), ' after the manner of the Greeks,' a word which is interesting as preparing the way for the Senecan *scholastica*. Later in the work (III, 34, 81), he gives examples of

[1] *loc. cit.*, ' declamatorem aliquem de ludo aut rabulam de foro.' cf. St. Jerome, *Epp.* 52, 8, 1.
[2] c. 1, ' Cicero ad praeturam usque etiam Graece declamitavit, Latine vero senior quoque.'
[3] *Dig.* I, 8 'si quis violaverit muros, capite puniatur', cited by Cousin, *op. cit.* I, p. 376.
[4] *Contr.* I, 4, 7 ' ex illa Ciceronis sententia tractus, quam in simili controversia dixit, cum abdicaretur is, qui adulteram matrem occidendam acceperat et dimiserat.'

such exercises, which are all philosophical—on poverty and the humble life, on exile, the ruin of one's country, and servitude ; they were far removed from the rhetorical exercises of his youth, and this adherence to the philosophical side of declamation is understandable when we realise that he was using it to beguile some of the saddest hours of his life, after his daughter's death.

The last picture we have of Cicero declaiming is at his villa at Puteoli in April, 44 B.C., when Caesar's murder had thrown everything into confusion. There he declaimed for, and listened to the declamations of, his ' grown-up pupils,'[1] Hirtius and Pansa, both of whom were destined to meet a tragic end in battle almost exactly a year later. It is to this period that the elder Seneca refers when he says that the outbreak of the Civil War kept him in Spain, and just prevented him from hearing the one man whose genius matched the majesty of Rome. Seneca lived to see very different circumstances for such declamations ; to Cicero they afforded an occasional source of practice[2] or amusement, and especially a solace in difficult and anxious times, but they were essentially private, and delivered to a small audience of friends. Declamation among friends still survived after Cicero's day, but the private rehearsal and friendly demonstration were soon to give place to the more brilliant public exhibitionism of the Empire[3].

(ii) *The Declamations of the elder Seneca: their subjects and general social, political, and legal background*

It was in the very year of Cicero's death, the pathos of which gave historians and rhetoricians alike a fine subject for their disquisitions, that the ' elder ' Seneca, then a boy some 12 years of age, arrived in Rome from Corduba. He and his fellow-countryman, M. Porcius Latro, became pupils of Marullus, himself in all probability a native of Corduba ; and the first *controversia* in Seneca's collection was declaimed in the school of Marullus (*Contr.* I, *Praef.* 22). Seneca does not expressly say that this school was in Rome ; it may possibly have been in Corduba, but the

---

[1] 'grandes praetextatos' Sen., *Contr.* I *Praef.* 11, Suet., *De Rhet.* c. 1; cf. Cic., *Ad Att.* XIV, 11, 2; 12, 2; 20, 4; 22, 1; *De Fato* c. 2; Quint., XII, 11, 6. For an earlier occasion cf. *Ad Fam.* IX, 16, 7; IX, 18, (Hirtius and Dolabella).
[2] cf. *Phil.* II, 17, 42 ' vini exhalandi, non *ingenii acuendi causa* declamas.' cf. V. 7, 19.
[3] Other references to declamation in Cicero are *Ad Fam*, VII, 33, 1 ; XVI, 21, 5-6 ; (the latter regarding the declamation of Cicero's son at Athens). It may be added here that the deliberative speeches *ad C. Caesarem de ordinanda republica* and the invectives, *declamatio in M. T. Ciceronem* and *responsio in Sallustium*, all of which were printed in the older editions of Sallust, have been until recently regarded as of later date and cannot with certainty be taken as affording evidence of declamation under the Republic ; cf. Teuffel, *Gesch. der röm. Literatur* I, pp. 484 ff., Schanz-Hosius, *Gesch. d. röm. Lit.* I, 2, 185, Gwynn, *Roman Education*, pp. 161-2. See now, however, R. Syme's review of E. H. Clift, *Latin Pseudepigrapha*, in *J.R.S.* XXXVII (1947), pp. 200-201.

fact that Marullus is so often mentioned as contributing to other declamations along with the series of other declaimers leads one to suppose that he taught in Rome[1]. What, indeed, would be more likely than that the Spaniards had their own school or schools in Rome, to which the sons of their countrymen would be welcomed on their arrival at the great metropolis[2]? But wherever it was declaimed, this first exercise of Seneca shows a marked change from those we have met so far : it is true that it is the first example of the actual *treatment* of an exercise in some detail, but the subject itself has an air of unreality about it which suggests that the teaching of the schools was now beginning to sacrifice verisimilitude for, legal intricacy and highly flavoured themes. Its subject is as follows :, ' Two brothers, one of whom had a son, quarrelled ; the boy's uncle fell into poverty, and, against his father's wish, the boy supported him ; he was in consequence disinherited by his father, but accepted his lot ; he was adopted by the uncle. Later his uncle came into a legacy, and became rich. His father, on the other hand, began to grow poor ; against his uncle's wish the boy supported him, and consequently was disinherited again !' An elaborate concoction this, and not a situation likely to occur very often ; yet not without legal value, for, as the arguments in the *divisio* show (§§ 13 ff.), it would require a strict investigation to be made into the exact legal definition of ' adoption ' ; and the question of equity would arise—should a son be punished for an act which was in accord with the law ' Liberi parentes alant aut vinciantur ' (the law, drawn from Greek sources on which the exercise is based) ? But in the succeeding exercises of Seneca's collection we meet such characters as the pirate, the adulterer, and the tyrant-slayer. So, in *Contr.* I, 2, ' A girl was captured by pirates, sold, and bought by a pander and made a prostitute. She asked money of those who came to her, provided she was not compelled to earn it : a soldier approached her and not being able to persuade her, tried to use force : she killed him. Being tried and subsequently acquitted she was sent back to her own country. She then became a candidate for the priesthood !' An astonishing situation ! It was hardly necessary to invent so lurid a setting in order to exercise pupils in the application of the law ' Sacerdos

---

[1] cf. Bornecque, *Déclam.* p. 179.
[2] Other Spanish declaimers were Junius Gallio, Turrinus Clodius, Statorius Victor, Gavius Silo, and probably Catius Crispus, Cornelius Hispanus, Broccus, Quintilianus senex, and Seneca Grandio. See the articles of H. de la Ville de Mirmont, ' Les Déclamateurs Espagnols au temps d'Auguste et de Tibère ' (*Annales de la Faculté des Lettres de Bordeaux* [Bulletin Hispanique] XII (1910) pp. 1-22, XIV (1912) pp. 11-29 ; 229-243 ; 341-352, XV (1913) pp. 154-169 ; 237-267 ; 384-410), esp. in this connection xv 154-169). These articles appear to be too little known in England, and deserved mention in Edward's bibliography to his edition of the *Suasoriae* (Cambridge, 1928).

casta e castis, pura e puris sit '—a law which they would probably never need unless they joined the College of Pontiffs.

We proceed with the collection to find a brave man who had lost his hands in war returning to find his wife, by whom he had a son, with a paramour ; he ordered the son to kill the paramour, but he failed to do so and the latter got away. He thereupon disinherited the son (*Contr.* I, 4). In a further example a young man seduces two girls in a single night, one of whom demands his death and the other marriage, as each was entitled to do by the law : 'Rapta raptoris aut mortem aut indotatas nuptias optet ' ; the dilemma of the rhetoricians who declaimed this exercise may be imagined (*Contr.* I, 5). A priestess is thrown from the Tarpeian Rock for unchastity : she still lives and the question arises—should she be thrown down again ? (*Contr.* I, 3) And so on with the pirate's daughter and the tyrannicide and the thrice-heroic son. These exercises of the first book strike the keynote for the whole collection.

Two interesting questions, closely related to each other, are raised by these declamations. The first concerns the origins of the subjects—how far are they Greek, and how far Roman, and what kind of influences are noticeable in them ? The second is— To what extent, if at all, do they represent the contemporary life of Rome ? Are they purely imaginary, or may they be regarded as a mirror of Augustan life and conduct ?[1]

Only a minority of the subjects can be asserted with confidence to be particularly Greek or particularly Roman in origin. *Contr.* I, 3, and VI, 8, which involve Vestal Virgins, are obviously Roman, and were probably inspired by the defence of the Vestal Licinia by Crassus in 113 B.C., a famous speech.[2] Exercises concerning Metellus (IV, 2), Popillius (VII, 2), and Flamininus (IX, 2) clearly owe their origin to Roman rhetoricians, who do not, however, scruple to modify their own national history to suit their purpose[3].

---

[1] See T. S. Simonds, *Themes Treated by the Elder Seneca* (Diss., Baltimore, 1896) pp. 57 ff. ; Bornecque, *Déclam.*, pp. 75 ff. (useful parallels from later rhetoricians, followed by good criticism) ; Boissier, *op. cit.* (Eng. trans.) pp. 185-192 ; S. Rossi, ' Vita e Realtà nelle Controversie di Seneca il Retore ' (*Rivista Indo-Graeco-Italica di Filologia* II, (1918) 203 ff., and III, (1919) 13 ff. ; N. Deratani, 'Le réalisme dans les Declamationes' (*Revue de Philologie* LV [1929] pp. 184-9); M. Schamberger, *De declamationum Romanorum argumentis* (Halle, 1917) (collects parallels for a number of Senecan themes from Greek and Roman history and legend, and is useful, though not always convincing); E. Patrick Parks, *The Roman Rhetorical Schools as a Preparation for the Courts under the Early Empire* (Johns Hopkins University Studies in Historical and Political Science, Series LXIII, No. 2, Baltimore, 1945), pp. 88-97.
[2] *Ad Herennium* IV, 35, 47, (cf. Marx, *Prolegomena*, p. 106); Cic., *Brut.* 43, 160.
[3] Schamberger, p. 68, compares *Contr.* VI, 8 with the case of Postumia (334 B.C.), recounted by Livy IV, 44, *sub fin*. On Metellus (241 B.C.), cf. Cic., *Pro Scauro* 23, 48, and see O. Leuze, ' Metellus caecatus ' (*Philologus*, LXIV, 1905, pp. 95 ff.). On Popillius and Flamininus, see Bornecque vol. II, notes 60 and 182. The latter case may have been drawn from Valerius Antias.

Suas. VI and VII, on the murder of Cicero, are evidently recent inventions of Roman schools. *Contr.* IV, 8, and X, 3 are also definitely placed in the period of the Civil War, and VI, 4 refers to proscription. On the other hand, exercises concerning the Olynthian father (III, 8), the brother 'pancratiasts' (V, 3), Iphicrates (VI, 5) Phidias (VIII, 2), Parrhasius and Prometheus (X, 5), are most probably of Greek origin, as are *Suas.* I, and IV (on Alexander), II and V (on the Persian Wars) and III (on the Trojan War). *Contr.* IX, 1 (on Cimon), though historically inexact, may originally have been formed from a conflation of the accounts of Ephorus and Stesimbrotus.[1]

It has been observed[2] that themes involving tyrants and tyrannicides and pirates are more likely to have been invented in Greek than in Roman schools, on the ground that tyrants were more characteristic of Hellenistic Greece than Augustan Rome, and that pirates had ceased to be a menace since Pompey's day. This is probably fairly true as a whole, though it is not a certain criterion. The career of Caesar would give new point to discussions on tyranny[3], and there was a recrudescence of piracy under Sextus Pompeius, and again in 6-9 A.D.[4]. Exercises involving tyrants (I, 6 and 7; II, 5; III, 6; IV, 7; V, 8; VII, 6; and IX, 4) and pirates (I, 2, 6, 7; III, 3; VII, 1 and 4) also contain a good deal of evidence of contemporary Roman life, as, for instance, the *beata uxor* of *Contr.* I, 6[5], so common in Horace (*Odes* III, 24, 19; *Epp.* I, 2, 43-4; I, 6, 36 etc.), the stress laid on contemporary feminine luxury, and the Roman formula of divorce in *Contr.* II, 5, 7 and 9, the use of the genuine provisions of the *Lex Aquilia* in *Contr.* III, 6, and the allusion in § 2 to the constant danger of fire in Rome ('periculosum urbi'). Bornecque[6] gives to the credit of Roman rhetoricians those exercises which are based upon a genuine Roman law, mentioning *Contr.* I, 4, IV, 4, V, 6, X, 1, and 6; and an attempt will be made below[7] to show that there is rather more genuine Roman law in other exercises than has commonly been supposed. Furthermore, it sometimes happens that although the exercise is on a Greek subject, the controlling law contains, at least, elements of Roman legal phraseology, as in III, 8[8]. The most, in fact, that can be said is that, although such subjects were

---

[1] Schamberger, p. 15.
[2] By Bornecque, *Déclam.*, p. 77; cf. Deratani, *op. cit.*, p. 187.
[3] cf. above, p. 10, and below, p. 43.
[4] Dio Cassius, lv, 28. H. A. Ormerod, *Piracy in the Ancient World* (Liverpool, 1924), pp. 264-5, observes that the letter sent by the pirates to the relatives was probably based on actual practice, but refers the themes to New Comedy.
[5] On this exercise, see esp. S. Rossi, *op. cit.*, who considers that it reflects contemporary conditions.
[6] *Déclam.*, p. 78.
[7] pp. 108 ff.
[8] See below, p. 113, for the phrase 'coetus concursus.' Another example is IX, 1.

probably originally due to Greek ingenuity, the Romans probably took over merely the conventional characters and settings, but thoroughly Romanised the treatment of them, and adapted them to their own legal thinking.

The evidence of the declamations on the prevalence of cases of poisoning finds support in actual incidents cited by Roman historians of the Empire. The famous Cluentius case of 66 B.C. was by no means an isolated instance. In the Augustan Age there were, for example, the case involving L. Nonius Asprenas (c. 9 B.C.) who was accused by Cassius Severus[1] (particularly interesting as both were declaimers), and the *cause célèbre* (c. 19 B.C.) of Moschus, (another declaimer), defended by Pollio[2]. Tacitus (*Ann* IV, 10) reports a story of an alleged attempt by Drusus to poison his father Tiberius —an account which has been compared[3] with the theme of *Contr.* VII, 3. The declamatory cases are on the whole not far-fetched (except for the 'ter abdicatus' element in the last-named). It may be added that *Contr.* III, 9, involving poisoning, has a clearly Roman reference to appeal to the tribunes and a direct invocation of the *Lex Cornelia de sicariis et veneficis*. *Contr.* VI, 4, also concerned with poison, has a 'proscriptus' as its subject, and *Contr.* VII, 3, which deals with the question of the justification of suicide by poisoning (*pertrita quaestio*, § 7), is very similar to it in theme. Closely connected with poisoning is the subject of adultery; cf. VI, 6 (Adultera venefica); and as the elder Cato had observed that every adulteress is a potential poisoner[4], so the elder Seneca in *Contr.* VII, 3, 6, notes the close connection between the two. That adultery was prevalent in the early Empire is clear from Augustus' restrictive measure of 17 B.C. (*Lex Iulia de adulteriis*) and from the censure of Horace[5], designed to aid the Emperor's programme of moral reform. Latro's description of the subject in *Contr.* II, 7 is no doubt a rhetorical disquisition on the favourite theme of 'prolapsi mores' and 'castigatio saeculi'; but that it represents a fairly accurate picture of contemporary Rome can hardly be doubted. Augustus would have fully approved of Latro's exhortation to the Roman matron to dress with becoming modesty, mix with friends of her own age and station, lower her glance towards the ground and sacrifice politeness rather than *pudor*; though if he had a sense of humour, he might have thought it rather too much to ask her to blush to order when addressed[6].

[1] Suet., *Aug.* c. 56, 3.
[2] *Contr.* II, 5, 13 ; cf. Porphyrio on Horace, *Epp.*, I, 5, 9.
[3] By Casimir Morawski, in *Wiener Studien*, IV, (1882) p. 166. See also Simonds, *op. cit.*, pp. 89-92, Deratani, *op. cit.*, p. 185, and Parks, p. 90.
[4] Quint., V, 11, 39 ; cf. *Ad Herennium*, IV, 16, 23.
[5] *Odes*, III, 6, 17 ff., and cf. *Sat.* I, 2 for disreputable escapades; cf. Carcopino's *Daily Life in Ancient Rome* (trans. Lorimer, London, 1941) pp. 93-95.
[6] *Contr.* II, 7, 3 ' etiam in necessaria resalutandi vice multo rubore confusa sit.'

The not-quite-transparent garb of the chief offenders, noted by Latro in an indignant rhetorical expostulation, finds numerous parallels in the 'Coae vestes' of Augustan poets[1]. Several of the declamations involve moral delinquency of some kind, and although we can hardly believe that rape was anything like as common as its frequency in the exercises would suggest, there is probably more truth than imagination in the general picture of contemporary morals which they supply[2]. Indeed, a genuine *cause célèbre* sometimes was just as extraordinary as a declamatory subject; the story of the prosecution of Octavius Sagitta in 58 A.D. for the murder of a woman with whom he had committed adultery, told by Tacitus (*Ann.* XIII, 44), has all the sensational elements of declamations on such subjects—the seduction by gifts, the *conscia ancilla*, the concealed weapon, the scene of the crime in the bedchamber; and Vacca's *Life of Lucan* tells us that Lucan declaimed this very case, both for and against. Exercises on poisoning and adultery at any rate may generally be regarded, if we allow a little for rhetorical exaggeration, as reflecting Roman life.

If one were to descend to detail, one would discover in the Senecan declamations a wealth of evidence of contemporary Roman life, which has been all but neglected by historians of the subject, owing to the all-too-prevalent attitude of suspicion towards everything savouring of rhetoric. It is perfectly true that, for instance, the denunciation of contemporary luxury is a familiar rhetorical commonplace; but, nevertheless, when declaimers expatiate on large estates cultivated by slave-labour in the absence of landlords, on sumptuous villas with elaborate ceilings and tesselated pavements, even encroaching upon the sea, or on the high buildings in Rome and the frequency of fires, or on love of jewellery, effeminate and costly dress, perfumes, gluttony and feasting—they are describing for us the Rome of their day[3]. The best proof of this is that every one of these points may be paralleled from Horace—a close contemporary, whose works are accepted as a valuable source of information on conditions in the Augustan Age[4].

It is also clear that the declaimers did not move entirely in a Hellenistic or imaginary world, from the fact that sometimes subjects

---

[1] Hor., *Sat.* I, 2, 101; *Odes*, IV, 13, 13; Prop., I, 2, 2, II, 1, 5-6, IV, 2, 23, etc.
[2] cf. Bornecque, *Déclam.*, p. 94, who, *en passant*, expresses surprise that Friedländer (*Darstellungen aus der Sittengeschichte Roms*, Eng. trans., *Roman Life and Manners*, London, 1908-13) makes so little use of the declamations. Marquardt, *Das Privatleben der Römer* (2nd edn., Leipzig, 1886) includes occasional references. F. Lanfranchi, *op. cit.*, p. 246, says 'rispecchiano quasi sempre esattamente la vita sociale del tempo'—an overstatement.
[3] The examples are mainly from *Contr.* II, 1 and V, 5.
[4] See J. F. D'Alton, *Horace and His Age* (London, 1917), ch. v 'Horace and Social Problems.'

of Senecan declamations, which at first sight might seem purely fictitious, find parallels in the contemporary work of Valerius Maximus, who, though a story-teller rather than a scientific investigator, is commonly accepted as an authority for Roman History. In *Contr.* vi, 7, a father of two sons, having remarried, finds one of them mentally ill, and extracts the confession that the son is the lover of his *noverca* ; whereupon he yields the woman to him, and is accused of madness by the other son. Valerius Maximus (v, 9, 1) tells the story of a certain L. Gellius (c. 170 B.C.), who discovered that his son had committed two great crimes, ' in novercam commissum stuprum ' and attempted parricide ; but after allowing the youth to defend himself in a much-enlarged family-council, absolved him of all blame, thereby gaining a name for paternal indulgence and restraint.[1] Again, *Contr.* vii, 6, deals with the faithful slave who did not take advantage of a tyrant's permission to seduce his mistress; while the rest of the slaves, who did so, were subsequently crucified, he won his lady in marriage. Valerius (vi, 1, 3) gives the case of a daughter of Pontius Aufidianus, seduced by her slave-tutor; both were put to death at his order, ' ne turpes . . . nuptias celebraret.' But in vi, 8 Valerius gives examples of the loyalty of slaves. In *Contr.* vii, 1, the son, convicted for attempted parricide, is placed on a frail craft (' exarmato navigio '), and exposed to the mercy of winds and waves. Bornecque[2] notes that this was a punishment inflicted on *delatores* under Trajan; but it was much earlier, for, according to Suetonius (*J.C.* c. 66), Julius Caesar threatened his troops with precisely this fate. There are, then, very considerable Roman elements in the exercises; but there is also a certain stereotyped form in which they appear, and this may be due to the Greek influence.

Readers of the Senecan declamations have often been struck by the remarkably limited scope of their subjects ; the declaimers ring the changes on a small number of stock characters and situations. There seems some reason to suppose that in this respect they owed a good deal to Greek New Comedy and its Roman counterpart[3]. Quintilian not only advises declaimers to study Menander, but makes special mention of the stock characters of comedy which recur in declamation[4]. This parallelism can hardly be fortuitous, and it seems probable that the frequent opposition of the rich man and the poor man (*Contr.* ii, 1 ; v, 2 and 5 ; viii, 6 ; x, 1), the father and the son (i, 1, 4, 6, 7 ; viii, 5 ; x, 2), the well-behaved son

[1] I think that this parallel is quite as close as that of Stratonice, cited by Schamberger, pp. 38-40, Bornecque, vol. i, n. 329, Mesk, *Rh. M.* lxviii, 380.
[2] vol. ii, n. 25.
[3] Particularly the mime, cf. *Contr.* vi, 7, 2, vii, 3, 8-9.
[4] x, 1, 71 ; cf. iii, 8, 51 ; cf. above, p. 21.

and the spendthrift son (III, 3, cf. Terence, *Adelphi*) is partly due to the influence of New Comedy[1]. Situations in which a young man becomes involved with a *meretrix* and is disinherited (II, 4), or abandons himself to riotous living (II, 6, III, 1, IV, 1), were probably suggested by the stage. Some of the themes, in fact, have quite a 'romantic' plot (see esp. I, 6 ; II, 4 and VII, 1, and 4) and exercised through their descendants in the Second Sophistic, considerable influence on the later Greek novel[2]. In the novels, the capture of heroines by pirates and brigands, descriptions of storm and shipwreck, the introduction of poison-philtres, the tendency to depict stock characters rather than individuals, the love of speechifying and elaborate description, are all evidence of rhetorical treatment which dates back to the declamations of the early Empire[3]. There is also evidence that the erotic themes of the rhetorical schools had their influence upon contemporary Roman elegy, as well as the later amatory epistle[4], and that they form one of the sources of the collection of monks' tales, known as *Gesta Romanorum*[5].

These are curious affinities for a type of study which originated in the need for preliminary exercise in oratory. Granted that there are often general parallels from Roman History or contemporary life, why did the practical Roman adopt this kind of highly-flavoured, romantic, unusual theme, dealing with types instead of persons, when he might have drawn upon themes so much more closely modelled on the work of the law-courts? Quintilian gives a hint of the reason ; in defending the practice of declamation[6], he observes 'alitur enim atque enitescit velut *pabulo laetiore* facundia '—that is, this is ' richer fare ' than that of the everyday courts. Much, indeed, of Roman Civil Law must have been dull and uninspiring, dealing as it did with questions of disputes over wills, contracts, ' stillicidia,' and all the minor subjects of day-to-day litigation, an excellent list of which, from the Centumviral Courts, is given by Crassus in Cicero's *De Oratore* (I, 38, 173). The declaimers were certainly familiar with these courts, which gave some scope to the orator, but preferred on the whole to go over to the more exciting field of criminal law, and further enhanced the study by inventing novel, and even fantastic, situations

---

[1] On the other hand, the evidence of Philostratus, *Vit. Soph.* p. 481, requires to be borne in mind ; cf. above, p. 12.

[2] cf. Rohde, *Die griechische Roman*, pp. 361 ff. Rohde instances, among others, *Contr.* VII, 5, as ' eine blutige Criminalnovelle.'

[3] See F. A. Todd, *Some Ancient Novels* (Oxford, 1940), pp. 15-18, 21-22, 29-30, 36, 55-6, 81-2 etc. On the pirate-theme in New Comedy, declamation, and the novel, see also H. A. Ormerod, *op. cit.*, pp. 261-266.

[4] See A. A. Day, *op. cit.*, ch. III, ' Rhetoric.'

[5] Some parallels in Friedländer, *op. cit.* (Eng. trans.) vol. IV, pp. 297-8.

[6] X, 5, 14 ; cf. II, 10, 5 ff. and see below, chapter IV.

to attract their pupils[1]. It is in fact, a gilding of the pill ; to many readers the gilt is so opprobrious that they fail to recognise the pill, which consists in the section of the exercises called the *divisio*, where, as Quintilian well knew, there is most valuable practice in logical thinking, legal interpretation, and clear co-ordination of argument. We must, in fact, not be too easily misled into taking these exercises at their face value and, on the strength of their general subject-matter, dismiss them as the wild imaginings of disordered brains[2].

But although the subject-matter of declamation underwent this great change, an even greater development took place in the circumstances under which it was conducted ; it became a social activity, much in the same way as did the *recitatio* of verse. The declamatory subjects propounded in the *Ad Herennium* and *De Inventione* are intended only for school-pupils, or at any rate for novices in the rhetorical art, but the Senecan declamations were mostly delivered at gatherings of quite mature people. It is true that the first *controversia* was declaimed in a school when Latro and Seneca were young[3] ; and it is also true that nearly all these themes were invented for and debated in the schools, as is witnessed by their survival in the *Lesser Declamations* attributed to Quintilian, where they are prefaced by the professorial *sermo*. But most of the Senecan declamations appear to have been based upon debates where rival professors used the school-subjects to exhibit their powers and win the plaudits (or be shamed by the ridicule) of their contemporaries[4]. The exact stages in this development are not easy to determine with certainty, but were probably somewhat as follows. At first, professors of rhetoric would declaim in their schools for the benefit of their pupils, and orators at home among a few friends. So we find that Pollio (*Contr.* IV *Praef.* 2), Labienus (*Contr.* X *Praef.* 4) and Scaurus (*Contr.* X *Praef.* 3), did not admit the public to their declamations ; they were all primarily orators, not teachers. Then the professors began to invite the public to their

[1] J. W. Duff, *Literary History of Rome in the Silver Age* (London, 1927), p. 54, classifies the types of case in the *Controversiae*, and notes that criminal charges predominate ; cf. T. S. Simonds *op. cit.*, p. 69.
[2] As does, for instance, M. Jerome Carcopino, who, in his *Daily Life in Ancient Rome* (English translation, London, 1941), an admirably vivid book, fulminates with Juvenalian indignation against the rhetors (pp. 114 ff. ' Impractical Rhetoric '). My own view is at many points in accord with that expressed by E. Patrick Parks, *op. cit.*, e.g. pp. 96-7, a study which did not become accessible to me until my own MS was almost complete. But I do not agree with his political argument (cf. below, pp. 44 ff.), or his view that these themes were made fictitious because the advocate had no serious need of legal knowledge.
[3] *Contr.* I, *Praef.* 24.
[4] On this distinction between the declamations of schoolboys and adults, cf. Parks, *op. cit.*, pp. 63-4, who criticises earlier scholars on this point. But J. de Decker, *Juvenalis declamans* (Ghent, 1913), pp. 15 ff., had already made it clear.

schools on special occasions. So Albucius opened his school thus five or six times a year (*Contr.* VII *Praef.* 1), and Seneca explains that this is why he did not hear him frequently. Professors with a flair for publicity then kept more or less open school ; so Cassius Severus ' drops in ' at Cestius ' school (*Contr.* III, *Praef.* 16), and the phrase ' apud Cestium ' is used by Seneca (*Contr.* I, 3, 11 ; *Suas.* VII, 12). The orators of the older school, however, such as Labienus, viewed such displays with contempt (*Contr.* X, *Praef.* 4 ' non admittebat populum, et quia nondum haec consuetudo erat inducta[1], et quia putabat frivolae ac turpis iactationis ') but Haterius admitted the public (*Contr.* IV *Praef.* 7). The professors also began to invite parents to listen to their sons' declamations (Persius III, 45, Quint., II, 7, 1, X, 5, 21). Finally, the presence of other professors would encourage the introduction of meetings for friendly competition ; these became popular social occasions, and probably took place often in other buildings than the school itself ; even those who did not declaim publicly came to listen, and joined in the criticism and discussion. Orators like Pollio and Cassius Severus, scholars like Messala, social figures like Ovid, men of affairs like Gallio and Fabius Maximus, historians like Livy and Bruttedius Niger, were present at these declamations, some of them were attended by Maecenas and Agrippa, and by Augustus himself. So it is clear from *Contr.* II, 4, 12 that Latro was declaiming the exercise in the presence of Augustus and Agrippa in 17 B.C. These are no mere gatherings of schoolboys[2]; the maturity of their mutual criticism, not to speak of their literary criticism, the constant reference to the leading declaimers as having established reputations and pupils of their own, the whole atmosphere of the Senecan declamations is that of men of standing who found therein a means of sharpening their wits, elaborating and exhibiting their legal knowledge, and spending their leisure hours in a friendly, amusing, and by no means futile intellectual exercise.

Quite apart from the extension of the subject-matter and change of the *milieu* of declamation, the exercises which in earlier generations had formed merely a part of rhetorical doctrine were, under the Empire, so far developed within the schools themselves as to take the main place in the education of the young Roman, in which legal studies were so prominent. It has already been remarked

[1] Bornecque, in his note on this passage (vol. II, n. 239) places the introduction of ' public ' declamation about 10 A.D., that is, the admission of anyone and everyone. *Contr.* II, 4, 12 (dated 17 B.C.) probably refers to a public occasion, with a select audience.

[2] Apart from such young prodigies as Alfius Flavus—cf. *Contr.* I, 1, 22. In I, 3, 10, Quintilius Varus is ' praetextatus,' but in § 11 Pastor Aietius is ' iam senator '; in I, 2, 22 we have a former praetor, in IX, 4, 18 a consul. (cf. Edward, *op. cit.*, p. xx).

that the *controversiae* had their origin in that section of the rhetorical τέχνη which was devoted to the classification of legal issues ; they may have been originally called συστάσεις, if our emendation of Suetonius is correct. As illustrative material for the various *constitutiones causae*, they were no more prominent in a rhetorical education than the study of many other aspects of invention, arrangement, and style. But under the Empire *controversiae* and *suasoriae* became the staple education, and the terms *controversia* and *declamatio* took on a much wider significance. Both now normally meant a whole oratorical exercise, whether spoken only, or spoken and subsequently written down or published[1]. With regard to subject-matter, it is hardly necessary to stress the bad effect upon the young pupil of this concentration on erotic and often sordid themes, this devotion to point and flamboyancy of style, whatever good he may have obtained from the logical presentation of a case and the invention of novel lines of argument. No doubt the adventurous escapades of youths and maidens among pirates, and mysterious murders and poisonings made a great appeal to the young imagination, but the recurrent treatment of adultery and divorce, rape and incest, strikes a modern student as an incredible foundation for education; as incredible as would be the adoption of a collection of 'cases' from the popular Press as material for study in our schools[2].

Finally, the development, or degeneration, of declamation is seen in the very motive of the declaimer himself. 'He who prepares a declamation,' said Votienus Montanus to Seneca, ' writes not to convince but to please, and so he casts about for every possible means of seduction ; arguments, because they are a nuisance and are least attractive, he omits; he is satisfied to please the listener with point and development ; for he desires to win approval for himself, not for his case '[3]. That there is a good deal of truth in this criticism is seen from the constant reference to the

---

[1] On extensions of meaning in Sen. Rhet., cf. H. Bardon, *Le Vocabulaire de la Critique Littéraire chez Sénèque le Rhéteur* (Paris, 1940) pp. 95-6.

[2] J. W. Duff, *op. cit.*, p. 56, considers that ' the pernicious influence of some of the subjects upon the morality of pupils may easily be overstated.' No doubt the declaimers did not permit their classrooms the same degree of liberty which they permitted themselves in their professional meetings ; but Parks, *op. cit.*, p. 78, claims : ' The moral sentiment expressed throughout these and other *controversiae* cannot but have had a wholesome effect on those engaged in such exercises.' ! Contrast Boissier, *op. cit.*, p. 188, n. 3. See, more generally, the lively article of Pichon ' L'éducation romaine au Ier siècle ' (*Revue Universitaire*, IV, 1895, pp. 156-169). Mlle. Nougaro's work *L'éducation romaine au temps de Sénèque le Père* (Memoire de dipl. d' études supérieures—Faculté des Lettres de Paris, 1937) is inaccessible to me.

[3] *Contr.* IX, *Praef.* 1; cf. IX, 6, 12 (Cestius) ' multa autem dico non quia mihi placent sed quia audientibus placitura sunt.'

applause which greeted a successful sally, and from the way in which successful declaimers are idolised by their pupils. On the other hand, there is also keen rivalry, and criticism is sometimes severe; but the mutual admiration which Horace[1] found so obnoxious among contemporary poets was certainly a feature of their fellow-artists in prose.

The question which naturally suggests itself at this point is—why did declamation become so popular just at this time, and why did Augustus encourage it by his patronage? The answer is not far to seek—it lies in the changed condition of oratory which resulted from the rise of the imperial system. Many of the ancients themselves realised that their oratory had begun to suffer a decline after the fall of the Republic. 'All that Roman eloquence has to equal or surpass the arrogant claims of Greece,' says the elder Seneca[2], 'flourished in Cicero's day; all the great men who have made our studies illustrious, were born in that era, but since then the position has daily deteriorated.' His contemporary Velleius Paterculus[3] strikes the same note : ' Oratory and forensic eloquence and the perfected grace of prose style, provided that we omit Cato, (if I may say so despite Publius Crassus, Scipio, Laelius, the Gracchi, Fannius, and Servius Galba), sprang to such perfection in its principal exponent, Tullius, that one can take pleasure in very few of his predecessors, and one cannot admire anyone who either was not seen by him or did not see him.' That the imperial system 'ipsam quoque eloquentiam sicut omnia depacaverat' is the famous verdict of Messala, in the *Dialogus* ascribed to Tacitus (c.38 *sub fin.* cf. cc. 25 ff.), though Aper takes the opposite view.

Three possible causes of the decline are suggested by the elder Seneca[4]. One is that it is due to natural law ; rapid decay succeeds supreme efflorescence ; but this easy explanation is hardly satisfactory, and is, in any case, probably little more than a commonplace[5]. Albucius Silus gives a similar thought in the form of a *sententia* in *Suas.* I, 3—' quidquid ad summum pervenit incremento non relinquit (reliquit, mss) locum.'[6] Another reason given is that the general growth of luxury was responsible—a rhetorical theme[7] which Seneca expounds in some detail. His most convincing explanation is that which suggests that there was no longer, under the Empire, sufficient incentive to oratorical effort[8].

---

[1] *Epp.* II, 2, 99 ff.
[2] *Contr.* I, *Praef.* 6-7.
[3] I, 17, 3.
[4] *Contr.* I, *Praef.* 7 ff.
[5] Norden, *A.K.* I, 245 calls it ' eine weitverbreitete litterar-historische Maxime des Altertums.' cf. Vell. Pat., I, 16-17.
[6] cf. Edward's edition *ad loc.*
[7] cf. Sen., *Epp.* 114, 2; Petronius, *Sat.* 88; [Longinus], π. ὑψ. c. 44, 6-11.
[8] *loc. cit.* ' cum pretium (praemium, mss) pulcherrimae rei cecidisset, translatum est omne certamen ad turpia multo honore quaestuque vigentia.'

Under the Republic, oratory had been essential for success in public life, and the whole subject was alive and keenly debated ; but under the principate it had lost much of its political value. It was not so much that the courts had lost a great deal of their power ; there were still civil and criminal cases to attract the advocate. It was rather the lack of assured success in public life, which the good orator in Republican days could naturally expect. Under the principate, so much depended upon Imperial and Court patronage ; and it became necessary to choose one's words rather too carefully when speaking in public for the practice to be a popular one. Writing under Tiberius (if not Caligula) the elder Seneca could look back upon the Augustan Age as a time when there was ' so much liberty of speech '[1] ; but even then that freedom which the author of the *Dialogus*[2] and the philosopher in Longinus[3] consider so essential for good oratory, was fast disappearing from Roman public life[4].

And so oratory betook itself to the safer arena of the schools, where a man might air his Republicanism without fear of consequences[5], and where one might be recompensed for the loss of political prestige by the plaudits of one's fellow-citizens. The term *scholastica* came into vogue—a ' school-oration '[6] as opposed to the genuine public speech, and the exponents of these display-speeches became known as ' schoolmen '—*scholastici*. Such speeches often involved problems of interpretation of law, but the rift which Cicero had noticed between rhetorical preparation and practical oratory was widening ; and henceforth the critics of declamation constantly stress the difference between the training-ground of the schools and the battleground of real life, and between the *rhetor* and the *orator*. Some of the declaimers—men like Cassius Severus, T. Labienus, and Asinius Pollio, were also orators of great ability, but the failure in public of declaimers like Latro and Albucius only served to underline the difference of the atmosphere in which the exotic products of school-declamation were nurtured.

This is the commonly accepted explanation of the popularity of declamation in the early Empire. But it should be added at this

[1] *Contr.* II, iv, 13 ' Tanta autem sub divo Augusto libertas fuit.'
[2] c. 28.
[3] c. 44, init.
[4] cf. W. A. Edward, Introduction to his edn. of the *Suasoriae*, pp. xvi ff.
[5] At any rate under Augustus ; cf. *Contr.* x, *Praef.* 5 ' qui Pompeianos spiritus nondum in tanta pace posuisset.' Eulogies of Cato and Cicero were common. But later, from Tiberius onwards, the risks were greater; cf. Dio Cassius 59, 20, 6 and 67, 12, 5 (exile and death penalties for using school-themes on tyrants to convey anti-monarchical sentiments). cf. Boissier, *L'opposition sous les Césars* (Paris³, 1892), pp. 93-7.
[6] In *C.R.* LXI (1947), p. 86, I have endeavoured to show that this word is a feminine singular, not a neuter plural, as it is generally said to be in the Lexica.

point that in a recent work[1] on the relationship between the rhetorical schools and the courts of law, this view has been challenged. The arguments there advanced[2] are as follows : ' (i) the courts continued to function under the emperors with little established evidence of restriction, and were even over-worked ; (ii) the advocates found ample opportunity for eloquence, (iii) the rhetorical schools . . . continued to offer a practical preparation for these advocates.' This view contains much truth, but (ii) is based on the doubtful assumption that there was equal opportunity for great oratory in the courts of law which dealt with non-political cases and in the major criminal courts and the public assemblies. It deserves, however, careful consideration.

There was undeniably a great amount of legal activity under the early Empire, and the extension of the *fora*[3] is good evidence for it. That there were considerable financial advantages for advocates[4] is probable, though the evidence for it is rather later than the period of the Senecan declamations, and Augustus did revive the *Lex Cincia*, which forbade the taking of fees[5]. It is argued[6] that the Emperor did not interfere with the course of justice, but actively furthered it; this is largely true of Augustus, though he was checked on one occasion for undue severity[7], but it is not quite so certain of his ministers[8], and it is even less certain, for political cases, under Tiberius. It is implied, in support of this belief in non-interference, that much of the legal business transacted, particularly in the civil courts, was of too trifling a character to merit the Emperor's attention[9]. This is true, but it is also the strongest argument against the belief that great oratory is equally likely on such restricted themes.

In defence of this last opinion, the author says[10] that Cicero's *Pro Caecina*, which is concerned with a minor civil case, ' compares very well with the other speeches of Cicero, and manifests the usual eloquence of the author, which is definite proof that the highest eloquence was very possible even through a strictly limited legal medium.' No doubt it may be possible, but it is extremely unlikely, and the purely personal opinion expressed of the *Pro Caecina* is anything but 'definite proof,' especially in face of Tacitus'

[1] E. P. Parks, *op. cit.*
[2] p. 19.
[3] Suet., *Aug.* c. 29 ; Parks, p. 55.
[4] Parks, pp. 56 ff., relying mainly on Martial, Pliny's *Letters*, and the later books of Tacitus, *Annals*.
[5] Dio LIV, 18 ; Parks, p. 58, says this ' proved injudicious,' but it was nevertheless a restriction, though doubtless often evaded.
[6] pp. 32 ff.
[7] Dio LV, 7.
[8] e.g. Maecenas, Dio LIV, 30, 4 (actively aiding a man on trial).
[9] pp. 32, 36.
[10] p. 31.

statement[1], which has received strong modern approval[2], that the speech is an inordinately long one on a trifling subject, and that it is the *Verrines*, the *Catilinarians*, the *Pro Milone*, and the *Philippics* that make the orator's reputation.[3] These are mainly *criminal* cases of the highest political importance, and it is impossible to believe that they could have been treated with equal freedom under the Empire. The evidence of the author of the *Dialogus* cannot be thus lightly dismissed, even if the Tacitus of the *Annals* is biased. The author himself admits that the ordinary courts and the centumviral court in particular presented the most fertile fields of activity for the pleader, and that these courts dealt principally with non-political cases[4]. Now Messala says distinctly that none of the great orators of the Republican period made their reputation in the centumviral courts, although these courts were in existence at the time[5]. So Pliny, *Epp.* II, 14, says of centumviral cases : ' sunt enim pleraeque parvae et exiles, raro incidit vel personarum claritate vel negotii magnitudine insignis.'

We may now turn to the final argument, that the rhetorical schools were the only source of these pleaders at the bar[6]. If we accept the sharp distinction made by Schulz[7] between jurisconsults and advocates, this may be true. But it is at least worth while to remember that special schools of law existed under the early Empire, such as that instituted by Labeo, and that formed by Masurius Sabinus and Cassius ; the former began under Augustus, and the latter was flourishing long before the declamations ascribed to Quintilian were written[8]. They replaced the old Republican system whereby a young man attached himself to a distinguished lawyer and learnt his profession by apprenticeship and actual experience[9]. But if we believe that the advocates were not admitted to these newly-formed law-schools, the question still remains whether the training of the declamatory schools was a practical preparation for the courts, for very many young Romans certainly spent the formative years of their youth in them.[10]

The answer to this question will depend partly on the relationship of the declamatory 'laws' to Roman statutes and praetorian legislation, a full enquiry into which is made below[11]. But the chief

1 *Dial.* c. 20 (Aper), which Parks cites.
2 Forsyth, *Life of Cicero*, p. 52 ' it would be impossible to make the case interesting '; quoted by Sandys on Cic., *Orat.* 29, 102.
3 *Dial.* c. 37 (Messala).
4 p. 36.
5 *Dial.* c. 38.
6 Parks, p. 19.
7 *History of Roman Legal Science* (Oxford, 1946) p. 71.
8 *ib.*, pp. 119 ff.
9 Tac., *Dial.* c. 34 ; Schulz, pp. 57,8.
10 Even the *grammatici* produced successful advocates, acc. to Suet., *De Gramm.* c. 4.
11 Chapters v and vi.

argument used by Parks[1] is that the declamatory schools, gave a training in equity, and this is absolutely true. The practice of distinguishing in a given case between the strict wording of the law (*ius*) and the claims of equity (*aequitas*) would be of value to the advocate. Cicero tells us in the *Brutus* that Crassus won a case in the centumviral court, against the famous Q. Mucius Scaevola (pontifex), where the point was essentially one of law, by pressing the claims of equity[2]. This was the well-known *causa Curiana*, which came before the centumviral court (?, in 137 B.C.). It was the case of a man who instructed in his will that if his wife bore a son after his death the son should be his heir, but that if the son died before reaching maturity, the inheritance should revert to M'. Curius. No son was in fact born, but M'. Curius still claimed the inheritance ; this was contested by the nearest agnate, M. Coponius, but the case went in the favour of Curius. Scaevola, with the characteristic attitude of the Republican jurist, maintained, in Coponius' favour, the strict literal interpretation of the will. Crassus, on the other hand, pressed the *voluntas* of the testator. The case became celebrated because it involved a dramatic contest of two opposing principles. Cicero says[3] of Crassus that his strength lay ' in explicanda aequitate ' ; he defended ' aequum bonum ' against the letter, and argued that there was danger of ' in verbis captio, cum in ceteris rebus tum in testamentis, si neglegerentur voluntates.'[4] Similarly, Cicero himself in the *Pro Caecina*[5] bases his case on the intention of the interdict rather than on its exact verbal implication, and contrasts *ius* and *verborum vis* with *aequitas* and *voluntas*. Both of these examples are given by Stroux, in a well-known brochure[6] to which we shall recur. At any rate, it is so far clear that, although the declaimers may have been over-fond of dividing any and every case into *ius* and *aequitas*, they could hope, as advocates, to transfer that treatment to the courts with every chance of success. Quintilian[7] tells us that some judges were particularly inclined to favour arguments based on *aequitas*, and it was not for nothing that every schoolboy in Cicero's day was taught to argue for ' equity ' against the letter of the statute[8].

[1] pp. 78 ff.
[2] 39, 145 ff. ' ita enim multa tum contra scriptum pro aequo et bono dixit, ut hominem acutissimum Q. Scaevolam et in iure, in quo illa causa vertebatur, paratissimum obueret.'
[3] *ib.* 144.
[4] *ib.* 53, 198; cf. *De Orat.* I, 39, 180, II, 32, 140 ff.; *Pro Caecina* 18, 53.
[5] chapters 19-22.
[6] *Summum Ius Summa Iniuria* (Festschrift Paul Speiser-Sarasin, Leipzig, 1926), pp. 28-33.
[7] VII, 1, 63 ' nihil libentius iudices audiunt. '
[8] *De Orat.* I, 57, 244.

Can a similar claim for the value and influence of this kind of thinking be made for Roman jurisprudence, that is, not merely for the advocate and judge but for the jurisconsult, the member of that limited circle of men who gave official advice upon the law ? Here there is a sharp division of opinion among scholars. It is well-known that this treatment according to *ius* and *aequitas* is merely a general manifestation of the detailed doctrine of the στάσεις νομικαί, the origins of which are at least as old as Aristotle and the *Rhetorica ad Alexandrum*, and which were fully formulated by Hermagoras long before they appeared in Cicero's youthful *De Inventione*[1]. Stroux, expounding this theory from the *De Inventione*, maintained that it represented ' eine vollständige rhetorische Theorie der Gesetzesauslegung,'[2] and pointed not only to the *causa Curiana* and the *Pro Caecina*, but to the fact that a jurist such as S. Sulpicius Rufus was praised by Cicero (*Phil.* IX, 10) on account of ' paene divina eius in legibus interpretandis, *aequitate explicanda* scientia,' for ' semper ad facilitatem *aequitatemque* referebat[3]. ' Similarly, Stroux[4] observes that Cicero's own *Topica*, addressed to the jurist Trebatius, is declared useful ' iuris etiam peritis.' Stroux, however, produced little evidence from the legal sources and his citations are not free from suspicion of interpolation (e.g. *Dig.* I, 3 ; L, 16, 116). The criticism with which his arguments met at the time[5] has recently been supported by Schulz[6], who argues that such appeals to the hypothetical intention of the legislator simply reflect Greek philosophical and rhetorical thought and would be merely misleading in the solution of a given case ; he adds that *aequitas* does not occur in Republican legal texts. Buckland[7], though not altogether unfavourable, was not disposed to rate highly the *aequitas* arguments, and noted that Cicero's own ideas of what constituted *aequitas* seemed to fluctuate.

The evidence of the legal sources has not yet been fully examined, but the useful dissertation of Himmelschein[8] analyses passages from several books of the *Digest* from this point of view. He rightly argues that the antithesis *verba*) (*voluntas* is one of the main keynotes of the rhetorical system and shows that, quite apart

1 See above, p. 14; Quint., VII, chapters 6-9, is a good account of them.
2 *op. cit.* pp. 18-19.
3 *ib.* p. 41.
4 p. 36.
5 *Z.S.S.* XLVIII (1927) 668 ff. (Levy) ; *Phil. Woch.* XLVII (1927) 915 ff. (Kübler). Riccobono, in *Gnomon* V (1929) 65-87, and *Annali del Seminario Giuridico di Palermo* XII (1929) pp. 639-647, was most favourable. See, also, however, H. F. Jolowicz, ' Academic Elements in Roman Law ' (*L.Q.R.* XLVIII, 1932, pp. 171 ff.); add Steinwenter in *Z.S.S.* LXV (1947) (too late for use).
6 *op. cit.* pp. 74-5.
7 *Text Book*, pp. 52-55. But see further his *Equity in Roman Law* (London, 1911).
8 *Studien zu der antiken Hermeneutica Iuris* (Leipzig, 1935).

from the tendency of rhetorically-influenced Byzantine glossators to stress *voluntas* in any case, many of the passages where the antithesis occurs are probably interpolated[1]. But he admits that there are several perfectly sound texts, and it is interesting to note (in view of the *causa Curiana*) that these texts generally refer either to cases of will or to cases of contract (cf. Pliny, *Epp.* II, 16). Such are *Dig.* XXXIII, 10, 7, 2 where Servius stresses the literal interpretation and Tubero the intention of the testator ('quorsum nomina, inquit, nisi ut demonstrarent voluntatem dicentis ?'); Papinian, XXXV, 1, 101 pr. 'cum in condicionibus testamentorum voluntatem potius quam verba considerari oporteat'; *Dig.* L, 16, 219 (again Papinian) 'in conventionibus contrahentium voluntatem potius quam verba spectari placuit.' Similarly, not all texts dealing with *ambiguitas* are interpolated[2] e.g. XXXIV, 5, 26 (27) 'cum quaeritur in stipulatione, quid acti sit, ambiguitas contra stipulatorem est' ('ein Musterbeispiel rein juristischer Behandlung')[3]. The essential part of XXXII, 62, 1 is not interpolated and is remarkably close in spirit to the examples of *ambiguitas* cited by Quintilian : 'qui duos mulos habebat ita legavit : ' mulos duos qui mei erunt cum moriar [Seio] heres dato '; idem nullos mulos sed duas mulas reliquerat. Respondit Servius deberi legatum.'[4] Himmelschein finds little or no juristic evidence for *contrariae leges* and the syllogism[5], but leaves the general question open, noting that the practical Roman jurist did not normally think in rhetorical categories, but adding that in the study of conflict between *verba* and *voluntas* 'ist die Denkweise der römischen Juristen von den Rhetoren nicht unbeeinflusst geblieben.'[6] Finally Lanfranchi[7] maintains the view of Stroux, using the declamations as further evidence. But, in spite of modern disagreements, perhaps the strongest testimony of all is that of Quintilian[8], who says expressly : ' scripti et voluntatis frequentissima inter *consultos* quaestio est, et pars magna controversi iuris hinc pendet ; quo minus id accidere in scholis mirum est, ubi etiam ex industria fingitur.'[9]

But, although the rhetorical schools were preparing their pupils to be advocates, there were, of course, certain differences of

[1] pp. 393-6, 398-409.
[2] Himmelschein, pp. 409-417; but many passages, as he shows, are suspect.
[3] p. 412.
[4] p. 410.
[5] pp. 418-9.
[6] p. 423-4. See, likewise, Cousin, *op. cit.* I, p. 378.
[7] *Il Diritto nei Retori Romani* (Milan, 1938) pp. 65 ff., 108 ff. He likewise refers the consilium) (eventus division to the legal sources, e.g. in *Contr.* x, 3 (pp. 96 ff.).
[8] VII, 6, 1.
[9] cf. XII, 3, 7 'at quae *consultorum responsis* explicantur, aut in verborum interpretatione sunt posita aut in recti pravique discrimine.'

treatment between the school declamation and the court case. The element of display[1] in the schools was so marked that it led to digressions and verbal sophistries which could hardly have been tolerated in the courts, even by judges who had an ear for an occasional *bon mot*. Declamatory appeals to the emotions could likewise hardly have been effective, for Cicero[2] in an interesting passage, makes a distinction between the type of pleading one uses before a judge, based on evidence, and the type of pleading one uses before a parent, based on emotion. His example of the latter is 'ignoscite, iudices ; erravit, lapsus est, non putavit ; si umquam posthac... etc' —phraseology which is precisely similar to that used by the declaimers when they press their favourite excuses in defence of a disinherited son. Nor can we ignore the many points made by the adverse critics of declamation throughout the first century A.D.[3]. Even though we may find that there was considerable legal knowledge among the declaimers, to argue that the schools were the one and only source of advocates would be to stress unduly the serious side of this σπουδαιογέλοιον and to ignore the pleasantries, not to say the follies, of what had become a social rather than a purely legal activity.

When young pupils declaimed, it is probable that they competed before a master, who criticised their efforts, and then gave them a model of his own composition[4]; and when the practice extended to public gatherings of adults the whole approach became even more competitive. A considerable number of speakers declaimed on the same subject, which might extend over some days[5], their aim being to excel their predecessors in brilliance of epigram, originality of comment, vividness of description, ingenuity of argument, and subtlety of misrepresentation. Improvisation became a useful gift, and an increasingly common feature of declamation[6].

Very often 'comments' passed from one speaker to another with little real change of point, but with slight variety of expression. Sometimes a saying was taken up with eagerness (*exceptus*) and bandied about the city as the latest example of wit or concentrated brilliance[7]. But the repetition of subjects and the succession of speakers caused them frequently to express the same idea in more

[1] cf. Quint., II, 10, 12 'aliquid in se habet ἐπιδεικτικόν' (sc. declamatio).
[2] *Pro Ligario*, 10, 30.
[3] cf. below, c. IV; cf. p. 52 below, for impersonation replacing advocacy.
[4] Quint., I, 2, 23-4; II, 4, 12; II, 6, 1 ff. cf. Edward, *op. cit.*, *Introd.* p. xxi, for a sketch of class-room procedure.
[5] *Contr.* I, 7, 13 'cum postero die declamaret,' II, 1, 26 'postero die quam erat a Fabiano dicta declamavit.'
[6] *Contr.* IV, *Praef.* 7, VII, *Praef.* 2; cf. J. F. D'Alton, *op. cit.*, p. 210 and n. 10.
[7] For *exceptus* cf. *Contr.* II, 1, 28; II, 2, 9; *Suas.* V, 6; VI, 9; cf. *Contr.* II, 4, 9, 'sententiam quam Fabius Maximus *circumferebat*.'

and more heightened fashion until ultimately it reached the absurd[1]. The later a speaker came in the series, the more difficult it was for him to be both original and sensible; the audience had a keen sense of this difficulty, and although a successful effort received their acclamation[2], any over-stepping of the line aroused their derision[3]. So declamation had become a kind of game, but, in its way, a highly intellectual game, which called for ingenuity and agility of mind and considerable legal skill, and was even at this stage by no means without practical value. What, then, were the rules of the game?

---

[1] A good example is *Contr.* VII, 2, 14 regarding the arrival of Cicero's assassin, Popillius. Latro says simply 'Popillius, ut venit, admissus est'; Cestius goes one better, and makes Cicero say 'Popillio semper vaco'; Cornelius Hispanus makes him actually complain 'Popilli, tam sero ?'! See further, Boissier, *op. cit.*, p. 187.
[2] *Contr.* I, 8, 12 'valde laudata,' II, 1, 36 'magnis excepta clamoribus'; II, 3, 19 'summo fragore'; II, 4, 8 etc. See further C. Morawski, *De rhetoribus latinis observationes* (Cracow, 1892), pp. 2-5.
[3] *Contr.* I, 7, 10 'Haec sententia deridebatur a Latrone tamquam puerilis'; I, 7, 18 'sententiam dixit dubiam inter admirantes et deridentes.'

CHAPTER III

THE PROCEDURE OF THE DEVELOPED DECLAMATION AND ITS CHIEF RHETORICAL CHARACTERISTICS

When the company had assembled, in a school or hall hired for the purpose if the declamation was to be public, or perhaps in the house of one of the professors if it was to be private[1], a subject would first be selected by general agreement; sometimes a number of alternatives would be offered by a particular declaimer who was to display his powers[2]. Once the subject (*thema*[3] or *materia*) was clearly announced, it would be the duty of each declaimer to abide strictly by the set of circumstances (*positio*) envisaged; he would be at liberty to use the utmost ingenuity in alleging motive, in relating one act to another within the theme, in explaining away an awkward situation, provided he did not alter the facts of the case; this would be to upset the theme (*thema evertere*)[4] and defeat the object of the declamation. To avoid this, the rhetoricians trained in the school of Apollodorus particularly insisted that the themes should be precise and well-determined[5]; but the general practice was for the theme to be sufficiently loose to allow latitude for interpretation and originality[6]. The same speakers often debated the same theme both for and against, in Latin and then in Greek[7], and it was a sign of ability to adopt the more difficult side[8].

Once the subject had been announced, the first speaker would make a few preliminary remarks (*praelocutio, praefatio*)[9], while still seated, but would normally rise to make the speech itself. It was regarded as unusual and worthy of comment that Latro outlined his main points while still seated (*Contr.* I, *Praef.* 21), and that Albucius only rose when carried away by his own

---

1 The exact *locale* is extremely difficult to assess (cf. O. Gruppe, *Quaestiones Annaeanae* [Sedini, 1873] pp. 26-7), but phrases like 'apud Cestium' (*Contr*, I, 3, 11, *Suas.* VII, 12 etc.) probably refer to the school. The important distinction is between public and private gatherings—cf. *Contr.* IV, *Praef.* 7 'admisso populo,' X, *Praef.* 4 'non admittebat populum.'
2 cf. Pliny, *Epp.* II, 3, 2, 'poscit (ponit) controversias plures, electionem auditoribus permittit.'
3 cf. Quint., VII, 1, 4 'nam in schola certa sunt et pauca et ante declamationem exponuntur quae themata Graeci vocant, Cicero proposita.'
4 *Contr* IX, 5, 10-11, cf. II, 3, 11; Quint., IV, 2, 28, 90, XII, 8, 6.
5 *Contr.* I, 2, 14.
6 cf. Quint., II, 10, 14-15.
7 *Contr.* IX, 3, 13 'illos semper admiraretur, qui non contenti unius linguae eloquentia, cum Latine declamaverant, toga posita sumpto pallio quasi persona mutata redibant et Graece declamabant' etc. cf. Pliny, *Epp.* IV, 11, 3.
8 cf. *Contr.* X, 4, 17, Bornecque, *Déclam.* p. 90.
9 *Contr.* III, *Praef.* 11 'Silo Pompeius sedens et facundus et litteratus est et haberetur disertus, si a praelocutione dimitteret; declamat tam male ut videar belle optasse cum dixi: numquam surgas.' Pliny, *Epp.* II, 3, 1, 'praefationes tersae.' Gellius IX, 15, 4 implies that the *praefatio* sometimes had little to do with the exercise itself.

exuberance (*Contr.* VII, *Praef.* 1, Suet. *de Rhet.* c. 6). Normally, in his preliminary remarks, the speaker would give a brief sketch of the case, and indicate which side he intended to take. This practice of giving a preliminary sketch had its dangers in actual pleading, for Quintilian tells us (IV 1, 3-4) that it led declaimers to omit relevant information in the proem, and to assume in court that the judge was already familiar with the case. A point of some consequence was whether the speaker should use the first or third person[1]. According to Quintilian (IV, 1, 46), a free choice was allowed in the schools between adopting the character of a party to the suit and acting as an advocate; in actual practice an advocate would generally be employed. In most *controversiae* the speaker would imagine himself in the position of the accuser or defendant and act the part[2], but there were certain circumstances in which it was the custom to 'grant an advocate' (*patronum dare*)[3], and to defend or, less commonly, to accuse in the third person. If, for instance, the person bringing the action should be a woman, she would not speak for herself in a declamation any more than she would, normally, in actual practice, as this would offend the Roman sense of decorum[4]. This is a rule which appears to be generally observed not only in the declamations of Seneca but also in those ascribed to Quintilian. Similarly, a slave would not conduct his own case either in court or in a declamation[5]; and even a citizen who had forfeited his right to speak through being a depraved character, or who was on trial for treason[6], would not declaim *in propria persona*, but would require to be represented by a 'patronus.' These instances conform to legal practice. A further example of the general sense of decorum is the fact that in certain circumstances, even a free citizen might prefer not to speak for himself, if, for instance, as a son, he should have to attack his own father and thereby offend the Roman conception of the dignity of the *pater familias*[7]. The practice of the declaimers is clearly summed up in the professorial advice (*sermo*) given in the 260th of the lesser declamations ascribed to Quintilian. 'In

---

[1] cf. W. Hoffa, *De Seneca patre quaestiones selectae* (Diss. Göttingen, 1909) pp. 46 ff.
[2] Quint., III, 8, 51 'declamatoribus ... qui paucissimas controversias ita dicunt ut advocati.'
[3] *Contr.* I, 7, 13; II, 6, 10; VII, 2, 13.
[4] With certain exceptions in practice—e.g. a woman could act as accuser in the case of the murder of her husband. Valerius Maximus VIII 3 gives an account of women who 'apud magistratus pro se aut pro aliis causas egerunt.' cf. also Juvenal's attack in *Sat.* VI, 242 ff.
[5] cf. *Contr.* III, 9.
[6] *Contr.* IX, 2, X, 4, 15 ff., X, 5, 17.
[7] cf. *Contr.* II, 6, 10, where Silo Pompeius grants the son a *patronus*, but Latro dispenses with this device; so in I, 7, 13.

many exercises we generally make a point of inquiring whether we should speak in our own person or in the character of an advocate ; either on account of the sex, as in the case of women, or on account of some unpleasantness in the general life of the character concerned or in the nature of the act under consideration.' Even when the declaimer spoke as a *patronus* he was frequently able to enhance the vividness of his speech by direct quotation of alleged remarks of his client—a favourite device—but the use of the first person would be particularly desirable in declamations which turn largely on emotional features.

A similar choice, between the first and second person, lay before the declaimer of a *suasoria*, though the purpose of that exercise—to train the speaker in deliberative oratory—occasioned a much wider use of the direct address ; the object of a *suasoria* was ' consilium dare '[1]—to give advice to a person in a dilemma : only in one of the seven Senecan *suasoriae* do the speakers act the part of the person himself, viz. III (' Deliberat Agamemnon an Iphigeniam immolet, negante Calchante aliter navigari fas esse '), and the exercise becomes thereby a soliloquy, known as *prosopopoeia*[2]. Isidore[3] indeed only allows the former type to be called *suasoria* and distinguishes the latter by the name of *deliberativa*. But in *controversiae* the declaimer would generally find himself taking the part of a father or a son, a rich man or a poor man, a tyrannicide or an injured husband, and he would particularly seek to represent that character as faithfully as possible ; to do so was to speak *ethicos* and to earn the compliments of one's fellow-rhetoricians[4].

After the preliminary remarks came the declamation proper. It is unfortunate that the works of the elder Seneca do not contain any example of a complete declamation[5] ; he gives citations and general comments which are of inestimable value for our knowledge of the subject, but his division of his work into 'sententiae, divisiones et colores' tends to obscure the original form of the speeches as they were delivered. For this it is necessary to read the collections ascribed to Quintilian, which include complete

---

[1] *Suas.* VI, 11, ' itaque Cassius Severus aiebat alios declamasse, Varium Geminum unum *consilium dedisse*.' So Juvenal I, 16, is using strictly correct rhetorical terminology when he says ' *consilium dedimus* Sullae . . . .' cf. Quint., III, 8, 46. ' unum ' (as opposed to ' alios ') is more likely to be the right reading in Seneca than ' vivum,' read by Kiessling and Edward. ' consilium dedisse ' as a technical phrase does not need ' vivum ' to qualify it.
[2] cf. Quint., III, 8, 49 ; Theon, *Progymn.* c. 10 (= II, 115, Spengel).
[3] *De Rhet.* IV, 4 (*R.L.M.* p. 508).
[4] *Contr.* II, 3, 23 ; II, 4, 8, ' Albucius ethicos, ut multi putant, dixit (certe laudatum est cum diceret)'; *Suas.* I, 13 ; Quint., III, 8, 51, IV, 1, 47.
[5] *Contr.* II, 7 is the nearest approach to it; it is the best example of Latro's consecutive prose that has survived, but even so is incomplete. Schoolboys, and others, kept notebooks of approved passages, cf. Quint., II, 11, 7.

speeches. But the 'Lesser Declamations' ascribed to Quintilian are merely school-models prepared by the master for his pupils, and neither they nor the 'Longer Declamations' quite capture the wit and brilliance which must have characterised a speech of Latro or Gallio. It is clear from Seneca's occasional comments that the declamation itself followed the oratorical form laid down in rhetorical handbooks for many centuries, namely the four-fold division into proem, narrative, proofs, and peroration[1]. So his quotations are mentioned as having occurred *in prooemio* (VII, 1, 26; X, 1, 13) *in narratione*[2] (I, 1, 21; II, 6, 9; IX, 4, 16) *in argumentis* (I, 6, 9; VII, 1, 21; X, 3, 16; X, 4, 15; X, 5, 17), or *in epilogo* (I, 7, 15; VII, 4, 6; [*in epilogis*]; VII, 4, 8; IX, 6, 12). The declaimers did not always make their speech-divisions obvious, but sought to effect neat transitions from one section to another, cf. *Contr.* I, 1, 25 'transiit a prooemio in narrationem eleganter,' 8, 1 'sic descendit in narrationem.' But some overdid this practice by trying to make every transition by means of a *sententia*[3], and the common expedient of using such stereotyped formulae as ' quid porro ?' ' quid quod ?' ' quid referam ?' in passing from one topic to another was by no means elegant[4].

The question which immediately arises is: 'What exactly were the *sententiae*, *divisiones*, and *colores*, and how were they related to the four major divisions of a declamation ?' The *sententia*, the brief pointed comment, aptly summing up some aspect of life or of the case, which became so characteristic of post-Augustan prose and poetry, could occur in any or all of the four subdivisions; the speeches of the declaimers scintillated with *sententiae*, and Quintilian's criticism of their excessive use (VIII, 5, 31 ' nec multas plerique sententias dicunt, sed omnia tamquam sententias ') is well applicable to many of them[5]. A few examples from the many *sententiae* which are found in the pages of the elder Seneca may be given at this point :—*Contr.* I, 1, 3 ' omnis instabilis et incerta felicitas est '; I, 2, 10 ' nulla satis pudica est, de qua quaeritur,' I, 6, 5 ' omnes uxores divites servitutem exigunt,' *ib.* 7 ' impotens malum est beata uxor,' I, 8, 3 ' optimus virtutis finis est antequam deficias desinere,' II, 1, 28 ' nihil est indecentius novicio divite,' II, 6, 4 ' non coercet vitia qui provocat,' II, 7, Exc., ' muliebrium vitiorum fundamentum avaritia est,' V, 1, 1 ' spes est ultimum adversarum rerum solacium,' VII, 1, 10 ' magnum praesidium

---

[1] Dating back to Isocrates; cf. Dion. Hal., *De Lysia*, c. 16, sub fin.; Arist., *Rhet.* III, 13.
[2] cf. Quintilian's strictures on the declaimers' over-fondness for narration, in IV, 2, 28-9, and 128.
[3] Quint., IV, 1, 77.
[4] See J. de Decker, *op. cit.*, pp. 127-8.
[5] cf. Norden, *A.K.* I, 280 ff.; de Decker, *op. cit.*, pp. 155 ff.

in periculis innocentia,' IX, 1, 2 'non potest generosus animus contumeliam pati,' IX, 4, 5 'necessitas magnum humanae imbecillitatis patrocinium est,' X, 3, 5 ' optima civilis belli defensio oblivio est,' *ib.* 14 'ne mitissimus quidem victor statim ignovit' etc. These are closely allied to the proverb; occasionally, indeed, a proverb appears, as II, 6, 4 'navem in portu mergis', *Suas.* II,13 'hic meus est dies'; but they probably owe more to the mime, as written by Publilius Syrus, for Seneca makes special mention of the *Publiliana sententia* in connection with declamation[1].

But the declamations would make poor reading if they consisted merely of *sententiae* of this gnomic type. Frequently they have a purely local rather than a universal application, and are sharpened by antithesis or subtle allusiveness. 'Non quaerimus orbem sed amittimus,' says Alexander's adviser at the shores of Ocean (*Suas.* I, 2); 'quantum suspicor, ne rapta quidem es', hints Cestius of the girl whose option was for marriage (*Contr.* I, 5, 1). The desire for novelty led often to improbability and obscurity, one result of the search for sententious brevity being the cultivation of paradox, of which *Contr.* I, 5, 2 'perieras, raptor, nisi bis perire meruisses' is a typical example[2]. Almost Gorgianic in its paradox and antithesis is *Suas.* VII, 4 'causa illis vivendi fuit fortiter mori [velle]'; quite ridiculous is *Contr.* III, 7, 2 'ipse sui et alimentum erat et damnum.'

The term *color* had, before Seneca's day, been applied only as a general word for 'cast' or 'tone' of style[3], and was clearly used to represent the Greek χρῶμα[4]. But in Seneca it takes on the quite different meaning[5] of 'twist of argument,' 'plea,' 'excuse'; and it is very interesting to note, in view of the legal associations of the *controversiae*, that the term 'color insaniae' survives in the *Digest*[6], meaning a 'plea of insanity,' in connection with the *querela inofficiosi testamenti*. The *colores*, though often so expressed that they were themselves *sententiae*, would mainly occur in the section devoted to *argumenta*, though they would be foreshadowed in the *narratio* (*Contr.* IV, 3, 3, cf. VII, 1, 20). They were arguments, often pithily expressed, which threw a different light on the actions of the defendant or accuser. Making black white and the reverse was the age-old prerogative of the pleader, but the *colores* of the

---

[1] *Contr.* VII, 3, 8-9; cf. Sen. phil., *Epp.* 8, 8.
[2] cf. Bornecque, *Déclam.*, pp. 108 and 112.
[3] cf. Cic., *De Orat.* III, 25, 96; 52, 199 (both qualified with *quasi* and/or *quidam*; *Brut.* 44, 162; 46, 171; so likewise *colorare*, *De Orat.* II, 14, 60; *Orat.* 13, 42; *Brut.* 46, 170.
[4] Dion. Hal., *De Thuc.* c. 42; *Ep. ad Amm.* II, c. 2; *De Comp. Verb.* cc. 4, 20, et al.
[5] cf. Bardon, *op. cit.*, pp. 19-20 and p. 96. In *Contr.* X, *Praef.* 5 it bears the meaning 'cast of style.' Ovid, *Trist.* I, 9, 63, Juv., *Sat.* VI, 280, VII, 155 are exx. of the new usage in Latin; [Dion. Hal.], *Ars Rhet.* VIII, 3 in Greek.
[6] V, 2, 5; cf. Just. *Inst.* II, 18, init.; Buckland, *Text-Book* pp. 324 ff. See below, pp. 93-4.

declaimers were something more subtle ; by a slight shift of argument, by an added insinuation, or a guileless plea, they tone down the guilt or represent it in even more glaring colours. The *colores* are the Persian carpet of the declaimer ; look at it from one angle and the colours are bright and clear, the pattern simple, but observe it from another angle, and the shade deepens, the pattern changes, and the whole appears in a different light.

The really clever *colores* are those which depend on insinuation for their effect : but many of them were stupid, unconvincing, the products of exhausted ingenuity[1]. So the defendant will excuse his action by saying that he had a dream which induced him to do what he did—an old device so overdone in the books of *colores* published by Junius Otho that they earned the ridicule of more sensible declaimers like Gallio (*Contr.* II, 1, 33)[2]. ' It is ridiculous,' says Seneca, apropos of this, ' to invent arguments which cannot be proved,' though he does Otho justice by showing that he was well able to invent *colores* of a more subtle and convincing kind (*ib.* 37 ' solebat hos colores, qui silentium et significationem desiderant, bene dicere '). Or again, the argument would be used that the culprit had been deterred by omens (*Contr.* I, 8, 15 ; II, 1, 27) or other supernatural manifestation (I, 2, 21), or overcome by emotion (I, 8, 5), or that he was really only intending to test the other person (II, 2, 7; VII, 3, 7), or that he thought he himself was being tested (VII, 1, 7, 21; VIII, 3, 1), or that he thought the other person didn't really mean what he said (I, 1, 18), or that he himself didn't really mean it (V, 3, 2), or that someone else had persuaded him (II, 3, 20), or even that he was intoxicated at the time (IX, 2, 20). Any port in a storm ; after hours of listening to every possible argument that could be raked up to throw a different light on the case, it is small wonder that the mental exhaustion of the declaimers restricted their output to these weak and futile points.

More important than either *sententiae* or *colores* was the *divisio*, for this was the skeleton plan of the whole argument—its function was ' ostendere ossa et nervos controversiae,' as the author of *Decl. Min.* 270 says. Its normal place would, of course, be immediately after the narrative, for the name *divisio* signifies the dividing up of the various arguments and the placing of them in the most effective order—cf. the remarks of Quint., VII, 10, 6. Latro seems to have sketched out in his prefatory remarks the general plan of argument which he intended to follow[3] ; but he

[1] Bornecque, *Déclam.*, pp. 101-2, gives some good examples.
[2] cf. Petron., *Sat.* 10 ' somniorum interpretamenta' ; Quint., IV, 2, 94.
[3] *Contr.* I, *Praef.* 21, ' antequam dicere inciperet, sedens, quaestiones eius, quam dicturus erat, controversiae proponebat.' Cicero, *Brutus,* 88, 303 tells us that Hortensius sketched out beforehand ' partitiones quibus de rebus dicturus esset ' ; cf. Quint., IV, 5, 24.

would almost certainly expand that preliminary sketch in the declamation itself. The main division of argument, which is closely observed in the Senecan exercises and recurs in those attributed to Quintilian, is into (i) *ius* and (ii) *aequitas*. The first consideration is given to the strictly legal position : is the defendant empowered by law to act as he did (*an liceat, an possit*) ? Secondly, even supposing his actions to have been legally correct, was he morally justified in acting as he did ? (*an debeat, an oportuerit*)[1]. Each of these main sections would involve a number of questions, one dependent on another, for the issue was not often a simple one ; these questions, if of strict law, were entitled *iuris quaestiones*, if of equity, *tractationes* (though occasionally Seneca uses *quaestiones* loosely of both)[2]. Latro was particularly fond of treatment according to *ius* and *aequitas*, to which he often subjoined consideration of mitigating circumstances. The main division was a natural one, used by Cicero[3] and ascribed by Seneca (*Contr.* I, 1, 13) to ' veteres ' ; but he implies that the younger declaimers of his day made the subordinate *quaestiones* more numerous and intricate—a natural tendency which may be observed in other branches of rhetorical doctrine[4].

That the arguments should first proceed, wherever possible, from a careful examination of the wording of the law concerned, had been laid down as a precept in Seneca's day, for he says in *Contr.* I, 2, 15 ' praeceptum sequitur, quo iubemur ut, quotiens possumus, de omnibus legis verbis controversiam faciamus,' cf. I, 4, 6 ' quaestionem ... ex verbo legis natam '; and in the declamations ascribed to Quintilian we observe the same practice (cf. *Decl. min.* 272 ' quam quidem ego postea adfectus necessitate merito defendam [viz. " aequitas "] ; interim defendere *verbis legis* volo.'). That the general order of arguments was fairly stereotyped appears from Seneca's criticism of Haterius (*Contr.* IV, *Praef.* 9)—' is illi erat ordo, quem impetus dederat ; *non dirigebat se ad declamatoriam legem* '—sufficient indication of the encroachment of routine on an exercise which should have continued to give full scope for individual treatment.

Such was the general relationship between the *sententiae*, *divisiones* and *colores* given by Seneca and the four-fold division of the declamation itself. The declaimers were not, however,

[1] cf. *Contr.* I, 1, 13 'divisit in ius et aequitatem, an abdicari possit, an debeat'; I, 4, 6 ' an licuerit filio tunc vindicare, an oportuerit ' ; II, 5, 16 ; VII, 1, 16, *et saep.*; so 'Quint.', *Decl.* 251, 254 etc. H. Bardon, *op. cit.*, pp. 68-77, analyses several of Seneca's exercises from this point of view.
[2] cf. Bornecque, *op. cit.*, pp. 51-2 and 103-4.
[3] cf. above, p. 46.
[4] e.g. that of the virtues of style, which became ever more subject to subdivision; cf. my *Literary Treatises of Dionysius of Halicarnassus* (Cambridge, 1939) pp. 17-18. On the subdivision of *quaestiones*, see Hoffa, pp. 8 ff.

restricted completely to that division; for their speech would almost always contain one or two rhetorical descriptions, arising sometimes naturally from the narrative, but frequently dragged in for the purpose of display. The *descriptio* thus became a digression, and that it was regarded as an integral part of the speech is clear from the fact that Seneca says (*Contr.* I, 4, 8-9) 'et *in descriptione* dixit' and 'et illud *post descriptionem* adiecit' exactly as he uses *in narratione* and *in argumentis*. So in II, *Praef.* 1, he says of Arellius Fuscus 'principia, argumenta, narrationes aride dicebantur, in descriptionibus extra legem omnibus verbis, dummodo niterent, permissa libertas.' Of Fabianus, Seneca notes (*ib.* 3) that he described, more lavishly than any other declaimer, natural scenery, the course of rivers, the sites of cities, and the customs of different peoples, and the long quotation given in the first *controversia* of Book II (§§ 10-13) is not only an admirable example of his style, but also shows how loosely these *descriptiones* were attached to the real subject-matter of the speech[1]. The theme was as follows: 'A rich man had disinherited three sons; he then asked a poor man to allow him to adopt his son. The poor man was willing; but the son refused to go; whereupon his father disinherited him.' Fabianus begins (*ab ovo*) with a grandiloquent opening describing the horror of the civil war; he proceeds to inveigh against the luxury and greed which caused that war. What, he asks, has not wealth corrupted? What, indeed? He proceeds to enumerate, describes the prevalent craze for lofty buildings and lavish decoration; his account sparkles with gold and marbles and precious jewels. He pauses to lament, sententiously, 'O paupertas, quam ignotum bonum es,' and continues with a description of the gardens of the villas of the wealthy, masonry piled up on the shore, the sea itself channelled, nothing natural, everything a misguided distortion of Nature. And so to a superb example of anti-climax: 'And do you wonder, if men who so crave to alter nature are not satisfied except with someone else's children?'... Parturiunt montes...Yet, despite the way in which this *purpureus pannus* is introduced, there are passages in it which, in another context, would ring true, and which cause one to wonder how much even of the best Roman prose is inspired by genuine feeling, and how much is rhetoric in disguise. Suppose the following passage had occurred in a reputable author: 'I can scarce believe that any of them ever saw the forests and wide rolling plains and the stream dashing headlong from the hills or peacefully winding through the level country or that they ever climbed a hill to see the waves moving drowsily, or whipped into fury by a winter wind.' Would not the critics extol it as indicative of their author's deep sensibility to Nature?

[1] cf. Norden, *A.K.* I, 276-7 and 285-6; Bornecque, *Déclam.*, pp.96 ff.

But this is Fabianus speaking ; it is, alas, only rhetoric ; its label—
descriptio locorum, or ἔκφρασις τόπων[1].

So anxious was Fabianus that the audience should not miss his descriptions that he prepared the way by introducing the passage with some such phrase as ' describam nunc ego . . . ' (*Contr.* II, 5, 6), a practice which Vibius Gallus carried to absurd lengths by raising his voice to a sing-song and warning the audience ' amorem describere volo ' or ' divitias describere volo ' (*Contr.* II, 1, 26)—a clear indication of their divorce from the real subject-matter of the exercise.

One of the favourite subjects was the description of storm and shipwreck ; so Haterius in *Contr*, VII, 1, 4 (cf. 26) makes a dramatic setting for the abandonment of a man accused of parricide. ' From the thick clouds lightning flashed on all sides, and with a terrible thunder-clap the awful storm had blotted out the light of day ; everywhere drenching rain and everything seething in the gale ; the sea, I said to myself, awaits a parricide.' But the frail craft survived the storm, and Cestius draws the moral (*ib*, 10) : ' A mighty bulwark in time of peril is innocence. The cruel sea rolls, the gale sweeps the foaming waves against the sides of the craft, the ship is beset on all sides with perils ; but innocence is safe '—quite a ' Danae' touch ; so in VIII, 6, 2 the ' pauper naufragus ' takes the opportunity for a similar description and in *Suas.* III, 2 we read : ' describe nunc tempestatem.'

The *controversia* of the woman who was tortured by the tyrant gave the declaimers a glorious opportunity of describing the various instruments of torture and the sufferings of the poor woman, which they proceeded to do with great relish (II, 5, 4, 6). ' Describam nunc ego cruciatus ' says Fabianus with gusto[2]. In fact, a morbid love of the horrible is a characteristic of their effusions, a characteristic which was not without its influence on the literature of their time[3]. Similarly, their lack of taste is nowhere better displayed than in the description of a drunken orgy in *Contr.* IX, 2, 4. An interesting comparison may be made between the description of such an occasion quoted by Quintilian (VIII, 3, 66) from the lost *Pro Gallio* of Cicero, and that of Julius Bassus the declaimer. Cicero says : ' videbar videre alios intrantes, alios autem exeuntes, quosdam ex vino vacillantes, quosdam hesterna ex potatione oscitantes. Humus erat immunda, lutulenta vino, coronis languidulis et spinis cooperta piscium '—a restrained account which, as Quintilian says, pictures the scene itself with

---
[1] cf. Horace, *A.P.* 14-19 ; [Dion. Hal.] *Ars Rhet.* x, 17 ; Theon, *Progymn.* c. 11 (II, 118, Spengel). See also D'Alton, *op. cit.*, pp. 507-8.
[2] cf. *Suas.* VI, 10 ' cum descripsisset contumelias insultantium Ciceroni et verbera et tormenta ' ; *Contr.* IX, 6, 18 ' cum descripsisset tormenta ' etc.
[3] See below, pp. 162, 165.

admirable vividness[1]. Contrast the declaimer : ' inter temulentas reliquias sumptuosissimae cenae et fastidiosos ob ebrietatem cibos modo excisum humanum caput fertur : inter purgamenta et iactus cenantium et sparsam in convivio scobem humanus sanguis everritur.' Another example of description of the horrible is that of Cicero's head on the rostra (*Suas.* VI, 20).[2]

Another favourite description, which frequently formed one of the *colores*, was that of a swoon ; to Latro particularly it frequently provided a very acceptable way of avoiding responsibility, and to judge from the elder Seneca his clients must have suffered from a quite Victorian susceptibility in this respect. ' My senses left me ' he says, taking the part of the youth who was disinherited for helping a poverty-stricken father, ' I lost all control ; my feet refused to support my body ; my eyes were shrouded in sudden darkness ' (*Contr.* I, 1, 16) and again in I, 4, 7 ' Latro descripsit stuporem totius corporis . . . et cum oculorum caliginem, animi defectionem, membrorum omnium torporem descripsisset, adiecit': and yet again in VII, 1, 20 ' cum descripsisset ingenti spiritu titubantem et inter cogitationem fratris occidendi concidentem, dixit . . . ' So Blandus in VII, 1, 6.

Sometimes Seneca cannot find time to do more than indicate the subject of a description[3]. Particularly in *suasoriae* he introduces a number of the ' celebres descriptiunculas ' (*Suas.* II. 10) of Arellius Fuscus ; though he admits (*Suas.* III, 4) that some of them were not only unnecessary but ill-befitted the subject-matter— ' valde autem longe petiit et paene repugnante materia, certe non desiderante, inseruit.'[4] The style of the *descriptio* was frequently poetical, and Fuscus was particularly fond of imitations of Virgil ; and in the first *Suasoria* Seneca himself quotes a passage from a poem of Albinovanus Pedo as a model for the description of the Ocean, which that exercise naturally invited.

Equally loosely attached[5] to the main subject of the declamation were the *loci communes* or ' common-places ' which had long been current in rhetorical theory, and provided useful little disquisitions on a large variety of topics ; they were generally

---

[1] cf. Quint., IV, 2, 123-4—an excerpt from Caelius' speech against Antony, on a similar theme.

[2] It is noteworthy that Quint., IX, 2, 42 ff. declares the love of vivid description to be particularly characteristic of declamation. Libanius gives several examples of ἔκφρασις (vol. VIII, pp. 460 ff., Foerster).

[3] cf. *Contr.* I, 4, 2 ' descriptio pugnantis viri fortis,' *ib.* 12 ; *Suas.* II, 8 ' descriptio Thermopylarum.'

[4] cf. Quint., IV, 3, 2 ff. on the influence on court-speeches of the declamatory digression, and see also Bornecque, *Déclam.*, pp. 96-7.

[5] cf. Bornecque, pp. 94 and 97-8, Pichon, pp. 161-2.

learnt up beforehand, and inserted as desired[1]. So in one passage (*Contr.* I, *Praef.* 23) Seneca calls them ' *tralaticiae* sententiae' because they are not part and parcel of the *controversia* but are equally applicable elsewhere (' nihil habent cum ipsa controversia implicitum, sed satis apte et alio *transferuntur* ')[2]. He instances as subjects, the fickleness of fortune (cf. I, 1, 3, 5 ; I, 8, 16 ; II, 1, 7 ; V, 1, 1 etc.) cruelty (cf. I, 2, 8) the degeneracy of the age (' convicium saeculi' or ' insectatio temporum ') (II, *Praef.* 2 ; II, 1, 11 ff. ; II, 5, 7 ; II, 7, 1 ff. ; X, 4, 17-18) and wealth (II, 1, 4, 11, 17, 21, 29 ; II, 6, 2).[3]

Other *loci* which appear in the declaimers are on envy (I, 8, 10; VII, 6, 20), on humble birth (I, 6, 3 ff.), on adoption (II, 1, 17 ; II, 4, 13), on poison (II, 1, 29), on filial affection (VII, 5, 13), on the tolerance of Rome towards its generals (IX, 2, 19), on the desire of criminal parents for innocent children (IX, 6, 19), against those who professed to prophesy (*Suas.* III, 4), and against belief in dreams and providence (*Suas.* IV, 4). The number of *loci* was evidently constantly expanding; those of the *Ad Herennium* and Cicero, *De Inventione*, were mainly concerned with forensic practice—e.g. on the trust that may be placed in witnesses, in torture, in rumours, but a considerable addition to them was made by topics on moral subjects, such as avarice, envy, adultery, profligacy ; though even these were accepted by Quintilian as useful in the lawcourts (II, 1, 11 ; 4, 22). So Albucius, whose fondness for utilising philosophy in his declamations was notorious (*Contr.* I, 3, 8 ; VII, *Praef.* 1 ; VII, 6, 18) introduces in I, 7, 17 what is called a ' philosophumenon locum.' But Quintilian (II, 4, 28 ff.), with characteristic shrewdness and commonsense, realised the fatal weakness of the *locus communis*; it became too ' communis ' and was trotted out on so many occasions that it became a wretched piece of furniture (' infelix supellex ')[4] which no one ever wanted to set eyes on again. Yet it is surprising how many of these pieces have found their way into the showrooms of Latin literature, where, assiduously re-varnished and polished by the skill of literary craftsmen, they have frequently been mistaken, as they were perhaps intended to be mistaken, for the genuine article[5].

A regular feature of the development of a *locus communis* (technically known as ' implere locum,' cf. *Contr.* VII, *Praef.* 3)

[1] cf. Quint., II, 4, 27 ' scriptos eos memoriaeque diligentissime mandatos in promptu habuerint, ut quotiens esset occasio extemporales eorum dictiones his velut emblematis exornarentur ' ; and II, 11, 6 on their loose connection.
[2] cf. Cic., *De Inv.* II, 15, 48 ' argumenta, quae *transferri* in multas causas possunt, locos communes nominamus.'
[3] See de Decker, *op. cit.*, pp. 19-70 for a good exposition, and detailed illustrations of the influence of these declamatory topics on Juvenal.
[4] So Latro (*Contr.* I, *Praef.* 23) without the ' infelix '—' hoc genus sententiarum supellectilem vocabat.'
[5] See below, p. 163.

was the citation of historical examples ('exempla') to prove the point. 'Nemo sine vitio est' is a commonplace (*Contr.* II, 4, 4); it is proved by the fact that Cato lacked moderation, Cicero lacked steadfastness, Sulla lacked pity[1]. That some men have risen from humble birth to distinction is a commonplace (*Contr.* I, 6, 3-4); it is proved by the careers of Marius, Pompey, and especially King Servius Tullius, son of a slave girl (*ib.*; cf. III, 9, 2; VII, 6, 18). Fortune is fickle; Croesus (II, 1, 7), Marius (I, 1, 3, 5) and Crassus (II, 1, 7) all prove it[2]. In I, 8, 10, Blandus declaims on the power of envy and the great men it ruined; ' Hic exempla ' says Seneca. ' He had a profound knowledge of all history,' says Seneca proudly of Latro (I, *Praef.* 18) and that this was the ideal of the declaimers is seen from the frequency of these historical examples. Aristides, Phocion, Demosthenes, Horatius, Decius, Fabricius, Coruncanius, Scipio Africanus, and Aemilianus, the elder and younger Cato, Mithridates, Lucullus, Virginia, Lucretia, Cornelia, and many others serve to point a moral or adorn a narration; perhaps the best example of a display of historical knowledge is *Contr.* VII, 2, 6, 7, where we have a gallery of national heroes. But, as usual, some declaimers spoiled the effect by going out of their way to drag in historical illustrations (*Contr.* VII, 5, 12-13).

Every good rhetorician in antiquity was expected to be a master of ἦθος, characterisation, and πάθος, emotional appeal; the scope for characterisation in declamation has already been mentioned, but the appeals to the emotions are so characteristic that they deserve fuller treatment. It was obviously difficult to work up any genuine emotion for the stock characters of the declamations, or even for their historical personages[3], and the fact that the reader realises that these are only exercises does not put him in a frame of mind to appreciate the efforts of the declaimers; but it is not pathos, merely pseudo-pathos. Here is the poor starving father of *Contr.* I, 1, 8: ' Venit immissa barba capilloque deformi, non senectute sed fame membris trementibus, semesa facie, et tenui atque elisa ieiunio voce, ut vix exaudiri posset, introrsus conditos oculos vix allevans: alui'; and again (§ 17), helped out by apostrophe, chiasmus, triple repetition, and climax: ' venit subito

---

[1] cf. *Contr.* IX, 2, 19 'in Manlio impotentiam... in Sulla crudelitatem... in Lucullo luxuriam.'

[2] cf. Bornecque, *Déclam.* p. 95; on this subject, see further H. W. Litchfield, 'National *Exempla Virtutis* in Roman Literature' in *Harvard Studies in Classical Philology* XXV (1914) pp. 1 ff., and de Decker, *op. cit.*, pp. 107-110, who well compares Quint., XII, 2, 30.

[3] cf. Pichon, *op. cit.*, p. 158 ' il ne peut pas se passioner pour des gens qui n'ont jamais existé, ou qui sont morts il y a quatre cents ans.'

deformis squalore, lacrimis. O graves, Fortuna, vices tuas !' (we imagine the horrified declaimer lifting his hands—but this is also *verb. sap.*—a hint of the ensuing *locus communis*—on the fickleness of Fortune)—' Ille dives modo modo superbus ' (chiasmus), ' rogavit alimenta, rogavit filium suum, rogavit abdicatum suum ' (*repetitio* and *gradatio*). ' Cucurri miser ad ferrum, quasi manus haberem ' laments the hero who had lost his hands in battle and been unable to kill his wife taken in adultery (*Contr.* I, 4, 2).

The last moments of a disinherited son, commending to his father a child by a courtesan, afford the opportunity of a touching death-bed scene (II, 4, 3) : ' Assidebat mulier tristi vultu, affecta, aegrae simillima ipsa, demissis in terram oculis . . . ille magni modo successor patrimoni natus in lectulo precario moriebatur ; non servorum turba circumstabat, non amicorum ; inter infantem et mulierculam deficientis adulescentis spiritus in adventum meum sustinebatur. Ut intravi, cadentes iam oculos ad nomen meum erexit fugientemque animam retinuit.' This is Fabianus again ; but in case it should seem that real emotion is being decried, it is perhaps worthy of remark that his comment, ' in sinu meo et filium et animam deposuit ' is a good example of zeugma, a figure which does not normally occur to the distraught.

Although there was clearly a ' declamatory ' style, individual declaimers differed considerably in diction and composition[1]. Some were professed Asianists, as Craton (X, 5, 21,) and the Asiatic style is conspicuous.[2] A few, particularly those designated by the elder Seneca as ' scholastici', were purists, and preferred the Attic correctness of language—cf. *Contr.* IV, *Praef.* 9 ' quaedam enim scholae iam quasi obscena refugiunt, nec, si qua sordidiora sunt aut ex cotidiano usu repetita, possunt pati. Ille (sc. Haterius) in hoc scholasticis morem gerebat, ne verbis calcatis et obscenis [obsoletis MSS] uteretur.' Seneca himself observes (*Contr.* I, 2, 23) ' longe recedendum est ab omni obscenitate et verborum et sensuum,' and criticises Albucius (*Contr.* VII, *Praef.* 3) for his use of words with trivial or sordid associations like ' acetum,' 'latrina,' and ' spongia.' But the very subjects of some of the exercises encouraged the use of vulgar and erotic vocabulary, and the declaimers, who had no wish to gain a reputation for either pedantry or prudishness, were not slow to extend the use of words *sensu obsceno*. Examples are 'paparium facere ' (*Contr.* II, 1, 35), ' dupondiariae ' (X, 1, 14), ' virgo desultrix ' (I, 3, 11), 'volutare' and 'volutatio' (*sens. obsc.* I, 2, 6 ; I, 4, 3)

---

[1] cf. J. F. D'Alton, *op. cit.*, pp. 213-4 and p. 330 ; and see Norden, *A.K.* I, 286.
[2] cf. U.v. Wilamowitz-Möllendorf, ' Asianismus and Attizismus', *Hermes* XXXV (1900) pp. 1 ff.

'reludere' (*sens. obsc.* II, 2, 7), 'fornix' (I, 2, 21, IX, 2, 28) etc. The declamations sometimes provide useful evidence of contemporary colloquial Latin. So we are told that 'rivalis,' 'a rival in love,' is 'cotidianum verbum' (*Contr.* VII, 5, 9 ; cf. II, 4, 5 ; II, 6, 9 ; cf. Plautus, *Stichus* 434, 729 etc.). The expression 'domi est' (*Contr.* II, 3, 21), meaning here much the same as the English slang, 'it is in the bag,' is called by Seneca 'bellus idiotismus,' and may be paralleled from Cicero's *Letters* (*Ad Att.* X, 14, 2 ' nam id quidem domi est '—' ready to hand ') and Latin Comedy (Plautus, *Mil.* 191, Terence, *Ad.* 413 etc.). The colloquial ' malum habebis '— 'you're in for trouble' (*Contr.* II, 4, 13) is likewise a familiar expression in Plautus (*Amph.* 721 etc.) and Cicero's correspondence (*Ad Att.* VII, 2, 4)[1]. Most characteristic of all is the very frequent use of the adverb 'belle' and the adjective 'bellus[2].'

The fact that many of the declaimers came from the provinces did not tend to improve the accuracy of their Latin—at any rate by pure *Romano* standards. So Messala, whom Seneca styles 'Latini sermonis observator diligentissimus,' said of Latro, 'sua lingua disertus est' (*Contr.* II, 4, 8), much as Cicero had described the poets of Corduba as 'pingue quiddam sonantes atque peregrinum' (*Pro Arch.* 10, 26, cf. *Suas.* VI, 27). Rare or poetical words were not infrequently used to secure novelty and effect, generally without much success according to modern judgment, e.g. cicatricosus (*Contr.* I, 8, 3—Plautine), ossifragus (X, 4, 2), emancare (I, 7, 6), delumbare (X, 4, 2), repluere (X, *Praef.* 9), inhorrere (I, 3, 3), indenuntiatus (*Suas.* II, 2 ; V, 2). Particularly in the *descriptio* is this licence noticeable. Virgilian echoes are characteristic of Arellius Fuscus' *explicationes* in the *Suasoriae*, and typical of his semi-poetical style is *Suas.* VI, 6, where his expression (of the soul) 'ad sedes suas et cognata sidera recurret' could easily be transformed into a line of verse (e.g. ' adque suas sedes cognataque sidera curret'—cf. Ovid, *Met.* XV, 10, 839 ' aetherias sedes cognataque sidera tanget ')[3]. Bombastic language is common, and the elder Seneca has an amusing satire on the tendency of a namesake to use large words—this won him the name of Seneca Grandio (*Suas.* II, 17); cf. Horace's 'ampullas et sesquipedalia verba ' (*A.P.* 97).

In their technical terms of rhetoric and criticism both Seneca and the declaimers use a vocabulary which is much more Greek

[1] The program of Karsten, *De elocutione rhetorica qualis invenitur in Annaei Senecae Suasoriis et Controversiis* (Rotterdam, 1881) is inaccessible, and known to me only from Bornecque p. 114 (q.v.). But O. Rebling, *Versuch einer Characteristik der römischen Umgangssprache* (Kiel[2], 1882), pp. 36-48 has some interesting evidence from the declaimers (this section being the most useful of an otherwise out-of-date work, cf. J. B. Hofman, *Lateinische Umgangssprache* (Heidelberg, 1926), *Vorwort*).
[2] Bardon, *op. cit.*, p. 16, has noted 21 instances of the former ; cf. below, p. 79.
[3] See Edward's notes on this *Suasoria*, and cf. R. G. Austin on Quint., XII, 2, 28.

than that of Cicero and his contemporaries[1]. Latinised words which appear for the first time in his works are: anthypophora (*Contr.* I, 7, 17), cacozelos and cacozelia (*Suas.* II, 16; VII, 11; *Contr.* IX, 1, 15; IX, 2, 28), epiphonema (I, *Praef.* 23), hermeneuma (IX, 3, 14), ethicos (II, 3, 23, *Suas.* I, 13), hexis (*Contr.* VII, *Praef.* 2), idiotismus (II, 3, 21; VII, *Praef.* 5), metaphrasis (*Suas.* I, 12), phantasia (*Suas.* II, 14), phrasis (*Contr.* III, *Praef.* 7), problema (I, 3, 8), schema (I, *Praef.* 23; I, 1, 25 etc.), scholastica (II, 3, 13; III *Praef.* 12; VII *Praef.* 8; X, 5, 12), thema (I, 2, 14; VII, 2, 12; VII, 5, 12 etc.), thesis (I, *Praef.* 12; VII, 4, 3) tricolum and tetracolon (II, 4, 12; IX, 2, 27).

The declaimers are not deterred from the boldest extensions of the normal meaning of words. So Gargonius in *Suas.* VII, 14 says 'mortes feneraverunt,' Albucius speaks of the girl's ravisher in *Contr.* I, 2, 17 as 'piratae sui,' and Asprenas in I, 4, 2 speaks of 'matris leno.' But apart from these characteristics their diction is much the same as that of contemporary writers, and is typical of the earliest 'Silver Latin.'

In composition, the chief faults are the excessive use of short and disjointed sentences, giving an abrupt effect to the style, the rarity of well-balanced periods, and the use by some declaimers of weak and ineffective rhythms. The style of these extracts is what the Greek critics would have called κατακεκομμένη or κεκερματισμένη[2]; as an antidote to periodic structure, this feature would have been most effective, but it is so frequently used that the mind wearies of the repeated pungency and point. The famous criticism of Macaulay[3]—himself a master in the art of heightening the periodic style by the occasional epigram—that reading the philosopher Seneca was like living on nothing but anchovy sauce, is even more applicable to the contemporaries of his less distinguished father. In *Contr.* IX, 2, 22 Seneca criticises the style of Argentarius because 'in quae solebat schemata minuta tractationem violentissimam infregit,' (cf. Quint., X, 1, 130 on the younger Seneca 'si rerum pondera minutissimis sententiis non fregisset'); and the following may serve as examples of this common trait: *Contr.* I, 1, 2 'fatendum est crimen meum; tardius miseritus sum; itaque do poenas; egeo'; I, 2, 1 'deducta es in lupanar; accepisti locum; pretium constitutum est; titulus inscriptus est; hactenus in te inquiri potest; cetera nescio.' II, 4, 10 'nihil, inquit, peccaverat; amat meretricem; solet fieri; adulescens est, exspecta, emendabitur, ducet uxorem,' an effort of which Mr. Jingle might have approved.

---

[1] See H. Bardon, *op. cit.*, s.vv. cf. p. 108.
[2] Demetrius, π. ἑρμ. § 4; [Longinus], π. ὕψ. c. 42; cf. Cic., *Orat.* 67, 226; 69, 230 (Hegesias).
[3] *Essay on Bacon* (*Life and Letters*, May 25, 1836).

On the other hand the period was still used in descriptive passages, as may be seen e.g. from I, 3, 1 'constitit et, circumlatis in frequentiam oculis, sanctissimum numen, quasi parum violasset inter altaria, coepit in ipso, quo vindicabatur, violare supplicio,' and the consecutive prose of Fabianus in *Contr.* II, 1, and Latro in II, 7. The chief offenders in rhythm were the extreme Asianists, whose prose was weakened by allowing an excessive number of short syllables together[1], a fault censured by Quintilian (IX, 4, 66) as producing an effect like a child's rattle, and by a modern critic[2] as reminiscent of 'a flock of twittering sparrows.' An example (from Arellius Fuscus) is: 'trŭcēs quŏquĕ ănĭmōs mĭsĕrĭcōrs nātūrā dēbĭlĭtăt' (*Contr.* I, 4, 5). But the declaimers were by no means entirely insensible to the rhythm of their *clausulae*[3], although Quintilian (VIII, 5, 13-14) says they were much too fond of trying to end with tiny epigrams ('minuti corruptique sensiculi et extra rem petiti').

Alliteration was a favourite device which deserves special mention; its use with the letter 'p' is especially common, much more so than with any other letter: cf. especially II, 1, 37 'non possum, inquit, pati sine patre. me autem sine te putas pati posse? quemquam autem patrem putas pati sine liberis posse?'—a horror of Ennian proportions. So I, 1, 6 'si tam pertinacia placent odia, parcite'; I, 5, 1, 'producitur publicus pudicitiae hostis'; I, 6, 12 ὅρκος ἐστὶν πεῖσμα καὶ παρὰ πειραταῖς πεπιστευμένον; I, 7, 8 'qui patriam posset opprimere'; II, 2, 7 'eo se loco praecipitasse, ex quo praecipitata perire non posset' etc. These are curious examples of the exaggerated effects which sometimes characterise these odd but interesting products of the Roman genius[4].

Rhetorical figures, as might be expected, abound in the declamations. Seneca informs us (I, *Praef.* 23) that Latro made a practice of sketching out numbers of them, to suit various *controversiae*, though he adds that Latro took the view that there was no point in using figures just for the sake of display; they were invented as an aid to argument. Latro himself (I, 1, 25) distinguishes 'schema quod vulnerat' from 'schema quod titillat,' and the seductive type proved too tempting to many of his contemporaries, much of whose prose might have been written as an illustration for a rhetorical handbook like the *Ad Herennium*. Only the dull declaimers avoided figures (II, 1, 24); but the famous story of the sad failure of Albucius in a public speech (VII, *Praef.* 7-8) shows

---

[1] See Norden, *A.K.* 290 ff.
[2] Sir Walter Raleigh, *On Style*, (London, 1897), p. 16.
[3] See Bornecque's analysis, *Déclam.* pp. 26-28.
[4] On the other hand undue use of assonance is criticised in a clever parody by Cestius in *Contr.* II, 6, 8.

how ill-adapted a school *schema* could be to the needs of genuine oratory.

In a generation so devoted to point, it is not surprising that antithesis is exceedingly common ; sometimes it is neatly and effectively expressed : ' multis debeo misericordiam, multis tuli ' says Marullus, and ' etiamsi tu non odisti eum, qui mihi fecit injuriam, ego odi eum qui fecit tibi ' (I, 1, 12) particularly in the form of chiasmus e.g. ' nascimur uno modo, multis morimur ' (VII, 1, 9) ' adoptaui te cum abdicatus es ; cum adoptas abdico ' (I, 1, 11), ' qui alunt abdicantur, vindicantur qui non alunt' (*ib*. 6)'[1] But often the antithesis is frigid, being introduced just for the sake of contrast, without any real necessity, as I, 4, 3 ' vir fortis in civitate truncus integros adulteros spectat !' A typical example is II, 5, 9, of the woman tortured by the tyrant: ' deerat iam sanguis, supererat fides '—she had lost a lot of blood but had plenty of faith—enough and to spare, in fact. So again of the man on trial for seducing two girls in one night (I, 5, 2) ' toto die pereat qui tota nocte peccavit' Throughout I, 4, 9 is a fatuous contrast of ' pater ' and ' mater,' and 'unus') ('duo ' is insisted on wherever possible (cf. II, 6, 11 ; VII, 4, 2 ; IX, 3, 5 ; cf. I, 7, 3 duplam) (unico). A favourite device, which is worthy of special mention, is the antithesis of prepositions[2] ; cf. *Contr*. II, 1, 31 ' habebo hunc *cum* illis) (habebo hunc *pro* illis ' ; II, 2, 11 ' periit aliqua *cum* viro, periit aliqua *pro* viro ; II, 5, 8 ' haec non *cum* viro arsisset, quae *pro* viro arsit,? VII, 2, 2 ' hic *sub* Cicerone sedisti . . . hic *supra* Ciceronem stetisti'; VII, 7, 4 ' diutius nos *contra* filium rogasti quam *pro* filio hostem' ; *ib*. 9 ' ut filium pater spectem *in* cruce, filius patrem *de* cruce'; X, 3, 1 '*in* mortem) (*per* mortem'; *Suas*. II, 8 ' ait *in* his aut *cum* his.' Similarly when compounded with verbs[3], VII, 1, 11 '*in*iecit) (*e*iecistis,' VII, 7, 3 '*per*venerunt) (*con*venerunt.'

With antithesis, balance of clauses goes hand in hand ; parallelism (ἰσόκωλον) had scarcely been so popular since Isocrates' day. Examples are legion : e.g. I, 1, 9 ' homo est : non vis alam hominem ? civis est : non vis alam civem ? amicus est : non vis alam amicum ? propinquus est : non vis alam propinquum ?' I, 2, 2 ' sacerdoti pro libertate vota facienda sunt ; captivae mandabitis ? pro pudicitia vota facienda sunt : prostitutae mandabitis ? pro militibus vota facienda sunt ; isti mandabitis ?' II, 3, 10 ' servaturus es filium ? iam tempus fuit ; es occisurus ? iam tempus est.' X, 3, 4 'irato victore vivendum est, exorato patre

---

[1] cf. the structure of the refrain of the *Pervigilium Veneris*, ' cras amet qui numquam amavit, quique amavit cras amet.'
[2] This is also a common characteristic of the younger Seneca's style, probably derived from the declamations ; cf. *Epp*. 18, 6; 23, 6; 30, 5; 47, 4 etc. Summer's *Introd*. pp. lxxxv-lxxxvi.
[3] Quint., IX, 3, 71-2, classes this as a not inelegant form of play on words.

moriendum est' (triple antithesis and homœoteleuton), etc.
Clauses of three members (τρίκωλον) are mentioned by Seneca
(*Contr.* II, 4, 11 ff.) as having been 'the craze' in his day
('hunc novicium morbum ')[1]. As an example he gives 'accusatur
pater in ultimis annis, nepos in primis adoptatur, in mediis abdicatur
filius,' which is an extreme instance, as it contains also a triple
antithesis. Sentences like II, 3, 2 'ipse dispensasti triginta dies,
ut haberet primos socer, medios reus, novissimos pater'; I, 2, 3
'vendit pirata, emit leno, excipit lupanar'; VII, 1, 8 'maria iam
quiescunt, praedones iam miserentur, irati iam parcunt'; II, 3, 5
'hoc si reo dicis non curo ; si iudici, videbo ; si dementi, non
intellego' illustrate this trait, which is extremely common together
with a triple repetition (anaphora) of the leading word or phrase—
an interesting example of the respect paid in antiquity to that magic
number. A few of many are : I, 1, 12 'Scio quam acerbum sit
supplicare exteris ; scio quam grave sit repelli a domesticis ;
scio quam crudele sit cotidie et mortem optare et vitam rogare' ;
cf. I, 2, 2 ('age si quis' thrice repeated) II, 3, 6, ('deliberabo'
thrice) I, 1, 24, ('debuisti' thrice) I, 2, 4 ' (sacerdotis vestrae) summa
notitia est, quod prostitit ; summa virtus, quod occidit ; summa
felicitas, quod absoluta est' ;· II, 5, 7 'imputat tibi quod repudiata
est ; imputat tibi, quod torta est ; imputat tibi, quod sterilis est' ;
VII, 1, 12 'idem timuimus, idem doluimus, idem flevimus, eundem
patrem habuimus, eandem matrem, eandem novercam.' The
figure τρίκωλον was known to Seneca's contemporary, Dionysius
of Halicarnassus, who in *De Comp. Verb.* c. 9 attests the popularity[2] of an example from Aeschines : ' ἐπὶ σαυτὸν καλεῖς, ἐπὶ
τοὺς νόμους καλεῖς, ἐπὶ τὴν δημοκρατιάν καλεῖς.' He does
not entirely disapprove of the figure, but realises that it involves
additions which are not necessary to the sense (προσθήκας οὐκ
ἀναγκαίας ὡς πρὸς τὸν νοῦν, cf. *De Dem.* c. 39 παραπληρώμασι
τῶν ὀνομάτων οὐκ ἀναγκαίοις)—exactly as Seneca says (*Contr.*
IX, 2, 27) 'curamus ut numerus constet, non curamus an sensus.'
Fourfold repetition also occurs (cf. 'quid si tantum ' . . . in I, 2, 5)
Fourfold parallelism (*tetracolon*) is also censured by Seneca (*loc.
cit.*) as corrupt ; his example 'serviebat forum cubiculo, praetor
meretrici, carcer convivio, dies nocti'[3] may be paralleled by e.g.
VII, 1, 7 'pater noster navigavit sereno die, tranquillo mari,
auspicato itinere, integra nave'; X, 1, 1 'quod sordidatus fui,

---
[1] On ἰσόκωλα, τρίκωλα and τετράκωλα, see also Bornecque, p. 109, and Norden, *A.K.* I, 289 and P. *Vergilius Maro Aeneis Buch vi* (Leipzig, Teubner, 1926) pp. 376 ff. ('Rhetorische Gliederung').
[2] τρίκωλον ἐν τοῖς πάνυ ἐπαινούμενον. Quintilian IX, 3, 77 has an example from Cic., *Pro Cluent.* 6, 15. cf. also *Ad Herennium*, IV. 19, 26.
[3] On this well-known example and the characteristics of declamatory style, cf. A. M. Guillemin, *Le Public et la Vie littéraire à Rome* (Paris, 1937) p. 60, and see below, p. 161.

luctus est ; quod flevi, pietatis est ; quod non accusavi, timoris est ; quod repulsus est, vestrum est'[1]. That a style so exactly balanced, so coldly intellectual, would never arouse an audience is observed by Quintilian[2] and proved by Dionysius' criticisms on Isocrates ; it was fully realised by Shakespeare, who puts in the mouth of the unimpassioned Brutus a speech that would have delighted the *scholasticus* of Seneca's day by its parallelism and antithesis (*Julius Caesar*, Act iii, Sc. 2). No declaimer could have desired a better example of *tetracolon* than :—' As Caesar loved me, I weep for him ; as he was fortunate, I rejoice at it ; as he was valiant, I honour him ; but as he was ambitious, I slew him. There is tears for his love ; joy for his fortune ; honour for his valour ; and death for his ambition.'[3]

Apostrophe is another favourite figure, natural enough to those who so revelled in pseudo-pathos. The *raptor* in *Contr.* II, 3, 1 thus addresses himself : ' Quid contremescis, pectus ? Quid, lingua, trepidas ? Quid, oculi, extimuistis ?' and (§ 4) ' Quid, me intempestivae proditis lacrimae ?' and again (§ 6) 'Dura, anime, dura ; heri fortior eras ' (cf. Quint., IX, 2, 91). Mention may be made here of the sudden turn to apostrophe after direct narration, as *Contr.* X, 2, 3 ' dum cogito mecum Horatium ... et Mucium ... et dum *te, Deci,* cogito ' ; *Suas.* V, 2 ' Quid dicam Salamina ? Quid Cynaegiron referam et *te, Polyzele* ?'; for this form of securing variety, though not unknown in Augustan poetry, becomes particularly common in that of the 1st century A.D. onwards[4].

Play on words (*paronomasia*) is also common[5]. Again Seneca shows that the figure had been overdone in this day (*Contr.* VII, 3, 9) ' huius vitii, quod ex captione unius verbi plura significantis nascitur ' (cf. Quint., IX, 3, 69), and gives an interesting historical sketch, tracing it back through Cicero and Laberius to the Atellane farces. Examples are I, 2, 5, where ' communis locus ' may have the *double entendre* of (*a*) the lupanar (*b*) the rhetorical commonplace ; I, 3, 11 (' desultrix ') ; VI, 1, 1 ' fides ' (' trust ' and ' financial credit ') ; VI, 7, 1 ' sanus ' (' sane ' and ' in good health '); X, 6, 2 ' furtum ' (' theft ' and ' stratagem '). Closely allied to this is the trick of contrasting a simple with a compound verb, a form of *cacozelia*[6]

---

1 Cestius (*Contr.* VII, 2, 3) quotes Cic., *pro Rosc. Am.* 26, 72, itself a tetracolon : but Cicero later disparaged the style of his earlier speeches.
2 IX, 3, 102 ' ubi vero atrocitate, invidia, miseratione pugnandum est, quis ferat contrapositis et pariter cadentibus et consimilibus irascentem, flentem, rogantem ?' cf. Demetrius, π. ἑρμ. §§ 27-28.
3 Probably a parody of the style of Lyly's *Euphues*.
4 See below, p. 166. Further exx. of apostrophe in de Decker, pp. 173 ff.
5 cf. W. C. Summers, *op. cit., Introd.* p. lxxxii, Norden, *op. cit.,* I, 290 n. 3.
6 For this common term for various kinds of affectation and bad taste in the declamations, cf. *Suas.* II, 16, *Contr.* IX, 1, 15 ; IX, 2, 28 ; Quint., II, 3, 9 ; VIII, 3, 56 ; VIII, 6, 73; Suet., *Aug.* c. 86, and Edward's note on pp. 112-3 of his edn. of the *Suasoriae*.

also deplored by Seneca (*Suas.* VII, 11 ' quod detractu aut adiectione syllabae facit sententiam ') his example being : ' peribit ergo quod Cicero *scripsit,* manebit quod Antonius *proscripsit.*' cf. *Contr.* VII, 7, 3 ' legati nostri aurum *ferebant,* pater *auferebat.*' Different forms of the verb are frequently contrasted, as I, 1, 3 ' alter . . . *servatus,* alter *servandus* est ' ; I, 1, 5 ' quis alimenta *rogetur* et quis *roget* ' ; II, 3, 17 ' tu *exorasse* te dicis, ego te *exoratum* puto ' ; II, 4, 6 ' quis illis nuptiis interfuit nisi *abdicatus* aut *abdicandus* ' ; VII, 1, 15 ' narra, pater, quomodo te *dimiserit* sic *dimissus* ' etc. So finally, with any words of similar sound e.g. I, 4, 3 ' ante *patriae* quam *patri* negavit manus' ; I, 8, 1 ' quod *patriae* superest, *patri* vindico'; *Suas.* II, 4 'electi')('relicti.'

Hyperbole is a normal refuge for the declaimer who desires to ' say something novel,' even if he is not already disposed, like Seneca Grandio (*Suas.* II, 17), to ' talk big.' Here is an example from the sufferings of the poor woman tortured by the tyrant (*Contr.* II, 5, 3) ; he sends his minions to fetch her, and ' iactatur misera inter satellitum manus et *toto itinere non ducitur, sed trahitur* !' The hero in *Contr.* I, 8, 3 is thus addressed : 'nullum iam tibi vulnus nisi per cicatricem imprimi potest.' Such rhetorical exaggerations are a source of that *tumor* which often characterised declamatory style. One of the best examples of extended exaggeration is the description of deformed beggars given by Cassius Severus (critic of the declamations !) in *Contr.* x, 4, 2. They are mangled and re-mangled out of all recognition, and even the anatomical descriptions of Lucan and the younger Seneca's *Tragedies* pale into comparative insignificance. Small wonder that the most popular of the many rhetorical questions in the declamations (*Contr.* IX, 2, 24, cf. I, 6, 12, x, 3, 3, x, 4, 3) is : ' Quid exhorruistis, iudices ?'

The list of figures might be almost indefinitely extended ;[1] so detailed was the treatment of this study in the schools of rhetoric ; the precepts of the 4th book of the *Ad Herennium* and the 8th and 9th books of Quintilian could be well illustrated with examples from the declaimers. But enough has been said to show that these exercises were works of conscious, if often misguided, artistry, and it will appear to any student of Silver Latin Literature how deeply these characteristics of the schools impressed themselves on the works of poets and prose authors alike in the generations which followed the rise of declamatory rhetoric[2].

---

[1] e.g. to include the *figura iurisiurandi*—cf. below, pp. 153-4 and the frequent use of interjections and vivid representations (cf. Bornecque, *Déclam.*, p. 105).
[2] See below, c. VIII, for some indications.

CHAPTER IV.

DECLAMATION AND ITS ANCIENT CRITICS

Now that the historical development and characteristics of declamation have been considered, it may be of interest to study the criticisms of the practice made by the Romans themselves[1]. Much of this criticism is adverse, and has found supporters among modern scholars; it may, indeed, be said that the general view of declamation still is that it was a rather futile pursuit[2]. But we shall find that the verdict of Quintilian, a man who, albeit the professional rhetorician *par excellence*, is distinguished by his commonsense and liberal educational outlook, is a much more balanced one, and more favourable than that generally prevailing among the critics of the first century A.D.

Although the elder Seneca makes numerous criticisms of the style and manner of individual declaimers, and has in his excellent Prefaces a wealth of critical comment and lively anecdote, he does not express his opinion of the value and purpose of declamation as fully as might have been expected in a work of such scope.[3] But his general attitude is clear; he looks back to the Republic, and is 'laudator temporis acti se puero.' He had heard all the great orators who lived on into the Empire (*Contr.* I, *Praef.* 11) and now, in extreme old age, brought forth for the benefit of his sons the treasures of his extraordinary memory. Passionately fond of eloquence, which he terms 'res pulcherrima' (I, *Praef.* 7) and 'pulcherrima disciplina' (II, *Praef.* 5), he laments that the decline has set in, and, connecting oratory with morals (I, *Praef.* 8-10), as did Cato before him and Quintilian (XII, 1) after him, is appalled at the decay both of oratory and of standards of conduct. Even so, he has faith in the practice of declamation, not only as a preparation for public speaking but as an aid to the acquisition of other forms of culture.[4] But he clearly sympathises with the older generation for whom the practice was a private rehearsal, rather than with the

---

[1] See also Bornecque, *Déclam.*, c. VI, 'Jugement sur les Déclamations.' In the present chapter the material is arranged mainly chronologically, and Quintilian's views are more fully treated.

[2] cf. Friedländer, *op. cit.* (Eng. trans.), vol. iii, pp. 12 ff.; Carcopino, *op. cit.* (Eng. trans.) pp. 114 ff.; Schanz-Hosius, *op. cit.* vol. II, § 335. Edward, Introd. to edn. of the *Suasoriae*, is rather more favourable, but does not take the practice seriously. Lanfranchi, *op. cit.* pp. 33 ff., sees considerable value in it; Parks, *op. cit.*, pp. 97-101 rightly stresses Quintilian's points, but tends to whitewash the whole system.

[3] See A. F. Sochatoff, *C. J.* XXXIV (1938-9), pp. 345 ff., for some indications of Seneca's attitude.

[4] *Contr.* II, *Praef.* 4 'sed proderit tibi in illa, quae tota mente agitas, declamandi exercitatio'; *ib.* 3 'facilis ab hac in omnes artes discursus est.'

'novi declamatores' and the pure 'scholastici,' who had made of it merely a means of display. He quotes Calvus (I, *Praef.* 12) as distinguishing between this 'domestica exercitatio' and the 'vera actio' of the lawcourts, and uses this very term—'has domesticas exercitationes'—himself (III, *Praef.* 1). He recognises the rift between declamation and forensic oratory in his frequent contrast of 'declamare' with 'agere' (IV, *Praef.* 3) and 'ostentatio' with 'exercitatio' (IX, *Praef.* 1, cf. IV, *Praef.* 2; X. *Praef.* 4). He seems not to have declaimed, or to have taught declamation, himself, and although he would probably have sympathised with the views of Pollio, who only declaimed in private (IV, *Praef.* 2), he would hardly have agreed with the sweeping condemnations of Cassius Severus and Votienus Montanus, who had no use for declamation at all. His most outspoken comment (X, *Praef.* 12) is: 'There is nothing more unseemly than the imitation by the schoolman of the forum, of which he knows nothing. That is why I liked Capito—he was a genuine school-orator.' He is, with good reason, severe on the insane effusions of some of his younger contemporaries.[1] He tells of the unfortunate experience of Albucius in a court-speech (VII *Praef.* 6-8), and records the failure of his close friend Latro in beginning a forensic speech with a solecism, of which Votienus Montanus reminded him (IX, *Praef.* 3, cf. Quint., X, 5, 18). But he informs us elsewhere that some declaimers made reputations as orators (X, *Praef.* 14 and 16). In short, the elder Seneca regarded declamation as in itself a good means of preparation, but spoiled and made ridiculous by the follies of many of his younger contemporaries.[2] These faults, it should be added, were mainly faults of expression or delivery, and Seneca does not criticise adversely the themes of the exercises themselves or the laws on which they are based. His criticism is levelled at sordid and commonplace diction, extravagance and bad taste, lack of order in arrangement and balanced consistency in style, and carelessness or undue speed in delivery.[3]

The criticisms of Asinius Pollio (c. 76 B.C.-5 A.D.), recorded by Seneca, also reflect the attitude of the older school, and are marked by shrewdness and commonsense. Pollio, himself an orator of great repute, was familiar with the working of the courts (cf. *Contr.* II, 5, 13; *Suas.* VI, 15), and his comments show that he frequently directed the declaimers to the contrast between their treatment

---

[1] *Contr.* I, 7, 15, 'hominem inter scholasticos sanum, inter sanos scholasticum.'
[2] He is particularly critical of the 'novi declamatores'; cf. *Contr.* I, 1, 14; I, 4, 6; I, 8, 11 and 16; II, 5, 13; VII, 1, 20. On these, see Hoffa, pp. 8 ff.
[3] cf. *Contr.* I, 2, 23; VII, *Praef.* 3-4 (diction); *Contr.* IX, 1, 15, IX, 2, 28, *Suas.* II, 16, VII, 11 ('cacozelia'); *Contr.* II, 2, 9, IV, *Praef.* 9 (arrangement); IV, *Praef.* 7 (delivery). cf. VII, 4, 10 (composition).

and legal practice. So in *Contr.* II, 3, 13, he observes that the declamatory ' actio dementiae,' though parallel to the demanding of a *curator* in law, was different in that a *curator* could not be demanded for such trivial reasons. Pollio's criticisms on arrangement of arguments are also good; he warns against risking the entire case on a single point (*Contr.* II, 5, 10), or putting all *colores* in one section (*Contr.* IV, 3, 3). He always has an eye on the judge (*Contr.* IV, 6, 3), and derides flowery narrations (*Suas.* II, 10 'hoc non esse suadere sed ludere '), or extravagant interpretations (*Contr.* VII, 4, 3). Even when all the declaimers applaud a *color*, Pollio alone ridicules it with shrewd wit (*Contr.* II, 3, 19, cf. VII, 6, 24). He himself declaimed in private, even in times of great stress (*Contr.* IV, *Praef.* 2-6), and brings an air of sanity and practical commonsense into the classrooms of the younger rhetoricians.

Cassius Severus (c. 40 B.C.—37 A.D.) was one of a number of gifted orators, whom Seneca mentions as having rarely achieved any success in declamation ; in the Preface (§§12 ff.) to the third book of the *Controversiae*, he tells us the reasons which Cassius gave for this failure. In the first place, he finds an immense difference between declaiming before an audience and pleading before a judge ; he misses the objections of his adversary, which keep him alert and on guard against saying anything which would damage his case. Declamation is superfluous, and he feels that any remark he makes is superfluous. In the forum, he feels he is ' getting somewhere ' (' aliquid ago ') ; in a declamation he is struggling in a dream. The schools, he proceeds, have always claimed that they are a training-ground for orators, but bring the schoolmen into the forum, and what happens ?, they are dazzled and bewildered ; they are like pilots training on a fish-pond. What makes matters worse, and annoys Cassius, is the fact that men like Cestius regard themselves as superior to genuine orators like Pollio, Messala, and Passienus, and his young pupils so idolise Cestius as to think him almost a second Cicero. Finally, Cassius tells how he embarrassed the boastful Cestius by a witty rejoinder, and proceeded to expose the declaimer's ignorance of law.

Very similar to the view of Cassius Severus, is that of Votienus Montanus, who died in 27-8 A.D. His criticisms are detailed and practical ; he regards declamation as pernicious for the following reasons.[1] First, the declaimer aims at giving pleasure and winning applause ; consequently he avoids argument, and omits the essential in his search for superficial brilliance. Secondly, he can invent any kind of reply to an imaginary objection and assume his adversary

---

[1] *Contr.* IX, *Praef.* cf. Philodemus, *Rhetorica*, II, pp. 256-8 (Sudhaus), for a similar attitude.

to be as stupid as he likes.[1] Thirdly, he always has the applause of
his supporters to encourage him, and is not interrupted. Fourthly,
he selects his own theme, and is not in any way at the mercy of
circumstances. Fifthly, he speaks among a silent and attentive
crowd, and has no noise to cope with. Finally, he discounts the
fact that in court a judge has to be convinced and won over, not
given instructions.

These are searching criticisms, and it is unfortunate that the elder
Seneca's reply to them, if he made one, is not extant, as the Preface
concerned is incomplete. In reply to the first criticism, it may be
observed that the best declaimers, such as Latro, Cestius, and
Gallio, do pay very considerable attention to argument, and the
divisiones of the exercises are full of close reasoning. The second
is undoubtedly true, and a very important argument, as is the third,
though the declaimers were sensible of unconvincing argument, and
far-fetched points, as is clear from Seneca's references to ' longe
arcessiti colores ' and the frequent adverse criticism to be found
in his work. The fourth and fifth criticisms are true, and the last
is also a good point, for the declaimers are far too fond of rhetorical
imperatives, and are evidently not conscious of the judge as a real
person to be won over, but aim chiefly at scoring rhetorical points.

Seneca the philosopher was, as we know from the *Controversiae*,
as well as from his references to the style of the declaimers Haterius,
Vinicius, and Fabianus (*Epp.* 40, 9 ff.), and from his allusion to the
declamatory craze for applause (*Epp.* 20, 2) very familiar with the
characteristics of the schools. His own style was influenced by them,
and Quintilian (x, 1, 130) censures it for features which are familiar
in the declamations.[2] Yet in a letter devoted to the thesis ' style is
the mirror of morals' (*Epp.* 114),[3] Seneca himself attacks the worst
features of contemporary style in language which is closely com-
parable to that used in his father's *Controversiae* and *Suasoriae*, and
which shows that he was by no means sympathetic with the more
startling features of declamatory style. He notes the current craze
for novelty (§10) ' quod novum est quaerit ' (cf. *Contr.* ix, 6, 16
' omnes declamatores aiebat voluisse aliquid novi dicere '), and the
desire to say ' something big ' (§11)—' aliquid grande temptanti ' (cf.
Suas ii, 17 ' cupiebat grandia dicere '). Faults of style are loved for
their own sake (ib.) ' ipsum vitium ament ' cf. *Contr.* ii, 2, 12 ' non
ignoravit vitia sua sed amavit.' *Sententiae* are often abrupt (§§1, 11,
—cf. *Contr.* ii, *Praef.* 2 ' tam subito desinunt ut non brevia sint sed

---

[1] cf. Quint., iv, 2, 92 ' libertas omnia enumerandi quae responderi potuissent.'
xii, 6, 5 ' adversarius obstrepit,' and below, p. 81.
[2] See J. F. D'Alton, *op. cit.*, pp. 332-5, and cf. below, pp. 160 ff.
[3] cf. W. C. Summers' notes ad loc. ; I have amplified his parallels.

abrupta') and curtailed (§17 ' amputatae')—cf. Ovid's drastic cutting-down of a line of Varro of Atax in *Contr.* VII, 1, 27.[1] They are popular if they imply more than they say (§1 and §11) ' suspiciosae, in quibus plus intellegendum esset quam audiendum '—cf. *Contr.* I, 5, 9, II, 1, 34 (' suspiciose '), but are frequently (§16) trivial and puerile (cf. *Contr.* I, 7, 10 ' puerilis '), or bold ('improbae')—cf. *Contr.* VII, 5, 14 (' improbam sententiam ')—and risqué (cf. *Contr.* I, 2, 21-2), or showy and too seductive (cf. *Contr.* IV, *Praef.* 3 ' floridior' ; and *Suas.* VII, 12 ' praedulces '), merely empty resounding phrases (cf. *Contr.* VII, 4, 10 ' belle sonantis sententiae '). Composition in style is either rough and abrupt (§15 ' praefractam et asperam '—cf. *Contr.* III, *Praef.* 18), or too smoothly-flowing (' molliter labitur' cf. *Contr.* II, *Praef.* 1 ' compositio verborum mollior ') and metaphors have become bold and frequent (§10). In this letter of Seneca, therefore, we have a detailed criticism of the declamatory style.[2]

As a sufferer under the rhetorical education, the satirist Persius[3] has a few scathing comments to make on the delivery of such exercises as ' the speech of the dying Cato,' but his contemporary Petronius[4] puts into the mouth of his young hero, Encolpius, a much more outspoken and detailed criticism. Encolpius attacks the subjects as romantic and wildly improbable,[5] and the style as either bombastic or insidiously sweet.[6] He instances, as subjects, ' pirates standing on the shore with chains in their hands,' ' tyrants scribbling edicts, by which sons are ordered to chop off their fathers heads,' and ' oracular responses advising the sacrifice of maidens to ward off pestilence.' Pirates and tyrants are common enough in the elder Seneca, and the exercise in which a tyrant commands a son to strike his father (*Contr.* IX, 4) is perhaps one of which Encolpius here gives an exaggerated version. There are no exercises in the elder Seneca's collection involving ' oracular responses ' and ' sacrifices to avert pestilence,' though they occur in the declamations ascribed to Quintilian[7]. A further allusion to declamation is later (c. 48) made by Trimalchio, who cleverly satirises the stock theme of the rich man and the poor man, and neatly employs the correct terminology (*peristasis*) for the circumstances of the case.

---

[1] cf. below, p. 141.
[2] cf. *Epp.* 100, 5-6.
[3] *Sat.* III, 44-7; cf. I, 85 ff. on rhetorical antithesis and figures in court.
[4] *Satyricon*, cc. 1-2. See A Collignon, *Étude sur Pétrone* (Paris, 1892), pp. 75 ff.
[5] c. 1 ' nihil ex his, quae in usu habemus, aut audiunt aut vident ' (sc. adulescentuli).
[6] ib. ' sententiarum vanissimo strepitu . . . mellitos verborum globulos.' cf. c. 10 ' sententias, id est vitrea fracta (i.e. ' cheap junk,' cf. W. R. Smyth in *C.R.* LXI, 46) et somniorum interpretamenta '; also, c. 118.
[7] *Decl. min.*, 326, 384.

The style of declamation, says Encolpius, is impure and turgid ('maculosa,' 'turgida'), full of bluster and exaggeration ('ventosa,' 'enormis') and he rightly complains of the addiction of declaimers to the faults of Asianism[1]—though, as we have seen[2], there were some purists among them. His clever parody of a declamation—' haec vulnera pro libertate publica excepi ; hunc oculum pro vobis impendi ; date mihi ducem, qui me ducat ad liberos meos ; nam succisi poplites membra non sustinent' is all too reminiscent of the pseudo-pathos of certain exercises involving the inevitable 'tyrannicida'; here the pathos is increased by making the hero blind, and it is small wonder that Encolpius says that the declaimer who proceeded from these subjects to the courts found himself in quite another world, and that declamation had ruined genuine eloquence.

A reply to this tirade is then made by the rhetorician, Agamemnon,[3] who asserts that it is not the teachers who are to blame, but the pupils and their parents. If the teachers failed to tempt their pupils with such alluring bait, they would soon find themselves declaiming to an empty classroom. Parents are the real culprits, who fail to insist on a severe mental training, and a course of study which could proceed from poetry and philosophy to the great works of Greek and Roman eloquence. As it is, they thrust their young and ill-prepared offspring into the courts at the earliest possible opportunity, with the result that after merely playing at school they are ridiculed in the forum, and, what is worse, carry their obstinate follies with them to old age.

Further discussion between Encolpius and Agamemnon is precluded by the arrival of a vast horde of declaimers,[4] fresh from a *suasoria* on Agamemnon, as Encolpius says, in a witty allusion to the exercise which appears third in the elder Seneca's collection[5]. The young hero disappears to encounter more exciting, if less reputable, adventures, but it is interesting that the remarks here made are echoed by the author of the *Dialogus*,[6] and pave the way for the verdict of Quintilian.

In the *Dialogus*[7] of Tacitus, the attack on the practice of declamation continues. In an expansive encomium on the

---

[1] *Sat.* c. 2.
[2] cf. above, p. 63.
[3] *Sat.* cc. 3-5; cf. Quint., II, 10, 3, quoted below, p. 80.
[4] ib. c. 6.
[5] Ernout, in the Budé edition, p. 5, n. 2, wrongly calls it a *controversia.*
[6] See the careful comparisons made by Collignon, *op. cit.*, pp. 95 ff., and E. Paratore, *Il Satyricon di Petronio* (Florence, 1933) vol. II, pp. 1-5.
[7] cc. 28 ff., esp. c. 31 and 35. See the editions of W. Peterson (Oxford, 1893) and A. Gudeman (Leipzig-Berlin,2 1914) *ad loc.*

superiority of the Republican training for eloquence, Messala (c. 28) ascribes the decline of oratory to the laziness of pupils, the carelessness of parents, the ignorance of teachers, and the degeneracy of contemporary morals. He has little use for rhetoricians, whose pupils merely acquire a superficial fluency in declaiming subjects far removed from real life. They would be better engaged in acquiring the old encyclopædic education, in which philosophy played so large a part (cc. 30-31). As it is, their ignorance, even of the law, is shameful, and their style cramps the flow of eloquence into the narrow confines of a few sententious observations (c. 32). Lamenting the lack of legal apprenticeship among young men preparing for public life (c. 34), Messala says (c. 35) : ' They are conducted to the schools of the rhetoricians, of which I find it difficult to say whether the place, the type of fellow-students, or the curriculum itself, has the worst influence on the development of their talents.' The place, he argues, commands no respect—the school is merely the haunt of the inexperienced ; the young declaimers speak only among their contemporaries, and are sure of a safe hearing ; and, finally, the themes are fanciful and far removed from court-practice. Of the latter, he instances ' the rewards given to tyrannicides,' ' the options allowed to ravished maidens,' ' the remedies of pestilence,' and ' the incestuous conduct of mothers.' The first two are quite common in Seneca, but not the third, though pestilence forms the subject of 'Quint.' *Decl, min.* 323, 326, 329, 384; the last-named theme is not commonly represented in Seneca's collection, though *Contr.* VI, 7 (Demens Quia Filio Cessit Uxorem) comes very close to it, and Quintilian (IX, 2, 42) records a similar case as from Seneca. Of the *suasoriae* Messala has little criticism to make, but the *controversiae* are, he exclaims, incredible concoctions (' quales per fidem et quam incredibiliter compositae '). Finally, his reference to ' ingentibus verbis ' is another allusion to the bombastic style, and his last words before the lacuna in the text at the end of c. 35 (' cum ad veros iudices ventum ') show that he developed the well-known theme of the helplessness of the academic declaimer in the practical life of the law-courts.

Meanwhile, it is interesting to note that the chorus of disapproval had by no means interrupted the flow of declamatory eloquence. Not only had the Emperor Nero[1] and the poet Lucan[2] coveted glory as declaimers and given fresh impetus to the practice, but the elder Pliny had produced a work entitled *Studiosus*, in which he collected, just as the elder Seneca had done before him, neat

---

[1] Suet., *Nero* 10 ' declamavitque saepius publice.'
[2] Vacca, *Vita Lucani*, mentions practice-speeches for and against Octavius Sagitta, and a declamation *de incendio urbis*; cf. Schanz-Hosius, II, pp. 494-5.

and witty points from the declamations. This information we owe to Aulus Gellius,[1] who quotes an exercise from it on the old theme of the reward of the *vir fortis*. Passing over, for the moment, the criticisms on declamation of Quintilian, which are by far the most numerous and have a special importance, the chronological survey may be continued beyond his day to that of his pupil, the younger Pliny.

In *Epistles* II, 3, Pliny has an interesting and appreciative account of the declaimer Isaeus, to whom Juvenal[2] refers in no very complimentary terms, but whose style and manner made a favourable impression on Pliny. After praising his pure Attic style, his neat or dignified prefaces, his concentrated wisdom, his artistic expression, his virtues in the divisions of his speech, his ἐνθυμήματα[3] and his wonderful memory, Pliny says, in words that recall those of the elder Seneca on Capito[4], that Isaeus is still a *scholasticus*—' quo genere hominum nihil aut sincerius aut simplicius aut melius.' Contrasting the old school-orators with the lawyer, who has learnt much mischief in the real life of the courts, he adds that 'the school, the audience, the fictitious theme, are innocuous and blameless, yet none the less enjoyable, especially for the old, even as they give greatest pleasure in youth.' It is clear that Pliny had, however, a less favourable opinion of young declaimers, for in a further letter (II, 14), he laments the degeneracy of the centumviral courts where inexperienced speakers, fresh from school, show no sense of shame, but are merely avid for hired applause. ' Scito,' he adds caustically, ' eum pessime dicere qui laudabitur maxime.' Pliny was evidently fully aware of the difference between the rhetorician and the practical orator, for in *Epp*. IV, 11 he says of the exiled orator, Valerius Licinianus, who had become a professor in Sicily, that he had fallen so low ' ut exul de senatore, *rhetor de oratore fieret*.' He tells amusingly how Licinianus prefaced his delcamation with remarks on the mockery of Fortune (the old *locus communis* again), and then, putting on a Greek cloak instead of the Roman toga (which he was no longer entitled to wear) declared ' Latine declamaturus sum ! '—a neat παρὰ προσδοκίαν which may be illustrated by *Contr*. IX, 3, 13.

Martial's allusions to declamation show that he was just as satirical on the subject as Juvenal, but he has a delicate and pretty wit which contrasts strongly with Juvenal's mordant sarcasm. In *Epigrams* II, 7 he cleverly satirises the declaimer's passion for winning applause by saying something ' smart ' (*Contr*. I, 4, 10, ' omnes

[1] IX, 16, 1 ; cf. Schanz-Hosius, II, p. 781.
[2] *Sat*. III, 73-4 ' sermo promptus et Isaeo torrentior.' But Mayor, Advertisement to his edn., p. xix, interprets differently.
[3] cf. Sen., *Contr*. I, *Praef*. 23.
[4] *Contr*. X, *Praef*. 12. cf. above p. 72.

aliquid belli dixerunt '). The adverb ' belle ' was extremely fashionable among declamatory audiences both as a favourable criticism and as a delighted ejaculation. A recent critic[1] has counted 21 instances in the elder Seneca alone. So Martial very aptly puts the declaimer Attalus in his place by using the adverb ' belle ' or the adjective ' bellus ' thirteen times in seven lines (cf. x, 46). *Epigrams* IV, 80 is equally devastating; Martial observes that if Maron, who declaims through fevers and agues, cannot find a better way of inducing a perspiration, well and good; but the sensible thing would be ' tacere ' (' to lie. still ' and ' hold his tongue ').

Juvenal, it has been well said,[2] ' uses the force of a steam-hammer to crack a nut ' ; and the delicate shell of Roman declamation hardly withstands the vehemence of his scathing attack. ' I demens et saevas curre per Alpes, ut pueris placeas et declamatio fias ' comments the master of sarcasm,[3] and follows up this allusion to Hannibal with a clear reference to the *suasoria* on Alexander the Great. In a longer passage[4] he gives further details of the stock-in-trade of contemporary teachers of rhetoric, not only the *suasoriae* on Hannibal (' cuius mihi sexta quaque die miserum caput Hannibal implet ') but the *controversiae* on tyrants, seducers, poison-cups, cruel and unfaithful husbands, and wonderful cures for the blind. The ' ingratus maritus ' reminds the reader of *Contr.* II, 5, where the wife brings an *actio ingrati* against her husband, and the ' malus ' of the frequent declamatory cases of ' mala tractatio.' But it is noticeable that there is no example in Seneca of ' quae iam veteres sanant mortaria caecos ' though the *caecus* himself appears in *Contr.* III, 1. Equally uncomplimentary is Juvenal's reference in his last satire to ' the mulish disposition of the declaimer Vagellius,'[5] and to the torrential eloquence of the declaimer Isaeus (III, 74). The satirist has also at least one parody of a favourite declamatory subject—the contest for the arms of Achilles[6]. He is clearly familiar with declamatory terms[7], and his work abounds in rhetorical *sententiae* and commonplaces[8]. But one

---

[1] H. Bardon, *op. cit.*, p. 16 ; cf. also Persius, *Sat.* I, 87.

[2] By J. D. Duff, Introduction to his edition (Cambridge, 1898, rpd. 1925), p. XXXII.

[3] *Sat.* x, 166-7 ; cf. Mayor *ad loc.*

[4] *Sat.* VII, 150 ff.; cf. Mayor, *ad loc.*

[5] XVI, 23.

[6] VII, 115; x, 83-5 is a probable, but not certain allusion; cf. Mayor, and Duff, *ad loc.*

[7] VI, 245 (principium, locus), 280 (color), 450 (enthymema); VII, 155-6 (color, quaestio); VIII, 125 (sententia).

[8] cf. J. de Decker, *op. cit.*, *passim.*

would hardly guess from his sardonic allusions that he himself was a declaimer until middle age[1].

These criticisms might be further illustrated by comparison with Lucian's cynical comments in his 'Ῥητόρων διδάσκαλος, §§18 ff., and with the anecdotes to be found in Philostratus' 'Lives of the Sophists,' but at this point we must bid farewell to the company of poets and satirists, letter-writers and essayists, not to speak of disgruntled orators, and ask, in conclusion, the question: ' Is there any reply to these voices of condemnation?' Apart from the brief defence of the rhetorician Agamemnon in Petronius, one writer only ventures to answer; but that writer held the original Chair of Rhetoric in Rome for twenty years, and became the most celebrated educator of his day. Quintilian[2] is fully aware of these criticisms, but still maintains that declamation can be of great value. ' The practice,' he agrees, ' has *through the fault of its teachers* so degenerated that the licence and ignorance of declaimers may be numbered among the chief causes of the decline of eloquence at Rome. But it is still possible to make good use of what is naturally good. We shall look, it is true, in vain for magicians, pestilences, oracular responses, stepmothers more cruel than those of tragedy, and other even more fabulous subjects, among guarantees and interdicts '—though even these may be used as a temporary outlet for the exuberance of youth. But, ' those who consider the whole practice of declamation alien to forensic life, quite fail to perceive the reason for the original invention of the exercise.' Its only justification lies in its use as a preparation for public life, and Quintilian maintains that if actual names[3] were used in the exercises, if their themes were more intricate[4] and their style more simple, and if a sense of humour were occasionally displayed, they would be of considerable value. But these themes should be as close as possible to real life, for declamation, properly treated, is ' iudiciorum consiliorumque imago.'

A further selection of Quintilian's criticisms of declamation, both favourable and adverse, will perhaps help to clarify the general

---

[1] *Vita Iuvenalis*, ' ad mediam fere aetatem declamavit animi magis causa quam quod se scholae aut foro praepararet.'

[2] II, 10, 1-12, cf. J. Cousin, *op. cit.*, I, pp. 127-9, and Parks, *op. cit.*, p. 99.

[3] Parks, *op. cit.*, p. 98 n. 124 (who again anticipates my general point of view) questions the value of the addition of names, and cites the use of place-names in the exercises quoted by Suetonius, *de Rhet.* 1. I think Quintilian probably meant names of actual persons, and that this would have tended to define the very vague stock characterisation of the themes.

[4] Even though some of Seneca's themes seem rather elaborate already, the circumstantial details which would be necessary in court-cases hardly appear: cf. Bornecque, *Déclam.* p. 114 fin. For a highly intricate theme, cf. Quint., III, 6, 96 ff.

picture which he thus presents. He repeatedly stresses the close connection, for good or ill, between the preparation of the schools and the practice of the courts; so, in IX, 2, 81 he says : ' nam et in his (sc. scholis) educatur orator, et in eo, quomodo declamatur, positum est etiam, quomodo agatur.' So in IV, 2, 29 declamation is, or should be, ' forensium actionum meditatio,' though declaimers spoil its value through over-fondness for narration. The inventors of themes, though far too prone to rhetorical subdivisions and rules, follow out those themes ' ad modum actionum ' (IV, 1, 43).

Theoretically, Quintilian may have agreed with the author of *Decl. min.* 338, who[1] declares ' scholastica controversia complectitur quidquid in foro fieri potest ' ; in practice, he points out (VII, 4, 11) that several favourite themes are modelled on similar types of court-case, and (VII, 6, 1) such recurrent questions as *scriptum*) (*voluntas* are quite as much legal as they are declamatory.[2] Sometimes he goes out of his way to tell us that a class of case is not only frequently treated in the schools but is of common occurrence in the forum (VII, 2, 24), and notes that what is not expedient in the courts is forbidden in the schools (IX, 2, 67).

But this is not the only side of the picture, for Time has brought degeneration in its train, and declamations have ceased to be the sharp weapon that once they were, and have replaced a genuine vigorous, forensic style with one that aims merely at a seductive attractiveness (V, 12, 17). It is the style and manner of declamation which generally arouse Quintilian's ire, as when he ridicules the unreal diction (VIII, 3, 23), or absurd expressions (VIII, 5, 22-5) or over-imaginative figures (VIII, 3, 76 ; IX, 2, 42, 98). In deliberative themes, particularly, they quite overstep the mark by affecting abrupt and impetuous openings (III, 8, 58 ff). Even in forensic themes, some of them make the whole practice absurd by leaping up the moment the subject is announced and demanding a word from which to start! (X, 7, 21). Some declaimers, not content with such stylistic aberrations, grow grey in the schools and spend their time inventing themes as far removed from reality as possible (II, 20, 4).

With several of the criticisms of Votienus Montanus, Quintilian would have agreed. He is fully aware of the danger of pleading without an adversary (VII, 3, 20 ; XII, 6, 5),[3] which declaimers tried to circumvent by imagining every possible reply (IV, 2, 92), and of the declaimer's freedom to assume that any detail not mentioned in the

---

[1] The *Decl. min.* may, of course, be genuinely his own, or, at any rate, based upon his teaching.
[2] cf. above, pp. 47 ff.
[3] cf. R. G. Austin's notes on the latter passage (*op. cit.*, p. 108).

theme was in his own favour (VII, 2, 54). In his excellent precepts on the education of the young in the first two books he makes special note of the futility of mutual applause (II, 2, 9 ff.), a feature which survived among the adults. He notes when a feature is ' res declamatoria magis quam forensis ' (IV, 2, 128), and admits the risk of using fictitious themes (X, 2, 12). He might have thought the views of the satirists exaggerated, but would certainly have sympathised with the experience of the young Persius, for he expresses disapproval of parents who value quantity of declamation more than quality (X, 5, 21). And theory must always be supplemented by legal experience (XII, 6, 6-7).

In evaluating these criticisms of Quintilian, we must always remember that he had not only spent a life-time in teaching and writing, but had also pleaded on numerous occasions in the courts (cf. II, 12, 12). There is every reason, therefore, why we should have faith in his judgment, when he claims (X, 5, 14)' that, provided the themes are reasonably restrained, the practice of declamation is useful not only to the young student but to the orator of established reputation, as a training in invention and arrangement of arguments—*quia inventionem et dispositionem pariter exercent* ; and adds that their ' richer ' subject-matter also provides a refreshing change after the dull minutiae of the courts.

To these points of Quintilian, the following observations may be added. Many of the adverse criticisms it will be noticed, are considerably later than the elder Seneca, and although they are largely true when applied to his work, they are not wholly so, for some types of subject, e.g., ' magicians,' ' remedies for pestilences,' ' miraculous cures,' are not to be found in his work, and clearly show that further degeneration took place after his day. But in the elder Seneca's day declamation still retained some of its original value. It encouraged quick-wittedness in argument, originality of attack and defence, and ability to create an appearance of sincerity and simplicity of character, or to blacken that of an opponent by subtle insinuation. It demanded careful interpretation of the letter and the spirit of the law, a judicious weighing-up of the relative value of arguments, and a logical marshalling of the salient points in the most effective order. It caused a student to consider difficult problems of civil and criminal law, particularly where ambiguity existed, or where there was a conflict between one law and another.[2]

---

[1] See the admirable comments of F. H. Colson in the Introduction to his edn. of Quintilian, Book I, (Cambridge, 1924), esp. pp. 36-7.

[2] Lanfranchi, *op. cit.*, pp. 1-176 (' Il diritto nei retori in linea generale ') has examined the declamations of all three authors from this point of view and stresses the recurrence of such genuinely legal features as *ius*) (*aequitas*, and *voluntas*) (*scriptum*. cf. above, pp. 46 ff.

In all the criticisms of declamation there is little or nothing to suggest that the laws on which the exercises are based were the products of pure fantasy. Finally, the study developed the power of memory, as may be seen from the phenomenal achievement of Seneca himself[1].

Even so, granted the reason for the stock characters and heightened atmosphere, and granted the value of the exercises as a kind of mental gymnastics, the question may still be asked : ' Why did the cases chosen so often represent circumstances which could, in one's opinion, so rarely occur in real life—even though Truth may be stranger than Fiction ? '

The answer to this question seems hardly to have been made, and it may be suggested that these are *test-cases* in more senses than one. They not only test the validity of a law by positing more and more extreme circumstances—e.g., ' children must support (or obey) their parents '—what if the parents are manifestly undeserving, ungrateful, indeed criminal, the children marked by every known virtue, models of piety, saviours indeed of their country ? Is the law still applicable ?[2] They also test the *powers* of the declaimer ; the harder the case is, the more removed from the circumstances of everyday life, where there is nearly always something to be said on both sides, the better the declaimer needs to be to cope successfully with it. If he can produce a reasonably good defence with heaven and earth against him, he should, theoretically, be able to tackle law-court cases with greater ease. That was the theory, but not always the practical result.

The principle is a sound one, and by it the declamations may be defended on the very grounds that their critics attacked them. ' Gladiatores gravioribus armis discunt quam pugnant ' says Votienus Montanus.[3] Certainly, the conditions of the courts were more arduous in one sense—they lacked the quiet atmosphere of the *vita umbratilis*, the chorus, of approval, the mutual admiration, and this was why good declaimers made bad lawyers ; but the cases they debated often demanded great thought and originality, as well as judgment, all the more because they were deliberately designed to provide an almost, but not quite, impossible hurdle.[4]

---

[1] cf. *Contr.* I, *Praef.* 2.
[2] cf. the argument of Quint., v, 10, 97.
[3] *Contr.* IX, *Praef.* 4.
[4] The only hint of this which I have seen elsewhere is in H. de la Ville de Mirmont's eminently readable work, *La Jeunesse d'Ovide* (Paris, 1905) p. 87 ' Qui peut le plus, peut le moins ; un élève habitué à se tirer des procès fictifs les plus extraordinaires, quand il sera avocat, se trouvera à l'aise en face des causes ordinaires du Forum,' though he does not apply this remark to the Senecan exercises. He well adds that the gymnast becomes an acrobat and ends sometimes in disaster.

CHAPTER V

THE LAWS IN THE SENECAN DECLAMATIONS

A question of the first importance for any student of declamation is clearly that of its relationship to contemporary legal practice, as a training for which it was originally designed. To assess this fully would require a separate study[1] taking into consideration the conditions under which the Roman courts were operating in the early Empire, so far as those conditions can be envisaged. It is proposed to examine here the 'laws' which are invoked at the head of the Senecan *controversiae*, with the particular object of deciding how far they represent genuine Roman tradition.

It is not uncommonly stated that the declamatory laws are mostly fictitious, or that they have little connection with Roman Law[2]. Boissier[3], in a well-known article, declared roundly 'It is an imaginary legislation which is nearly everywhere invoked.' Geib[4] had long before stated what has been the general position of legal scholars : 'The writings of the rhetors are quite the worst and the most useless sources from an historical point of view. A position stated only by them, and resting on no other authority, may be treated without exception as incorrect and invented.' Bornecque[5], improving upon the works of Dirksen[6] and Lécrivain[7], showed that a minority of the laws could be paralleled from Roman legislation, but looked generally to Greece for his analogies. Sprenger[8], in a valuable dissertation, sometimes had difficulty in deciding exactly how much is Roman and how much Greek, but found more Greek (and imaginary) Law than Roman Law on the whole. On the other hand, Jean Cousin[9], in a chapter devoted to Quintilian's legal orientation, added further Roman evidence for

1 cf. E. P. Parks, *op. cit.*, and above pp. 45-8.
2 Pichon, in *Revue Universitaire* IV (1895), p. 160 says : 'Les lois invoquées sont des lois inventées à plaisir, dont on composerait un Digeste des plus fantaisistes et des plus extravagants.' cf. Gwynn, *Roman Education*, p. 163; Edward, edn. of *Suasoriae* of the elder Seneca, Introd. p. XXXII; Carcopino, *op. cit.* p. 118.
3 *Revue des deux mondes* XI, 1902, pp. 480-508, reprinted in *Tacitus and Other Roman Studies* (London, 1906) pp. 163-194. See p. 178.
4 *Geschichte des römischen Criminalprozesses*, (Leipzig, 1842) p. 277, quoted by Greenidge, *Legal Procedure of Cicero's Time*, p. 464.
5 *Déclam.* pp. 59-74.
6 *Hinterlassene Schriften* I, 254-280 (Leipzig, 1871).
7 *N.R.H.* XV [1891] pp. 680-691. Mention should also be made of T. S. Simonds, *Themes Treated by the Elder Seneca* (Baltimore, 1896) pp. 82-98.
8 *Quaestiones in rhetorum Romanorum declamationes iuridicae*, (Diss., Halle, 1911).
9 *Études sur Quintilien*, vol. I, (Paris, 1936) pp. 685 ff. Cousin also admits Greek influence, of course.

some of the laws recurring in the *Institutio Oratoria*. But the extensive study of F. Lanfranchi[1] has re-opened the entire question, for he views the laws of both the Senecan and the later collections as very largely representative of Roman legal thought, and the following conclusions, reached independently, may perhaps be held to be substantiated by and also, as far as Seneca is concerned, to substantiate his investigation.

The fact that many of these declamatory laws do not appear in extant Roman legal sources should not necessarily be allowed to rule out any possibility of their genuineness, for those sources represent but a fraction of the mass of legislation and juridical commentary which Rome produced in the thousand and more years of her history. Rather should doubt arise on the following grounds : (i) when classical writers themselves state or imply that the laws are fictitious ; (ii) when the laws appear in two or more contradictory versions, though the possibility, hitherto ignored, must be considered that the earlier version (e.g. in Seneca) may be genuine and the later (e.g. in pseudo-Quintilian) concocted ; (iii) when open conflict with established Roman law can be shown, though here it must be remembered that law is a living and changing element, and what conflicts with the law of the late Empire may not necessarily have conflicted with the law of the late Republic ; (iv) when the parallelism with Greek Law is striking, and Roman evidence is inadequate, inconsistent, or entirely lacking. On these grounds the following investigation is made.

A preliminary word of caution[2] may, however, be advisable at this point regarding the form in which declamatory laws appear. The most common phraseology is 'sit actio,' and, of course, even if the declamatory action can be shown to be genuinely praetorian, the praetor would not express his edict in that form. For instance, where the declaimers say 'sepulchri violati sit actio,' the praetor uses the first person, and says ' cuius dolo malo sepulchrum violatum esse dicetur, in eum in factum iudicium dabo.' The same will be found to be true of the declamatory law on *vis* and *metus*. The declaimers put the gist of the law in an adapted or simplified form for the purposes of their exercise, but this does not mean that they may not represent genuine legislation, or even that they do not contain some genuine phraseology. Lanfranchi[3] rightly warns us not to be misled by ' the peremptory form in which these laws are couched.'

[1] *Il diritto nei retori romani* (Milan, 1938). This work did not come into my hands until my own MS was practically complete, but I add full references to it. Note also the remarks of Düll in *Z.S.S.* LXIII (1943), pp. 74 ff.
[2] I am indebted for this reminder to Professor H. F. Jolowicz and Mr. W. Geddes.
[3] *op. cit.*, p. 463.

(1) Laws stated or implied to be fictitious

Certain 'actions' permitted by the rhetors fall into this category, of which the first is :—

INSCRIPTI MALEFICII SIT ACTIO

(*Contr.* v, 1, cf. III, *Praef.* 17, 'Quint.', *Decl. min.*, 252, 344, 370; Walz, *Rhet. Graec.* VIII, 392-3).

The point of this law[1] is to enable cases which did not fall within the scope of the existing code to be brought to court. It has been argued that Quintilian (VII, 4, 36) declares this to be an invention of the schools ('finguntur in scholis et inscripti maleficii' etc), but the passage only proves that the rhetors were fond of concocting cases on this basis, not that the actual law which they used was itself necessarily fictitious.[2] Moreover, the language of the declaimer in *Decl. min.* 252 (p. 31, ll. 10 ff., Ritter) has a ring of truth about it when he says : 'Our ancestors seem to have thought out this law with the utmost care, since they realised that no human skill was so great, no prophecy indeed so sure, that the foresight of lawgivers could plan against every possible misdeed which could ever be plotted in the minds of evildoers.' The idea of an *actio inscripti maleficii* was, he proceeds to argue, to safeguard against offences which might just escape the existing regulations. But the only legal analogy which has been hitherto adduced is that of *stellionatus*[3], which appears to have had an equally undefined application in criminal law. In *Contr.* III, *Praef.* 17, Cassius Severus tells how he ridiculed Cestius' lack of legal knowledge by haling him before the praetor on a charge of *inscriptum maleficium*. This would imply that the action was either fictitious or quite obsolete ; if it was obsolete, it would evidently be praetorian. On the same occasion Cassius accused Cestius, in fun, of ingratitude, before the other praetor, and finally demanded a *curator* for him from the *praetor urbanus*. Now, as will be seen, both of these, though used here in jest, contain close analogies in actual law, and it may be that Lanfranchi is right in suspecting a germ of genuineness even in the above 'law,' though it has been more usual to refer it, for the terminology, at least, to the ἄγαφα ἀδικήματα (cf. Hesychius, s.v. ἄγραφος) of the Greeks. But the exercise in which

---

[1] cf. Mommsen, *Straf.* p. 387, n. 1, Bornecque, *Déclam.*, pp. 62-3, and edn. of Sen. rhet., vol. I, n. 273 ; Sprenger, pp. 228-30 ; Lanfranchi, pp. 504-7.
[2] cf. Aerodius on *Decl. Min.* 344 in P. Burman's variorum edition (Leyden, 1720).
[3] Noted by Cuiacius, *Observ.* IX, 13 ; x, 26; cf. *Dig.* XLVII, 20, 3, 1 'ubicumque igitur titulus criminis deficit illic stellionatus obiciemus,' on which see Mommsen, *Straf.*, p. 680. But E. Volterra, *Stellionatus* (Sassara, 1929) argues that these words are interpolated, that *stellionatus* was a creation of Antonine jurisprudence, and that its only proven application is in certain types of commercial fraud.

it appears, involving a law-suit instituted by a would-be suicide against the man who prevented him, is certainly far-fetched.

A second action of which the rhetors are fond is:—

INGRATI SIT ACTIO

(*Contr.* IX, 1, cf. II, 5; 'Quint.', *Decl. min.* 333, 368; cf. Quint., VII, 4, 37-8).

The younger Seneca (*De Ben.* III, 6, 1) refers to this as ' lex quae in scholis exercetur,' and it is generally regarded as a conventional fiction. Seneca adds that there is no such action anywhere except in Macedon (*ib.* § 2, cf. IV, 37, 3). As a general principle applying to free citizens this may have been true, although Xenophon (*Cyrop.*, I, 2, 7) says there was a δίκη ἀχαριστίας in Persia. But it is a misleading statement, for Valerius Maximus tells us that it existed in Marseilles (II, 6, 7), and also at Athens (II, 6, 6, V, 3, ext. 3), where, in fact, the basis of the δίκη ἀποστασίου brought by a master against a liberated slave was ingratitude or failure to show proper respect[1]. What is more, an *actio ingrati* did exist at Rome, for a freedman who failed to show gratitude to his former master could be charged by him[2], and, although he could not normally be reduced to slavery again, he could be legally punished in a variety of ways ; and the important fact is that the law authorising this procedure, the *Lex Aelia Sentia*[3], dates from A.D. 4,—the centre of the period of the Senecan declamations. Moreover, an action of this kind could have been taken, at any rate under the later Empire, by a father against an ungrateful emancipated son, with a view to reasserting his *potestas*[4]. Similar to these situations is that of *Decl. min.* 333 where a rich man sues a youth whom he had befriended and who subsequently used his talents against him. In Seneca, *Contr.* IX, 1, the case is brought by a ransomer against the man he had ransomed from prison, and although the setting is from Greek history, inaccurately transmitted, this position is not as far as it might seem from Roman law. Quite apart from the fact that the ransomer may have had a lien over the *redemptus ab hostibus*[5], the kind of argument

---

[1] See Beauchet, *Hist. du droit privé de la République Athénienne* (Paris, 1897), II, pp. 501.ff.
[2] Ulp., *Dig.* XXXVII, 14, 1; III, 3, 35, 1; Paul, *Dig.* XXXVII, 14, 19; Marcian., *Dig.* XXXVII, 15, 4; *Cod. Iust.*, VI, 7, 3; Iust., *Inst.*, I, 16, 1, cf. Sprenger, p. 221, Lanfranchi, p. 191. Bornecque, *Déclam.* p. 67, and edn. vol. I, n. 152 does not mention this.
[3] Ulp. *Dig.* XL, 9, 30. On this law, see further W. W. Buckland, *The Roman Law of Slavery* (Cambridge, 1908) pp. 422 ff ; A. M. Duff, *Freedmen in the Early Roman Empire* (Oxford, 1928) pp. 37 and 41-2.
[4] *Cod. Theod.* VIII, 14, 1 = *Cod. Iust.* VIII, 49, 1, Mommsen, *Straf.* p. 856.
[5] Buckland, *op. cit.*, pp. 311 ff. (for which reference I am indebted to Prof. Jolowicz). This, the common view, is challenged, as regards the Republic and early Empire, by Ernst Levy, ' Captivus Redemptus ' (*Class. Phil.* XXXVIII (1943) pp. 159-176). Daube (*Studies in Biblical Law*, Cambridge, 1947, p. 73) upholds it.

used regarding acts which, though legal in themselves, entail ingratitude to a benefactor, is such as must have been used in cases against ungrateful freedmen by advocates in the Roman courts. In II, 5 and *Decl. min.* 368 the action is brought by a divorced wife against an ungrateful husband[1], whom she had not betrayed, under torture, to a tyrant. Now we may be fairly sure that she could not have brought an *actio ingrati* against her former husband, but she could have brought an *actio rei uxoriae*, claiming restitution of her dowry, on the grounds of his culpability; and an important fact is that questions of *moral justification* were considered in this action by the judge, as it was originally *in bonum et aequum concepta*[2]. In view of these facts, it is unsatisfactory merely to point to a Greek δίκη ἀχαριστίας (if such existed) as basis[3]. Even though ingratitude cases were probably debated earlier in Greek schools, they would have a particular appropriateness in the Augustan Age.

(II) Laws appearing in contradictory versions

Laws involving heroes and rewards are very common in the declamations[4] and in Seneca we meet :

VIR FORTIS QVOD VOLET PRAEMIVM OPTET, SI PLVRES ERVNT, IVDICIO CONTENDANT
(*Contr.* VIII, 5, x, 2, cf. Quint., *Inst. Or.* VII, 1, 24-5 ; VII, 5, 4 ; *Decl. min.* 293, 304, 371, *Decl. maior.* IV ; Calp. Flacc., *Decl.* 26, 27, 35; Aul. Gell., IX, 16, 5, Fortunatianus, *R.L.M.* p. 84, Julius Victor, *ib.* p. 383, etc).

Not only do the rewards claimed by declamatory heroes take fantastic forms, but the conflict of this law with the version given by 'Quint.', *Decl.* 258 'Si duo aut plures fortiter fecerint, de praemio *armis* contendant. Vir fortis optet quod volet ' renders it open to grave suspicion[5]. Neither this nor the related law :

QVI TER FORTITER FECERIT, MILITIA VACET
(*Contr.* I, 8; Calp. Flacc., *Decl.* 15) is supported by legal evidence, and even though rewards and *vacatio militiae* were common enough in Rome, they would certainly not have given rise to the

---

[1] cf. Juvenal, *Sat.* VII, 169 ' malus ingratusque maritus.'
[2] cf. Cic., *Top.* 17, 66, *De Off.* III, 15, 61; Girard, *Manuel Elémentaire de Droit Romain*[4] (Paris, 1906), pp. 950 ff.
[3] As does Bornecque *Déclam.* p. 67 ; see Sprenger, pp. 220-221.
[4] cf. the lists in Sprenger, pp. 176-7, Lanfranchi, p. 388. cf. Bornecque, vol. II, n. 260.
[5] The declaimer, moreover, knew the Senecan form, cf. p. 53, l. 8 (Ritter) ' sane ita sit constituta lex, ut in *iudicio* contendamus.'

kind of litigation the declaimers envisage. The ἀριστεύς and τρισαριστεύς are also found in the exercises of Hermogenes.

We may next consider the Senecan rape-laws, which seem to conflict with one another; though there are elements in them which find some support in legal sources. They are as follows :—

RAPTA RAPTORIS AVT MORTEM AVT INDOTATAS NVPTIAS OPTET
(*Contr.* I, 5; III, 5; VII, 8; VIII, 6).

This law reappears in Calpurnius Flaccus, *Decl.* 34, and, without the word *indotatas*, several times in the lesser declamations, ascribed to Quintilian (262, 270, 280, 286), also in Hermogenes, π. στάσ (p. 41, l. 10, Rabe); though there are also variant forms such as 'rapta raptoris mortem aut *bona* optet' (276) and 'raptor decem milia solvat' (252). The existence of these variants diminishes confidence in the veracity of the law quoted. In addition, it seems to conflict with the law given in *Contr.* II, 3, 'raptor, nisi et suum et raptae patrem intra dies triginta exoraverit, pereat,' in that the decision is left to the girl herself, not to her parent[1].

Rape was punishable by death, as Bornecque[2] observes, in Lacedaemon; and we may add that Plato, *Laws* 871 c, states that the ravisher of a free woman may be slain with impunity. In Attic Law, the normal procedure was to institute either a γραφὴ ὕβρεως (criminal) or a δίκη βιαίων (civil); under the former, the death-penalty might occasionally be imposed (cf. Lysias I, 32 ἐφ' οἷσπερ ἀποκτείνειν ἔξεστιν; Dinarchus, I, 23), but under the latter it was more normal to inflict a fine, even if force was used (Plut. *Solon* c. 23; Lysias I, 32-3), and if this fine were not paid the seducer, it appears, could be ordered to marry the girl—a situation frequently reflected in New Comedy[3]. There are, therefore, elements in the Senecan law which could be related to Greece. But the Roman evidence is equally strong, and demands at least equal consideration. In Roman Law an *actio iniuriarum* was a normal civil remedy for these offences, but they were also punishable under the criminal law. The *Lex Iulia de Adulteriis* (c. 17 B.C.) imposed a penalty of confiscation of half of the offender's goods, if he was *honestus*

---

[1] cf. Bornecque, *Déclam.* p. 61.

[2] *ib.* p. 69, citing Walz, *Rhet. Graec.* IV, 293, 1; V, 269, 13; VII, 244, 16. The evidence is rhetorical, but probably true.

[3] J. J. Thonissen, *Le droit pénal de la République Athénienne* (Paris-Brussels 1875) pp. 319-324. Meier-Schömann-Lipsius, *Der Attische Process* (Berlin, 1883-7), p. 509. Beauchet, *Hist. du Droit privé de la République Athénienne* (Paris, 1897), I, pp. 138-9; Sprenger, p. 204; Fredershausen, 'Studien über das Recht bei Plautus und Terenz, (*Hermes*, XLVII (1912) pp. 210 ff.) (Plaut. *Aul.* 791 ff. *Truc.* 841, 845; Ter. *Ad.* 724 ff., *And.* 780).

and if force was not used[1]. But forcible *stuprum* was a much more serious offence, and was a crime punishable under the *Lex Iulia de vi publica*, which remained the standing law on the subject for centuries[2]. The penalty for offences under this law was normally *aquae et ignis interdictio*[3], but forcible *stuprum* could entail a death penalty *extra ordinem*. This we know from Marcianus[4], but find that Paul, though treating of the offence as a form of criminal *iniuria*, gives exactly the same information[5], and there is therefore every likelihood that it dates back to the *Lex Iulia de vi*, on which Marcianus is commenting[6]. Under Constantine rape became a statutory crime, involving capital punishment[7]. It is in the legislation of Justinian that we meet with an important legal allusion to the option on the part of the girl. Justinian refuses this option in *Cod.* IX, 13, 1, 2 'nec sit facultas raptae virgini . . . raptorem suum maritum sibi exposcere.'[8] Now this refusal to countenance marriage in such cases may date back at least to Constantine[9], and it may well imply that such an option was legal before the severely repressive legislation of that emperor.

In conclusion, there are elements in the declamatory law which may be paralleled from both Greek and Roman sources. The position seems to have been very similar in both, and may be reconstructed somewhat as follows. Unless the affair was settled out of court (e.g. in the Roman *domesticum consilium*), the parent (or master) of the girl would bring a private action against the culprit (δίκη βιαίων or *actio iniuriarum*). The sentence would be a fine, but the alternative of marriage without dowry may commonly have been agreed upon, always assuming that *conubium* was possible. If the culprit refused both alternatives, he would render himself liable to a criminal charge (γραφὴ ὕβρεως, or for *crimen vis*, if force had been used, or *stuprum* under the *Lex Iulia de Adulteriis* if it had not). In an extreme case he might incur the death-penalty. So what the declaimers have done is to telescope the civil and

---

[1] Just., *Inst.* IV, 18, 4. Sprenger, p. 204, is wrong in saying that Marcianus *Dig.* XLVIII, 6, 5, 2 (' raptus crimen legis Iuliae de adulteriis potestatem excedit') precludes this view. Marcianus is speaking of the *quinquennii praescriptio*, and means that it applied in cases of adultery, but not in cases of *raptus*.

[2] Marcian., *Dig.* XLVIII, 6, 3, 4; cf. *Cod. Iust.* IX 12, 3; IX, 13, 1, 5; Just., *Inst.* IV, 18, 8. Mommsen, *Straf.* pp. 664-5.

[3] Ulp. *Dig.* XLVIII, 6, 10, 2.

[4] Marcian., *Dig.* XLVIII, 6, 5, 2 (commenting on *Lex Iulia de vi publica*) ' qui vacantem mulierem rapuerit vel nuptam ultimo supplicio punitur.'

[5] *Sent.* V, 4, 4 ' quae res extra ordinem vindicatur ita ut pulsatio pudoris poena capitis vindicetur '; cf. *ib.* 14, which shows that ' caput ' means ' death.'

[6] cf. Lécrivain in Dar. Sag. s. v. *Raptus*.

[7] *Cod. Theod.* IX, 24, 1 ; cf. Ammian. Marcell. XVI, 5, 12 (under Julian).

[8] cf. Lanfranchi, *op. cit:* pp. 462 ff.

[9] *Cod. Theod.* IX, 24, 3 allows such marriages to be challenged.

criminal law (of either Greece or Rome), and present a highly dramatic position, seizing on the two most exciting features, and bringing them into a striking antithetical relationship. The balance is inclined slightly to the Roman side by the fact that the declamatory law 'Raptor decem milia solvat' (which reappears in Quintilian IV, 2, 69, and VII, 4, 42) is generally considered to represent the fine imposed under the *Lex Scantinia* for assaults upon youths[1].

RAPTOR, NISI ET SVVM ET RAPTAE PATREM INTRA DIES TRIGINTA EXORAVERIT, PEREAT
(*Contr.* II, 3, cf. Quint., *Inst. Or.* IX, 2, 90; *Decl. min.* 349, cf. Calp. Flacc., *Decl.* 25).

This law is considered imaginary by Bornecque[2] and Sprenger[3], though the latter has observed that there is a rather remarkable resemblance between it and the Marcianus passage of the *Digest* which mentions the possibility of the girl's parent condoning the offence, and thereby saving the ravisher from the death-penalty[4]. The recurrence of the verb 'exorare' in this connection is also noteworthy, but as the passage is much later than Seneca, this, the only evidence available, is insufficient to establish the genuineness of the law; and, in any case, no reference is found to the appeasement of the seducer's own father (though the offence would, of course, be felt to reflect on his family; as to the girl's parent, cf. Livy, III, 44, 10, of Virginia's father, 'ad quem maior pars eius iniuriae pertineat'), or to a specific period of 30 days[5]. But such a period occurs in many other connections in Roman Law.

(III) **Laws which conflict with the evidence of legal sources.**

Conflict with established legal evidence is seen in the Senecan law regarding false witness:

---

[1] Mommsen, *Straf.*, p. 703, Sprenger, p. 207. On the whole subject of *stuprum* see W. Rein, *Criminalrecht der Römer* (Leipzig, 1884), pp. 858-869.

[2] *Déclam.* p. 61.

[3] *op. cit.* p. 205.

[4] Marc., *Dig.* XLVIII, 6, 5, 2 'Qui vacantem mulierem rapuerit vel nuptam, ultimo supplicio punitur, et si pater iniuriam suam precibus exoratus remiserit, tamen sine quinquenni praescriptione reum postulare poterit.'

[5] See, however, Lanfranchi, pp. 462-6, who, on the question of the 30 days, compares Calp. Flacc. *Decl.* 25 'Poena raptoris in diem tricesimum differatur,' and 'Quint.,' *Decl. min.* 313 'Damnatorum supplicia in diem tricesimum differantur' with Sidonius, *Epp.* I, 7, 12 'nunc ex vetere senatus consulto *Tiberiano* triginta dierum vitam post sententiam trahit.' cf. Mommsen, *Straf.* p. 912.

QVI FALSVM TESTIMONIVM DIXERIT VINCIATVR APVD EVM IN QVEM DIXERIT
(*Contr.* v, 4).

According to the XII Tables, false testimony was punished by hurling from the Tarpeian Rock[1], but in the Sullan legislation the penalty was deportation, if the false evidence led to a death-sentence[2]. The declamatory law is clearly of the *talio* type and is commonly regarded as fictitious[3]; there is certainly little evidence in its support, although it should be observed that the idea of the surrender of the offender's person to the offended one is among the oldest in Roman Law, being a leading feature of the original law of debt, and this survived in Roman private law in the so-called 'noxal actions[4].' Such actions could involve the surrender of the guilty person, and in early times even a *filius familias* could thus be transferred to another *potestas*[5].

It is just possible that the declamatory law may represent the position between the XII Tables and the *Lex Cornelia de falsis*, for it has been argued[6] that in that period false witness may have been regarded mainly as a private offence. And it is noteworthy, incidentally, how accurate is the statement in the theme of *Contr.* v, 4 that execution on a capital charge was deferred during a period of public holiday[7]. In any case, the law is decidedly not Greek, for in Greek law the normal penalty for false witness was a fine, sometimes accompanied by civic degradation.[8]

Conflict with established tradition is again seen in :—
INCESTA DE SAXO DEICIATVR
(*Contr.* I, 3 cf. Quint., vII, 8, 3 and 5; Julius Victor, *R.L.M.* p. 384).

In itself this law is almost certainly genuine, for there is evidence that persons convicted of incest were thrown from the Rock even in Imperial times[9], and from a passage of Cicero[10] it

---

[1] Tab. vIII, 23 = Aul. Gell xx, 1, 53 'ex xII tabulis . . . qui falsum testimonium dixisse convictus esset, e saxo Tarpeio deiceretur.'

[2] *Coll.* vIII, 4, 1, 'falsumue testimonium dixerit, *quo quis periret*' cf. Paul, *Sent.* v, 15, 5 ; v, 25, 2 ; Rein, *op. cit.*, pp. 792-3.

[3] Sprenger p. 227 ; Lécrivain p. 681 ; Bornecque vol. I, n. 280.

[4] See F. de Visscher, *La Régime Romain de la Noxalité* (Brussels, 1947).

[5] Gaius IV, 75; Just. *Inst.* IV, 8, 7 ; de Visscher pp. 500 ff.

[6] By A. W. Zumpt, *Das Criminalrecht der Römischen Republik* (Berlin, 1865-9), vol. II, 2, pp. 63-4. So Mommsen, *Straf.* p. 931 says that there is no extant case of use of the Rock, and that the practice must have soon become obsolete.

[7] cf. Bornecque, *ad. loc.*

[8] cf. Thonissen, *op. cit.* pp. 383-391.

[9] Tac., *Ann.* vI, 19 (A.D. 33) ' defertur incestasse filiam et saxo Tarpeio deicitur ' ; Dio Cass., LVIII, 22.

[10] *De Leg.* II, 9, 22 ' incestum *pontifices* supremo supplicio sanciunto.' cf. Tac., *Ann.* xII, 8.

might be argued that it dates back to the oldest pontifical law. But the declaimers take the word *incesta* as meaning ' unchaste ' and apply its provisions to a faithless Vestal ; for this there is barely any evidence, for the faithless Vestal was normally buried alive[1]. Certain variants[2] are mentioned, but not the use of the Rock. The declaimers appear then to be taking liberties with the law, but it is important that that law appears, in itself, to be well-founded in fact[3].

(IV) Laws for which Roman evidence is lacking or inadequate and Greek evidence exists

The following laws appear to fall into this category :—

DEMENTIAE SIT ACTIO

(*Contr.* VI, 7; X, 3; cf. II, 3, 4, 6; VII, 6; 'Quint.', *Decl. Min.* 346).

It is generally agreed that there was no such action at Rome, and that the declaimers are probably translating the Greek δίκη παρανοίας[4]. In Roman Law there was no action for insanity, but the procedure was for the next of kin to take charge, or, failing this, to appeal to the praetor, and demand a *curator*[5]. But Quintilian[6] tells us that school-exercises involving an *actio dementiae* were closely parallel to this procedure of real life. In real life, however, a *curator* would only have been granted in cases of proven mental derangement (*curatio furiosi*) or of squandering the family property (*curatio prodigi*)[7], and, as Bornecque has pointed out, only one of the six Senecan exercises falls within this category[8]. In the others, a

---

[1] cf. Mommsen, *Straf.* 928-9; Simonds, *op. cit.* pp. 82-3; T. Cato Worsfold, *History of the Vestal Virgins of Rome* (London, 1932) pp. 59 ff.
[2] e.g. scourging to death (Dion. Hal., *Ant. Rom.* I, 78 sub fin.), and hanging (Orosius IV, 5, 9). But Suet., *Dom.* 8 speaks of an option to choose the manner of death she preferred. ' ... cum ... liberum mortis permisisset arbitrium.'
[3] See also Bornecque, *Déclam.*, p. 70, Sprenger, p. 220, Lanfranchi, pp. 436-7. Mommsen, *Straf.* p. 931, n. 1 denies the juridical value of *Contr.* I, 3, but Lanfranchi, p. 437, disagrees, as does Stroux, *op. cit.*, p. 14, n. 24 (' einen rechtlich entsprechenden Fall ').
[4] Bornecque, *Déclam.* p. 67 ; edn. vol. I, notes 128 and 330 ; Sprenger, pp. 184-5 ; Lécrivain, p. 688. On the Greek action, see Beauchet, *op. cit.*, II, pp. 382-392, who cites the case of Sophocles and Iophon.
[5] Ulp., *Reg.* XII, 2; Ulp., *Dig.* XXVII, 10, 1; cf. Horace, *Epp.* I, 1, 102-3.
[6] VII, 4, 11, cf. 29. cf. *Contr.* II, 3, 13 ' ego scio nulli a praetore curatorem dari, quia iniquus pater sit aut impius, sed semper quia furiosus; hoc autem in foro esse curatorem petere, quod in scholastica dementiae agere.'
[7] The praetorian interdiction of the prodigal is preserved by Paul, *Sent.* III, 4 A, 7 ; it includes the phrase ' liberosque tuos ad egestatem perducis,' which is the position in *Contr.* II, 6.
[8] *Contr.* II, 6.

father is generally alleged to be insane by his son[1] on the grounds of an adverse decision or an action affecting himself or his family, and even though Quintilian (VII, 4, 10) implies that a son might demand a *curator* where the family interests were threatened, the cases in the *Controversiae* seem to be as far-fetched as possible and in most of them a praetor would almost certainly have rejected the application. Yet even here, there is an underlying problem which must often have faced the Roman praetor—exactly on what grounds and at what stage can it be said that a man is ' insane ' ?[2]; a problem which would also face the *centumviri*[3], in a less acute form, when a testator was alleged to have been near insanity. Moreover, even when an exercise has a Greek parallel, as, for instance *Contr.* II, 4 has in the story of Sophocles and Iophon, there still may be Roman legal value, for Quintilian, XI, 1, 82 describes a very similar type as 'scholastica materia, sed *non quae in foro non possit accidere.*'

MALAE TRACTATIONIS SIT ACTIO

(*Contr.* V, 3, cf. I, 2, 22; III, 7; IV, 6; Quint., *Inst. Or.* IV, 2, 30; VII, 4, 11, 29; *Decl. maior.* VIII, X, XVIII; *Decl. min.* 363; Calp. Flacc. *Decl.* 51).

The nomenclature of this law clearly suggests the Greek γραφή or δίκη κακώσεως[4], but it should be observed that Quintilian (VII, 4, 11), whilst making it clear that it is a law of the schools, remarks that cases in which it is used are parallel to those cases in the Roman courts in which the divorced wife reclaimed her dowry (*actio rei uxoriae*), and the judge had to decide whose fault led to the divorce[5]. This is interesting evidence, but the problem is complicated by the fact that the exercises in which *actio malae tractationis* occurs in the elder Seneca (and 'Quintilian's' longer declamations) are generally concerned, not with divorce, but with some ill-treatment by the husband of the children[6]; and it cannot be proved that a wife could have

---

[1] 'Quint.,' *Decl. min.* 346 gives the 'law' as 'adversus patrem ne qua sit actio, nisi dementiae.' Paul, *Sent.* I, B. 1 says 'parentes naturales in ius vocare nemo potest ' (= *Dig.* II, 4, 6) ; there were exceptions in matters of grave public interest (Ulp. *Dig.* II, 4, 4, 1; XXXVII, 15, 5, 1), but not in such comparatively trivial cases as these.

[2] cf. Quint., VII, 4, 25, 'et quid sit dementia . . . . . *finitur.*' The variation of terminology from *furiosus* to *demens* is noteworthy, although Rein, *Privatrecht*, 259 ff. cited by Simonds, p. 93, attaches no importance to it. (See now Lanfranchi, pp. 196 ff. and the authorities there cited).

[3] See below, p. 102.

[4] On this, see Thonissen, pp. 287-294, Meier-Schömann-Lipsius pp. 353 ff., and Beauchet, I, pp. 229 ff.

[5] On the *actio rei uxoriae*, see P. E. Corbett, *The Roman Law of Marriage* (Oxford, 1930) pp. 182 ff; H. F. Jolowicz, *Hist. Introd. to Roman Law* (Cambridge, 1932) p. 243.

[6] *Decl. min.* 363 is a case brought by the wife to rebut a suspicion of adultery.

brought even an *actio rei uxoriae* on these grounds, in view of the paramountcy of the *patria potestas*. Do the declamatory cases then represent Greek Law ? Even here there is no certainty, for it is disputed whether a δίκη κακώσεως could have been brought by *any* wife or whether it was restricted to the heiress (ἐπίκληρος)[1]. But the Greek action may have lain in the case mentioned in *Contr.* I, 2, 22 (failure to consummate a marriage, cf. Plut. *Solon* c. 20, though this is again with an heiress)[2]. To sum up, the declamatory exercises may represent Romanised versions of Greek originals, but even if an *actio malae tractationis* was never heard of outside the rhetorical schools, the exercises concerned would well fit an era in which the rights of women were becoming ever more widely recognised, and the arguments used would be such as advocates could employ to advantage in cases of recovery of dowry.

LIBERI PARENTES ALANT AVT VINCIANTVR

(*Contr.* I, 1 and 7 ; VII, 4 ; cf. 'Quint.,' *Decl. maior.* V; Quint., V, 10, 97; VII, 1, 55; VII, 6, 5 ; Fortunatianus, *R.L.M.* p. 107 ; Ennodius, *Dictio* 21).

This law is also reminiscent of the Greek κάκωσις γονέων, for a son who failed to support his parents was liable to accusation in court under the νόμος κακώσεως attributed to Solon[3]. The normal punishment seems to have been ἀτιμία[4], but in the *Laws* (932 B), Plato empowers the νομοφύλακες to chastise such offenders πληγαῖς καὶ δεσμοῖς, and this agrees with a passage of Demosthenes[5] (who also uses the term δησάντων) and the expression *vinciantur* in the law.

In the law of Graeco-Roman Egypt as known from the papyri, the obligation of parents and children was mutual[6], and this is the position in Roman Law from the time of the Antonines[7]. Before then, the legal obligation is difficult to prove, though it may well

---

[1] Aristotle, *Resp. Ath.* 56, 5 classifies κάκωσις as (1) γονέων (2) ὀρφανῶν (3) ἐπικλήρου (4) οἴκου ὀρφανικοῦ but Dionysius, *Ant. Rom.* II, 25 seems to imply that any wife could bring an action for κάκωσις in his day : οὔτε γαμετῇ κατ' ἀνδρὸς αἰτιωμένῃ κάκωσιν ἢ ἄδικον ἀπόλειψιν i.e. Romulus did not permit this, as we do now. Indeed these words might almost be held to support the existence of a Roman equivalent of κάκωσις in Dionysius' day. See further on this subject Sprenger, pp. 192-4, Lanfranchi, pp. 235-9, and authorities there cited.

[2] cf. Beauchet, I, 459-60.

[3] Isaeus, VIII, 32 (ὁ τῆς κακώσεως νόμος) cf. I, 39 γηροτροφεῖν ἠναγκαζόμεθα, Plut., *Sol.* 22 ; Aesch., I, 28 ; Vitruv., VI, *Praef.* 3 ; cf. Thalheim in *P.-W.* X, 2, 152-6 ff. ; Beauchet, I, 368 ff., Sprenger, pp. 238-9, Lanfranchi, pp. 274-9.

[4] Diog. Laert., I, 55.

[5] XXIV, 105.

[6] Taubenschlag, *Die Alimentationspflicht im Recht der Papyri* (= *Studi Riccobono* p. 509) cited by Lanfranchi p. 275.

[7] *Dig.* XXV, 3, 5 ; XXXIV, 1, 3 ; *Cod. Iust.* V, 25, 1-3.

have existed[1]; but even if it did exist, there is no mention in Roman sources for imprisonment for failure to observe it. On the basis of the available evidence, the general consensus of opinion, that the law is Greek, is justified.

Greek, likewise, is such evidence as is presented in support of the very interesting law :

CAECVS DE PVBLICO MILLE DENARIOS ACCIPIAT (*Contr.* III, 1), which is generally referred to a law of Solon[2] by which a grant of a few obols a day was made to the infirm who had less than three minae. But the parallel is a weak one, for the law quoted clearly implies a single substantial gratuity, and refers only to the blind. Our knowledge of the awakening of social conscience at Rome is extremely limited before the time of the younger Pliny, and it would not be surprising if inscriptions or papyri yet yielded evidence much later than the Solonian legislation.

QVI PATREM PVLSAVERIT, MANVS EI PRAECIDANTVR (*Contr.* IX, 4 ; cf. ' Quint.', *Decl. Min.* 358, 362, 372, Theon, II, 130).

In the earliest period of Roman Law the striking of a parent was punishable by religious sanction ; the culprit became *devotus* to the gods presiding over parents[3]. The law applicable in the elder Seneca's day was the *Lex Cornelia de iniuriis* of Sulla, to which it has even been thought that this enactment might belong[4] ; but although a heavy penalty was prescribed for *iniuria atrox*, it was almost certainly pecuniary[5]. According to *Dig.* XXXVII, 15, 1, 2 such offences were dealt with by the *praefectus urbi*. Bornecque[6] regards the law as fictitious, and Sprenger sees in it a rhetorical imitation of the *lex talionis* by which the offending member was sacrificed. But this law occurs in the identical form in one of the earliest existing codes of laws, the Code of Hammurabi, drawn up in Babylon c. 2100 B.C.,[7] and reappears in the Homeric Allegories

---

[1] A full survey of the evidence is given by Albertario, *Sul diritto agli alimenti* (*Studi di diritto romano*, Milan, 1933, vol. I, pp. 251 ff.). Cousin, *op. cit.*, p. 693, considers it could have been contemporary with Quintilian. On the transition from the moral to the legal necessity to provide aliments, see the excellent remarks of Cornil in *N.R.H.* XXI, (1897) 477.

[2] Lysias, XXIV, 26, Schol. in Aesch. I, 103 ; Arist. *Resp. Ath.* 49, 4. Bornecque, *Déclam.* p. 63, Sprenger p. 258, Lanfranchi, p. 391.

[3] Festus s.v. *plorare*.

[4] Voigt, *Rom. Recht.* I, 706, referred to by Sprenger p. 240. Other scholars refer it to the Greek κάκωσις γονέων ; cf. Lysias XIII, 91.

[5] *Dig.* XLVII, 10, 7, 8, XLVIII, 19, 28, 8. Mommsen, *Straf.* pp. 789, 804-5. Simonds, p. 97, gives evidence only from the imperial epoch.

[6] Vol. II, n. 207. Contrast Lanfranchi, pp. 568-9.

[7] § 195. ' If a son has struck his father, his hands shall be cut off.' (Translation in C. Edwards, *The World's Earliest Laws* [Thinkers' Library] ; text and trans. by R. F. Harper, Chicago, 1904).

attributed to Heraclides Ponticus[1]. Even allowing for the parallel growth of law, particularly of the talion type, in primitive societies, it is remarkable that the precise punishment for the same offence should recur ; and one may hazard a conjecture that this law may have found its way into the early Greek criminal codes[2]. In any case, it is certainly not imaginary, and although the exercise concerned is far-fetched and probably based on a Greek model, the *divisio* shows evidence of sound legal thinking on the interpretation and applicability of the law[3].

We may next consider :—

(v) Laws for which the available evidence is Roman quite as much as Greek

REIPVBLICAE LAESAE SIT ACTIO

(*Contr.* x, 4 and 5, cf. v, 7); 'Quint.', *Decl. min.* 260, 326, *Decl. maior.* XII; Calp. Flacc., *Decl.* 5, Hermog., pp. 62, 17; 73, 20; 118, 20, Rabe).

Quintilian (VII, 4, 37) makes reference to this type of case, but it is not definitely ascertainable from the context whether he regards it as purely scholastic or as also occurring in court-practice. Some of the *cases* which he quotes in this section are clearly fictitious and invented in the schools; cf. §36 'finguntur in scholis et inscripti maleficii', §39 'finguntur et testamenta': others are closely allied to legal practice (e.g. §32 'iniuriarum' §35 'tutelae'). It is probable that he is primarily thinking of cases debated in the schools, but he does make a point of remarking when there is a divergence between the scholastic and the legal position, as in §35 ' cui simile est male gestae procurationis, quae *in foro* negotiorum gestorum ; nam et mandati actio est.' The inconclusive nature of this evidence renders it difficult to assess the genuineness of the law ; but the instances of its applicability given by Latro (x, 4, 11), *viz.* the destruction of the walls, burning of ships, or loss of an army[4], are fairly closely related to those given subsequently by 'Quintilian', *Decl. min.* 260 (p.62 R), viz. burning of public works, sabotage of

---

[1] § 18 ὥσπερ δὲ οἱ νομοθέται τοὺς πατροτύπτας χειροκοποῦσι, τὸ δυσσεβῆσαν αὐτῶν μέρος ἐξαιρέτως ἀποτέμνοντες, οὕτως Ὅμηρος ἐν ἥπατι κολάζει τὸν δι' ἧπαρ ἀσεβήσαντα. (This parallel was given by Schott).

[2] Thonissen, p. 291 finds it difficult to accept, though the Hammurabi parallel does not seem to have been adduced before.

[3] Lanfranchi, pp. 498-502 is inclined to accept this law as Roman on general grounds. His parallels for the cutting-off of the hands for military theft viz. Cato apud Frontinum *Strat.* IV, 1, 16, Val. Max., II, 7, 11, Caesar, *B.G.* VIII, 44, afford evidence for the Roman character of this penalty. cf. Suet., *Cal.* c. 32 (theft); *Claud.* c. 15 (forgery), though these are arbitrary.

[4] This would have been punishable under the law of *maiestas*.

docks, theft of weapons of war, or in general, any deliberate damage to public property. It is true that the Greeks severely punished such acts as harmed the State (ἀδικεῖν τὸν δῆμον)[1], but it is doubtful whether they had a special γραφή for them[2], as they would evidently be very close to προδοσία[3]. One of the Senecan exercises in which the law given above appears (*Contr.* x, 5) was evidently drawn from a Greek source[4], but on the other hand, the Roman law of damage to public property, as opposed to private property (so fully dealt with by the *Lex Aquilia*), has not survived to any substantial degree[5].

If a special law dealing with acts prejudicial to the State did exist at Rome, it must have been, like that of *maiestas*, of a somewhat indeterminate character. The exercises concerning it involve the crime of mutilation of (exposed) children for purposes of begging (a practice still common in India), the torture of an old man by the painter Parrhasius, who wished to obtain a lifelike reproduction of Prometheus, and the abandonment to the enemy by a general of 300 of his own men who had escaped from enemy hands and to whom he refused to open the city-gates at night. All these Senecan cases Bornecque[6] allows to have been actionable in Roman law. In the first two the question involves the degree of damage inflicted on the State—two *expositi* and a *senex* are concerned—and probably represent border-line cases where it was highly debatable whether the facts justified that particular kind of prosecution. The third could hardly be regarded as *maiestas*, for the *imperator* has *summa potestas* and yet does not act in defiance of an existing military law.

To sum up, such evidence as is available here is fairly equally balanced between Greece and Rome, but in neither legal sysetm have we quite sufficient information to place the declamatory law on a sure footing.

IMPRVDENTIS CAEDIS DAMNATVS QVINQVENNIO EXVLET

(*Contr.* IV, 3; VI, 2, Quint., VII, 4, 43; 'Quint.', *Decl. min.* 248, 305).

Distinction between deliberate and involuntary homicide was made in Greece as early as the Draconian Code, the penalty for

---

[1] Xen. *Hell.* I, 7, 20, Dem., XXIV, 173. cf. Thonissen, pp. 169 ff.
[2] Meier-Schömann-Lipsius, pp. 426-7.
[3] Hyperides, *pro Euxenipp.* c. 22 ἢ ἐάν τις πόλιν τινὰ προδῷ ἢ ναῦς ἢ πεζὴν ἢ ναυτικὴν στρατίαν ... (Sprenger, p. 233).
[4] Lécrivain, p. 689, classes the law as Greek, as does Lanfranchi, p. 423. cf. Sprenger, pp. 230-233.
[5] cf. Mommsen, *Straf.* pp. 822 ff. Dr. Daube points out that *Dig.* II, 14, 7, 14, is important, as showing that the notion of *respublica laesa*, as opposed to damage to private property, did exist among the lawyers; moreover, this decision proceeds from Labeo. In Dr. Daube's opinion, even the words 'et in ceteris igitur omnibus ad edictum praetoris pertinentibus, quae non ad publicam laesionem, sed ad rem familiarem respiciunt' are not necessarily interpolated.
[6] *Déclam.* p. 74.

involuntary homicide being banishment for an indeterminate period[1]. This banishment could, in Attic Law, be terminated only by agreement with the kinsfolk of the deceased[2]; limitations were, however, imposed on them, and they were not allowed to exercise this power beyond a term legally fixed; this period, was, according to some scholars, a year (ἀπενιαυτισμός), according to others, five years, the evidence being inconclusive[3]. Plato (*Laws* 866 c) gives the penalty as purification and one year's absence from the country, arrangements having to be made with the dead man's kin for return, and adds that if the slayer failed to observe this, he could be prosecuted by the kinsfolk; and if next of kin failed to prosecute, he himself incurred the μίασμα, and could be exiled for five years. There would seem, therefore, to be close agreement between the rhetoricians and Greek Law in respect of the penalty of banishment, but less certain agreement respecting the term, though five years is mentioned in this connection.

In Roman Law, distinction was made at least as early as the time of the XII Tables[4] between voluntary and involuntary homicide, and a form of expiation to the kinsmen is mentioned; but of the penalty of exile no trace remains at this period. The *Lex Cornelia de sicariis* appears only to have dealt with deliberate homicide[5]; for which the penalty was permanent exile. It is not until the time of Hadrian[6] that we meet with a judgment imposing exile for involuntary homicide, and although the duration is given as five years it is not certain that the existence of a law to that effect can be deduced, as the instance may have been an isolated one[7]. The principle seems to have been observed, nevertheless, that a milder penalty was imposed for involuntary homicide[8] in Hadrian's day,

---

[1] cf. R. J. Bonner and G. Smith, *The Administration of Justice from Homer to Aristotle* (Chicago, 1930 and 1938) vol. I, pp. 118 ff.

[2] Dem. XXI, 43, XXIII, 72, XXXVII, 59; Thonissen, pp. 250-1; Meier-Schömann-Lipsius, pp. 379 ff.; Bornecque, *Déclam.* p. 64; Sprenger, pp. 216 ff.

[3] See Bonner and Smith, II, 230 for a clear summary.

[4] *Tab.* VIII, 24 (Servius on Virgil, *Ecl.* IV, 43, Bruns, *Fontes* I, 10; II, 79) 'sane in Numae legibus cautum est ut si quis *imprudens* occidisset hominem pro capite occisi agnatis eius in contione offerret arietem'; Festus, p. 247, Lindsay, (law of Numa) ' si qui hominem liberum *dolo sciens* morti duit parricidas esto.'

[5] Mommsen, *Straf.* p. 626 citing *Dig.* 48, 8, 7; Lanfranchi, p. 471, adds *Coll.* IV, 9, 1.

[6] *Coll.* I, 11, 1, = *Dig.* XLVIII, 8, 4, 1 ' cum quidam per lasciviam causam mortis praebuisset, comprobatum est factum Egnatii Taurini, proconsulis Baeticae a divo Hadriano, quod eum in quinquennium relegasset'; here, however, serious negligence rather then mere involuntariness in implied.

[7] Sprenger, p. 217, criticises Rein, *Criminalrecht* p. 418 for relating this rescript to the Senecan Law.

[8] cf. Mommsen, *Straf.* 839, Sprenger *loc. cit.*

if not earlier, by the exercise of magisterial *cognitio, according to the degree of negligence.* Paul (*Sent.* v, 23, 3) says ' is qui *casu iactu teli hominem imprudenter occidit, absolvitur.*' But in *Dig.* IX, 3, 1 pr, a fine is imposed for manslaughter caused by throwing an object out of a window[1], and Paul himself says that the unintentional killing of a person in a brawl (*Sent.* v, 23, 4 = *Coll.* 1, 7, 2, cf. Marcian., *Dig.* 48, 8, 1, 3), or by medicine negligently administered (*Sent.* v, 23, 19) was punished by banishment. It is not impossible, therefore, to regard the declamatory law as based on magisterial decisions in cases of strong negligence, which fixed a limit to the period of exile.

Neither C. IV, 3 nor VI 2 is allowed as a possible court-case by Bornecque, but VI, 2, may be regarded with less suspicion when the evidence for the Roman law of exile, ignored by him, is considered[2]. On the whole, the evidence for this particular law (of homicide) inclines to Greek rather than Roman sources, but here again, this result may be due merely to the paucity of our evidence on the Roman law of murder[3].

HOMICIDA INSEPVLTVS ABICIATVR
(*Contr.* VIII, 4).

In Greece, if we may use Plato's *Laws*[4] as evidence, the penalty for deliberate homicide was death, and the murderer could not be buried in the land of the victim. At Rome the penalty for deliberate homicide, under the *Lex Cornelia de Sicariis*, was not death, but banishment, and there could therefore be no case of refusal of burial[5]. But the question may still arise whether the law quoted may not have existed prior to the time of Sulla. The terms *homicida* and *homicidium*, do not, it is true, appear to be commonly used in the Ciceronian Age[6], but this does not prove that they may not have existed earlier, and fallen into disuse. The forbidding of the burial of criminals was by no means a purely Greek idea, for as early as 270 B.C. a *senatus consultum* was passed that the legionaries responsible for the sacking of Rhegium without

---

[1] This passage was brought to my notice by Dr. Daube—cf. his remarks in *Cambridge Law Journal*, 1939, p. 43.

[2] See below, p. 110.

[3] cf. Jolowicz, *op. cit.*, p. 178, ' One of the very few things that we know about the law of murder is that a distinction was already made between intentional and unintentional killing ' (at the time of the XII Tables). Lanfranchi (p. 474) decides that the law must be referred to Greek sources. But Quint., VII, 4, 43 might be further adduced in favour of a Roman alignment.

[4] 871 D ὁ δὲ ὀφλὼν θανάτῳ ζημιούσθω καὶ μὴ ἐν τῇ τοῦ παθόντος χώρᾳ θαπτέσθω. cf. Sprenger, p. 217, but also p. 244.

[5] Bornecque, *Déclam.* p. 65.

[6] Mommsen, *Straf.* p. 613, n. 3, Dar.-Sag. II, 231 (s.v. homicidium). Lanfranchi, however, p. 470, shows how frequent the terms are in the declaimers.

orders should be put to death and neither buried nor mourned[1]. In this case, the criminals were decapitated[2], and Mommsen[3] has deduced from this and other evidence, that the forbidding of burial of a *decapitated* criminal was a general rule. Now the early penalty for deliberate homicide under the Republic was almost certainly decapitation[4], and it is therefore but a step farther in logical deduction that the law quoted may be a genuine one, though obsolete in the elder Seneca's day, or, at any rate, based upon a recognised custom.

The circumstances of the exercise complicate the position considerably, for the man concerned is a suicide, not a murderer, and suicides were forbidden burial in Greece[5], and, in some cases, in Rome[6]. But Quintilian[7], in a passage which forms the best commentary on this exercise, tells us that the question was debated whether a suicide could be classed as a *homicida*. It would therefore seem possible that declaimers here may be using an old Roman law, subjecting its text to careful interpretation, and perhaps endeavouring to bring it into line with the corresponding law of Greece.

ABDICATIO

One of the most frequent sources of declamatory debate is the repudiation of a son[8] (or, occasionally a daughter)[9], known to the declaimers as *abdicatio*. They commonly envisage a court-case arising from this by reason of the son's objection to the grounds of repudiation. The exercises concerned are often denied to have any legal value, chiefly because it is clearly stated in *Cod. Iust.* VIII, 46, 6 (a rescript of Diocletian 287 A.D.)[10] that *abdicatio* has no sanction in Roman Law, and because such repudiations were not common

---

[1] Frontinus IV, 1, 38; a similar idea underlies the Roman punishment of parricide; cf. Mommsen, *Straf.*, p. 922.
[2] Val. Max. II, 7, 15 ' securi percuti iussit eorumque corpora sepulturae mandari mortemque lugeri vetuit.'
[3] *Strafrecht*, p. 988 ; cf. Lanfranchi p. 478, who sees in the Senecan law ' un applicazione del generale principio vigente in diritto romano.'
[4] Dar.-Sag. *loc. cit.*
[5] cf. Plato, *Laws*, 873 D; Dio Chrys. *Orat.* 64 (Cyprus); Aelian *V.H.* III, 57 (Ceos); Val. Max. II, 6, 7 (Marseilles).
[6] CIL 1418 = XI 6528, and XIV 2112 (Sprenger p. 237 n. 6, Lanfranchi, p. 489). It seems mainly authenticated for cases of hanging.
[7] VII, 3, 7.
[8] *Contr.* I, 1, 4, 6, and 8; II, 1, and 4; III, 2, 3, and 4 ; IV, 3, and 5 ; V, 2, and 4; VI, 1, and 2 ; VII, 1 ; VIII, 3 and 5 ; X, 2, and frequently in ' Quintilian' and Calpurnius Flaccus.
[9] *Contr.* II, 2.
[10] 'Abdicatio, quae Graeco more ad alienandos liberos ursurpabatur et apokeryxis dicebatur, Romanis legibus non comprobatur' cf. Buckland, *Text-Book*, p. 132 n. 6.

in the late Republic. It is, therefore, usually argued[1] that the rhetors have in mind the Greek ἀποκήρυξις. But, as Sprenger[2] has shown, the Greek ἀποκήρυξις was a more serious step than the *abdicatio* of the rhetors; it certainly may have led to a court-action[3] for reinstatement, but its consequences were the public severance of the relationship of father and son, which destroyed the state of agnation as well as right of inheritance[4]. *Abdicatio* in the Senecan exercises, as in Roman life, may be tantamount to ultimate disinheritance, but it is more in the nature of a moral repudiation; the son was ordered to leave the house, but remained *in patria potestate* and could be recalled and reinstated[5]. Quintilian[6] puts us on the right lines when he refers us to purely Roman practice and says that declamatory cases of *abdicatio* were parallel to actual cases of *exheredatio* in the centumviral court. Now this extremely important passage is clearly an allusion to the *querela inofficiosi testamenti*, which would always be brought before the *centumviri* when it was desired to secure a change in the dispositions of the will on the grounds of unfair exclusion[7]. So Quintilian means that the arguments which would be made against *abdicatio* by a declaimer would be closely parallel to those used against an unfair *exheredatio* by an advocate[8]. The only differences would be (I) that in the exercises the parent was still alive, whereas in the court the dispositions of his will could only be challenged after his death; and (II) that whereas *abdicatio* was not a legal act, *exheredatio* was. The rhetorical cases,

---

[1] Bornecque, *Déclam.* p. 66; Lanfranchi, p. 266; H. Fränkel, *Ovid—a Poet between Two Worlds* (California, 1945) p. 172.

[2] pp. 171 ff. I am not altogether convinced by Lanfranchi's arguments that the effects of ἀποκήρυξις and *abdicatio* were the same; for the literature on this vexed question, see his bibliography on p. 254, to which may now be added R. Düll, 'Iudicium domesticum, abdicatio und apoceryxis,' in *Z.S.S.* LXIII, (1943) pp. 54-116, a thorough treatment supporting the Roman alignment of the declamations in respect of *abdicatio*.

[3] See the excellent account of Beauchet, *op. cit.*, II, pp. 128-146; also Düll, pp. 85-96 and literature there cited. But there are scarcely any recorded cases, and the non-rhetorical evidence is sparse.

[4] Dion. Hal., II, 26, Lucian, *Abdicatus*, 16; Sprenger, p. 179.

[5] cf. Val. Max., V, 8, 3 ' domo mea indignum iudico protinusque ex conspectu meo abire iubeo.' See Düll, pp. 96-105, who instances Cic., *Pro Rosc. Am.* 15, 42 ff., Val. Max., V, 7, 2, Suet., *Aug.* c. 65, Tac., *Ann.* I, 5 etc.

[6] VII, 4, 11 (a passage which Lanfranchi, p. 265 also stresses though he is impressed by the Greek evidence) ' nam quae in scholis abdicatorum, haec in foro exheredatorum a parentibus et bona apud centumviros repetentium ratio est.' Rightly valued by Düll, p. 83.

[7] Just., *Inst.* II, 18; *Dig.* V, 2; Paul, *Sent.* IV, 5; Girard, *Manuel*, pp. 857-864, Buckland, *Text-Book*, pp. 327 ff. The *querela* took the form of a plea of near-insanity on the part of the testator, the so-called *color insaniae*.

[8] I owe the reference to the *querela* to both Dr. Daube and Prof. Jolowicz. The former adds that *emancipatio* against the son's will may be a further root.

both in Greek and in Latin, are, of course, often rather far-fetched, but if Lucian's *Abdicatus* is accepted as a partial reflection of Greek Law, there is equal reason to regard the Senecan exercises as a reflection, even if a somewhat distorted reflection, of the Roman courts.

MAGISTRATVS DE CONFESSA SVMAT SVPPLICIVM.
(*Contr.* VIII, 1, cf. 'Quint.', *Decl. min.* 314, Calp. Flacc., *Decl.* 42, with the reading *confesso*).

The principle that the confession of the accused automatically ended the proceedings and led to the exaction of the penalty was accepted in Greek law[1]. In Roman Civil Law, the formula *confessus pro iudicato* was generally observed, although *confessio* did not *necessarily* always put a stop to the case[2]. Although doubt has been felt about the applicability of the rule in Roman criminal procedure[3] it receives strong support from a passage of Sallust[4] and is accepted by Mommsen[5] and more recent scholars[6] as genuine, in the sense that the magistrate might exercise his discretion as to closing the proceedings in such circumstances; this rule still allowed the magistrate freedom in deciding whether a confession was genuine or false (as for instance, when elicited by torture).

The two military rules quoted by the elder Seneca:—

IMPERATOR IN BELLO SVMMAM HABEAT POTESTATEM.
(*Contr.* V, 7; 'Quint.', *Decl. min.* 348) and

NOCTE IN BELLO PORTAS APERIRE NE LICEAT.
(*Contr.* V, 7; cf. Cic., *De Inv.* II, 42, 123; Hermog. π.εὑρ. p. 118 Rabe; Apsines, τέχνη c. 3, sub fin. [I, 348 Sp.]; Syrianus, Walz, IV, 698, 1, Syrianus and Sopater, Walz, IV, 246, 9) are both obviously enough in conformity with Roman practice, and the former may be compared with Cic., *De Leg.* III, 3, 6 ' militiae ab eo qui imperabit, provocatio nec esto, quodque is, qui bellum geret imperassit, ius ratumque esto '[7].

It may be convenient to add at this point that two declamatory laws concerning priests and priestesses, namely:—

SACERDOS INTEGER SIT.
(*Contr.* IV, 2; cf. Sulp. Vict., *R.L.M.* p. 338 Hermog., p. 65, 3, Rabe, etc.)

---

1 Demosth., XXIV, 65 τῶν περὶ τἆλλα κακούργων τοὺς ὁμολογοῦντας ἄνευ κρίσεως κολάʒειν οἱ νόμοι κελεύουσιν; Aesch., I, 91; Sprenger, p. 252.
2 Greenidge, *op. cit.*, pp. 252 ff.
3 Greenidge, *op. cit.*, p. 464.
4 *Cat.* c. 52 *sub fin.* ' de confessis, sicuti de manifestis rerum capitalium, more maiorum, supplicium sumendum.'
5 *Strafrecht,* p. 438.
6 Sprenger, p. 252 ' optime afferatur illud Catonis apud Sallustium,' Lanfranchi, p. 536 ' perfettamente conforme ai principi romani.'
7 cf. Bornecque, *Déclam.* p. 59, Sprenger, p. 213, Lanfranchi, p. 380.

SACERDOS CASTA E CASTIS, PVRA E PVRIS SIT

(*Contr.* I, 2; Sulp. Vict., *loc. cit.*, Syrianus, Walz, IV, 218, 8, etc.) are generally accepted as genuine pontifical rules[1], for although the integrity of the priest was as important in Greece as in Rome[2], the second law on the selection of priestesses well fits the Vestal Virgins, and finds strong support in the excerpt quoted by Aulus Gellius[3] from the *de virgine capienda of* Antistius Labeo, the most famous jurisconsult of Seneca's day, who wrote a great deal on pontifical law. The Vestal Virgin, he says, must not suffer any disability in speech or hearing or be marked by any physical defect; the condition of her father must be examined, and she cannot be accepted if he has been or is a slave or has been engaged in an unworthy occupation. In *Contr.* I, 2 the girl had previously been acquitted for killing an assailant in self-defence; this is perfectly in accord with Roman Law.[4]

TYRRANICIDAE PRAEMIVM

(*Contr.* IV, 7, cf. III, 6, Cic., *De Inv.* II, 49, 144).

Bornecque[1] rightly says that this was a Greek custom[5], the reward being fixed in advance, whereas in the declaimers the tyrannicide has the right to select his own reward ('*Tyrannicida optet quod volet*' 'Quint.' *Decl.* 282, 293, *et saep*. He notes that tyrants had not existed in Italy or Sicily for several centuries and that the enactment did not exist in Rome. But Cicero, in *Pro Milone* §§80-81, after stating that the Greeks honoured tyrannicides as gods, adds that Milo himself could have expected 'praemia laudis' and 'honores amplissimos' for slaying Clodius. Moreover, it should be observed that the murderers of Julius Caesar had been publicly hailed as 'tyrannicides' and that the Senate actually considered a proposal to reward them for their services cf. Appian, *B.C.* II, 127: ' εἶτα ἐπὶ διαπείρᾳ τῆς βουλῆς οἱ μὲν αὐτῶν μάλα θρασέως τὸ πεπραγμένον ἐπῄνουν ἄντικρυς καὶ τοὺς ἄνδρας ἐκάλουν τυραννοκτόνους καὶ γεραίρειν ἐκέλευον, οἱ δὲ τὰ μὲν γέρα περιῄρουν ' κ.τ.λ. The custom, then, existed in Rome in Seneca's own lifetime.

---

[1] See Bornecque, *Déclam.*, p. 60; and esp. Sprenger, pp. 256-7, followed by Lanfranchi, pp. 286-8.

[2] Aesch. I, 188, Plato, *Laws* 759c etc; for Rome, Dion. Hal., II, 21, 3; Aul. Gell. I, 12, 2-3.

[3] I, 12, 1; cf. Bremer, *Iurisprudentiae Antehadrianae quae supersunt* (Leipzig, Teubner, 1898) vol. II, 1, pp. 75 ff., Schulz, *op. cit.*, p. 138.

[4] Paul, *Sent.* V, 23, 8 'qui latronem caedem sibi inferentem vel alium quemlibet stuprum inferentem occiderit, puniri non placuit.' Mommsen, *Straf.*, p. 620.

[5] Vol. 1, notes 73, 266.

[6] cf. Lucian's Τυραννοκτόνος, *argumentum* αἰτεῖ . . . γέρας ὡς τυραννοκτόνος.

[7] Lanfranchi, pp. 381-2 considers the law Greek, and compares it with a fragment of the law of Ilium (*Recueil des Inscriptions juridiques grecques* ed. Dareste-Haussoullier-Reinach, Series ii, Fasc. 1 (Paris, 1898) pp. 25-57).

FVR CONTIONE PROHIBEATVR
(*Contr.* x, 6).

Although there is clear evidence that in Attic Law persons condemned for theft suffered ἀτιμία, and therefore were forbidden to address public meetings, or to speak in court,[1] the fact that a similar enactment, inflicting *infamia*, existed at Rome,[2] and is contained in the *Lex Iulia municipalis*,[3] should be sufficient proof that the declaimers were not merely quoting a foreign law, but one which had a parallel in contemporary Roman Legislation.

IMPVDICVS CONTIONE PROHIBEATVR
(*Contr.* v, 6).

Sprenger[4] quoted only Greek evidence for this law, pointing out that in Attic Law those who practised certain kinds of vice suffered curtailment of their civic rights and were forbidden to address public assemblies. But as, Bornecque has observed,[5] at Rome, citizens condemned for *lenocinium* were not eligible to speak at municipal functions according to the *Lex Iulia municipalis*,[6] though the restriction does not apply to a general *contio*; and citizens condemned for such acts by the censors were deprived of electoral rights.[7]

Before proceeding to laws which seem to have a markedly Roman character, a brief account may be given of :—

(vi) Laws for which the ancient evidence is slight

COMPETITORI LICEAT IN COMPETITOREM DICERE
(*Contr.* v, 8, cf., vii, 7, 4 ; Quint., *Inst. Or.* ix, 2, 97).

In this law scholars see a simple usage elevated to law by the rhetors[8], but whereas Bornecque[9] refers it to Greek custom, it is compared by subsequent writers with a rule of the Emperor Alexander Severus, allowing recommendations for appointments to be challenged[10]. But it is hardly necessary to proceed to so late a

---

[1] Andoc., i, 74; Lysias, vi, 24; Dem., xxi, 87; Meier-Schömann-Lipsius pp. 454 and 755-6, cited by Sprenger, p. 219.

[2] Gaius, iv, 182; Paul, *Sent.* ii, 31, 15; Mommsen, *Straf.* p. 754.

[3] 108-110, Girard, *Textes de Droit Romain*,[3] p. 85 ; cf. Lanfranchi, p. 417.

[4] *op. cit.* p. 219, citing Aesch., i, 19 ff. 29, Demosth., xxii, 30; cf. Thonissen, pp. 327-335. So Cousin, i, p. 376, (on Quint. vii, 6, 3) compares Aesch., i, 56 ' τούτους (sc. τοὺς πεπορνευμένους ἢ ἡταιρηκότας) ἀπαγορεύει μὴ δημηγορεῖν.'

[5] Vol. i, n. 290.

[6] 120-125 ' queive corpore quaestum fecit fecerit.'

[7] cf. Mommsen, *Straf.* p. 994, Lanfranchi, p. 462. See Greenidge, *Infamia in Roman Law* (Oxford, 1894), p. 57.

[8] Lécrivain, p. 681.

[9] *Déclam.* pp. 59-60.

[10] *Hist. Aug. Alex. Sev.* 45, 6 cited by Sprenger, p. 258; cf. Lanfranchi, p. 389.

date, for the President of the Roman elections could refuse to accept a candidature on the grounds of legal incapacity, age, or immoral conduct[1], and it is natural to suppose that such information would often be laid before him by the competing candidate. The 'law' may be taken from an enactment on the conduct of elections, such as the Lex Iulia de Ambitu of 18 B.C.,[2] or may merely reflect custom.

CVM TRICENARIO FILIO PATER PATRIMONIVM DIVIDAT.
(Contr. III, 3).

Little evidence is to be found for this law. It is commonly regarded as fictitious[3], but it should be noted that the other declamatory law on division of patrimony ('Maior dividat, minor eligat') has considerable likelihood of genuineness.

SACRILEGO MANVS PRAECIDANTVR.
(Contr. VIII, 2).

Sacrilege, in the sense of temple-robbery, was in Roman Law punishable by death[4], as it was in Attic Law[5]. Under the Lex Iulia peculatus the penalty of aquae et ignis interdictio appears to have been substituted, and, later, deportation for honestiores and forced labour in the mines for humiliores were common, though the death-penalty subsisted for grave offences[6]. Nowhere is there a law prescribing the cutting-off of the hands for this offence—a punishment which again recalls the practice of talio common to many peoples[7]. At Rome, mutilation of this kind was not generally prescribed in classical law after the period of the early Republic.

SERVATVS CONTRA SERVATOREM NE QVAM HABEAT ACTIONEM
(Contr. III, 4).

The evidence available in support of this law is practically negligible. The opinion has been expressed[8] that the rhetors here imitated the praetorian edict which forbade a freedman to take legal

---

[1] Dar.-Sag. s.v. Comitia.
[2] Suet., Aug. c. 34 ; Dio, LIV, 16 ; Dig. XLVIII, 14.
[3] Lécrivain, p. 681, Sprenger, p. 187. Lanfranchi, p. 267, compares the Athenian law by which the youth of 18 years was allowed free disposition of his goods, and Daube's remarks in Z.S.S. LXV (1947), pp. 303 ff. have some relevance.
[4] Cic., De Leg. II, 9, 22 ; Sen., De Ben. VII ,7, 1 ; Dig. XLVIII, 19, 16, 4; Mommsen, Straf. 769 ff. Latro rightly says in Contr. I, 4, 5, 'si sacrilegium fecerit, occidetur.' cf. VIII, 1.
[5] Meier-Schömann-Lipsius, p. 459; Thonissen, pp. 182 ff.
[6] Ulp., Dig. XLVIII, 13, 7 and 11 ; cf. Simonds, op. cit. pp. 94-5.
[7] An inscription of the late 4th or early 5th century A.D. (C.I.L. v 8761) gives this penalty for profanation of sepulchre—cf. Mommsen, Straf. p. 821, n. 7. Lécrivain, p. 681, Bornecque, p. 62, Sprenger, p. 244, and Lanfranchi, p.503 all doubt the genuineness of this law.
[8] Bornecque, Déclam. p. 70, Sprenger, p. 189. But see Lanfranchi, pp. 526-7, who refers it to the debated question of the legal status of the redemptus ab hostibus. He well cites Cod. Iust. VIII, 50, 17 to show that there was no lien if the redemption was dictated purely by considerations of pietas.

action against his patron[1]. In the exercise concerned a father disinherits a son who had saved his life, and the son takes legal action against him; the case hinges on the problem whether *abdicatio* constitutes an *actio* or not, a problem which, although the answer would seem to modern scholars to be clearly in the negative, evidently merited the consideration of Roman lawyers, for Quintilian makes special mention of it[2].

CONCLUSIONS

So far we have considered just over one half of the Senecan 'laws'; in this half we have one which is quite possibly fictitious (*actio inscripti maleficii*), one which is often considered fictitious but did in fact exist (*actio ingrati*), four which have some conflict within themselves (the hero-laws and the rape-laws), of which the latter contain genuine elements, two which conflict with established Roman Law (on false witness, and Vestals), five in which the balance clearly suggests Greek influence (on insanity, maltreatment, parental support, gratuities to the blind, striking a parent), twelve for which there is as good Roman evidence as Greek (on damage to the State, involuntary homicide, deprivation of sepulchre, repudiation of children, confession in law, two military and two sacerdotal laws, tyrannicide, theft, and immorality) and four for which the evidence is slight (on election-candidates, division of patrimony, sacrilege, and action against a rescuer). Even in those categories in which no special claim is laid for Roman evidence, there are important statements in Quintilian which draw Roman parallels (particularly on insanity and maltreatment), and in a number of laws there is tantalising, but not quite sufficient, Roman evidence. Sometimes, the declaimers seem to take liberties with existing laws, as on ingratitude, and incest. At any rate, the case for belief in pure fiction is not at all strong, and the case for Greek originals is not as strong as might have been supposed. In the next chapter, the balance will incline very much more on the Roman side.

---

[1] Gaius, IV, 46; Ulp. *Dig.* II, 4, 4, 1. Lenel, *Ed. Perp.* (French trans.) I, 76.
[2] III, 6, 77.

Chapter VI.

THE LAWS IN THE SENECAN DECLAMATIONS (cont'd)

(vii) Laws for which there are strong Roman parallels

MAIESTATIS LAESAE SIT ACTIO
(*Contr.* ix, 2).

The exercise in question refers to the case of the proconsul Flamininus, who, according to the account of the declaimers, which is highly-coloured but based on a historical fact[1], slew a condemned man in order to gratify the whim of a courtesan at a feast. He is accused, in the exercise, of lèse-majesté, though in actual fact, he was degraded by the censor, Cato, for the offence. It has been argued[2] that the declaimers are, strictly, inaccurate in using the term *actio* of *maiestas*, for the offence was a criminal one, and *actio* normally designates a civil action ; but this is a common looseness of terminology with them, and it should be noticed that Cicero (*pro Mil.* 14, 36) says ' *actionem* perduellionis intenderat ' and Quintilian (v, 10, 39) ' maiestatis *actio* est.'[3] Moreover, it is clear that they rightly understood the essence of *maiestas* as residing in acts calculated to diminish the dignity or authority of the Roman State. Votienus Montanus defines it as any offence committed under the aegis of state authority[4], and maintains that in Flamininus' case, ' nihil detractum est populi Romani magnitudini.' This agrees well with the definitions given of *maiestas* by the treatise *Ad Herennium*[5] and Cicero[6]. It has been frequently observed[7] that definitions of ' *maiestas* ' are vague ; but the examples which Montanus gives are in accord with the evidence of Roman legal practice. He cites (§15) the signing by a Roman commander of a humiliating treaty which has the effect of binding the Roman people ; this may be borne out by the case of C. Popilius Laenas, legate of the consul L. Cassius Longinus in Gaul

---

[1] Cic., *De Sen.* 42 ; Livy, xxxix, 42-3 ; Val. Max., ii, 9, 2 ; Plut., *Cato maior*, 17, *Flamininus*, 18; cf. Bornecque, vol. ii, n. 182. The declaimers evidently used the account of Valerius Antias, recorded by Livy, *l.c.*

[2] Bornecque, vol. ii. n. 180.

[3] cf. below ' proditionis actio,' etc. Dr. Daube cites also *Dig.* xlviii, 16, 15, 3 ' actio ... veluti *maiestatis*.' Note Lanfranchi's remarks, pp. 510-511.

[4] C. ix, 2, 14 ' in eo autem, quod sub praetexto publicae maiestatis agitur, quid quid peccatur maiestatis actione vindicandum est.'

[5] ii, 12, 17 ; iv, 25, 35.

[6] *De inv.* ii, 17, 53.

Mommsen, *Straf.* p. 556 ; Schisas, *Offences against the State in Roman Law* (London, 1926), pp. 12-13. Jolowicz, *op. cit.* p. 323 ; Heitland, edn. of Cicero, *Pro C. Rabirio* (Cambridge, 1882) p. 7, n. 4, compares the lack of definition of Treason in old English Law.

in 107 B.C., who entered into a disgraceful treaty with the enemy and was accused of *maiestas*[1]. Breaches of magisterial duty formed a definite branch of the law of treason, and other examples are the trial of Norbanus[2] in 94 B.C., and that, in 54 B.C., of Gabinius[3], who, as governor of Syria, had led his army into Egypt 'iniussu populi aut senatus.' Now in the case of Norbanus, Antonius informs us in the *De Oratore* that he based his whole defence of him on the precise interpretation of the word *maiestas* in the *Lex Appuleia*, then in force, on that subject[4]. This is the problem which exercises the declaimer, and he rightly asks (§13) ' Exactly what offences committed by a magistrate during his term of office—surely, not *all*—are punishable under the *lex maiestatis* ? Supposing he murders his father or poisons his wife—is he to be charged with *maiestas*, and not *parricidium* or *veneficium* ? ' If he ascends the tribunal in festal garb (§14) or if, as praetor, he has the *fasces* carried before him to a house of ill fame (which he may visit as a private individual), or gives judgment when unsuitably dressed, he is clearly guilty (§17). But the case of Flamininus is less certain ; for (it may be added) the victim was a man already condemned, and, after all, Flamininus was *imperator* with power of life and death. The position is therefore neatly balanced ; it involves a classification of the law of *maiestas* and a nice discrimination between the rights and wrongs of the case. Cases of *maiestas* occurred frequently under the principate[5], the law of Appuleius (103 B.C.) and the *lex Varia* (90 B.C.) had been superseded by the *Lex Cornelia de maiestate* (81 B.C.) and subsequently by the *Lex Iulia* of either Caesar (46 B.C.) or Augustus[6], and a training on the lines of Seneca's declamation would not have been without value for a future member of the *quaestio de maiestate*, which continued to exist under the Empire[7].

PRODITIONIS SIT ACTIO
(*Contr.* VII, 7).

Treason (*proditio*) formed one of the many branches of offences against the state known as *maiestas* or *perduellio*[1].

---

1 *Ad Herenn.* I, 15, 25 ; IV, 24, 34 ; Cic., *de leg.* III, 16, 36.
2 Cic., *de off.* II, 14, 49 ; *de orat.* II, 21, 89 ; 25, 107 ; Val. Max., VII, 5. 2.
3 Cic., *In Pis.* 21, 50.
4 *De orat.* II, 25, 107, cf. 49, 201 ; cf. *Ad Herenn.* I, 12, 21 'quaeritur, quid sit minuere maiestatem.'
5 cf. Schisas, pp. 192 ff.
6 Mommsen, p. 541 and n. 4, refers it to Augustus; Greenidge, *op. cit.*, p. 427, to Julius Caesar.
7 It would therefore seem misguided to argue, as does Bornecque vol. II, n. 180, that the declaimers have in mind the γραφὴ ἀπατήσεως τοῦ δήμου of the Greeks. Lécrivain, p. 694, accepts the law as Roman. See the remarks of Kübler in *P.-W.* XIV, 546, and Lanfranchi, pp. 422-3. cf. Düll, *op. cit.*, p. 74.

It consisted not only in the surrender of a Roman position or person to the enemy, but in desertion, incitement to war, or any form of culpable relations with him, by message, letter, or other form of communication[2]. The crime was a capital one under the early Republic[3], and again under the Empire[4], though the *Lex Cornelia* and *Lex Iulia* substituted *aquae et ignis interdictio*[5]. There does not appear to be any evidence of an *actio proditionis* at Rome, as the offence is included in the wider scope of *maiestas* or *perduellio*, and it is possible that Bornecque[6] is right in referring, for the nomenclature, to the γραφὴ προδοσίας of the Greeks. On the other hand, the term *proditio* almost certainly occurred in the laws *de maiestate*[7] and that strong exception cannot be taken to the term *actio* has been shown by Cicero's use of *actio perduellionis*. The exercise itself, which still survived in Quintilian's day (see VII, 1, 29-31), is of the *constitutio coniecturalis* type, where there are strong indications of treason, but no definite proof, and it is admitted by Bornecque[8] that it could have taken place in a Roman court of law, and offers nothing contrary to contemporary social organisation. The case does not appear to occur in the Greek rhetoricians.

EXVLEM TECTO ET CIBO IVVARE NE LICEAT
(*Contr.* VI, 2).

Bornecque[9] refers this to Greek Law ('nothing of the kind at Rome ; on the other hand, in Greece whoever receives an exile exposes himself to the penalty of banishment '). Yet this provision was obviously an integral part of the *aquae et ignis interdictio*.

---

1 For the distinction between these terms, see Schisas, pp. 3 ff., Mommsen, *Straf.* p. 539, Heitland, *op. cit.* p. 24. Dr. Daube observes that Brecht, *Zur Abgrenzung des Begriffes Perduellio* etc (Munich, 1938) (reviewed by him in *J.R.S.*, 1941, pp. 180 ff.) argues that *proditio* was a crime different from, not subsumed under, *perduellio*. Daube does not think he has proved it, but agrees that the terminology was quite loose enough to admit of *proditionis actio*.

2 Marcianus, *Dig.* XLVIII, 4, 1, 1 'qui hostibus p. R. nuntium litterasve miserit, signumve dederit, feceritve dolo malo, quo hostes p.R. consilio iuventur'. Mommsen, p. 548, Sprenger, p. 235, Lanfranchi, p. 432, Brecht, pp. 27 ff.

3 Marcianus, *Dig.* XLVIII, 4. 3, 'Lex XII Tabularum iubet eum, qui hostem concitaverit, quive civem hosti tradiderit capite puniri.' cf. Simonds, pp. 93-4, Brecht, pp. 31 ff. for examples.

4 Mommsen, *Straf.*, p. 591.

5 *ib.* 592.

6 Vol. II, n. 124. Lécrivain, p. 682, considers it either Greek or Roman.

7 cf. Tac., *Ann.* I, 72 ' nam legem maiestatis reduxerat ... si quis proditione exercitum aut plebem seditionibus, denique male gesta republica maiestatem populi Romani minuisset.'

8 *Déclam.* p. 74, cf. p. 89.

9 *Déclam.* p. 65.

Voluntary exile to avoid capital punishment was normal at Rome, and the *exul* became a citizen of another state ; many cities had reciprocal obligations with Rome in this respect. But provision had to be made to prevent the exile from exercising this option a second time and returning to his native city, and the *aquae et ignis interdictio* was designed to this end. The exile who returned was regarded as a public enemy, and that those who received him also ran the risk of their lives is clear from the legislation concerning Cicero's exile[1]. The giving of asylum to a returning exile was punishable under the *Lex Iulia de vi*[2], and we are told that Augustus took vigorous measures against such accomplices[3]. The decree of banishment actually contained the word 'tecti'[4], and the Senecan law is therefore perfectly genuine[5]. So is the similar one of 'Quint.', *decl. min.*, 248, 296, 305, 351 ('exulem intra fines deprehensum liceat occidere'), though it may have existed more in theory than in practice[6], and was also true of Greece[7].

VENEFICII SIT ACTIO
(*Contr.* VI, 4 and 6; cf. III, 9, VII, 3, Calp. Flacc., *Decl.* 40).

Cases of poisoning in the elder Seneca's day would have come before the standing court established by Sulla's criminal legislation (*quaestio de sicariis et veneficis*), and the word *actio* is therefore again strictly inapplicable[8]. Before Sulla's day such crimes were still a matter for public investigation, and Livy uses the term *quaestio*, not *actio*, in his accounts of trials for poisoning in the 2nd century B.C.[9] The declaimers, therefore, are either using inaccurate terminology, or are rendering in Latin the γραφή φαρμάκων of Greek Law[10]. On the other hand, they are familiar with the terms of the *Lex Cornelia* which forbade the manufacture, sale, purchase, possession, or administering of poison[11], and on

---

1 *De Domo* 20, 51 ' poena est qui receperit ' ; Dio xxxvIII 17.
2 Paul, *Sent.* v, 26, 3.
3 Dio, LVI, 27.
4 Cic., *De Domo* 30, 78 '*tecti* et aquae et ignis interdictione'; Appian, *B.C.* I, 31 μηδένα Μετέλλῳ κοινωνεῖν πυρὸς ἢ ὕδατος ἢ στέγης.
5 See Mommsen, *Straf.* p. 936; *P.-W.* vI, 2, 1683 ff. I cannot agree with Sprenger p. 255 that the use of the term ' accusata ' in Seneca's argument does not square with the legal position. The woman could have been brought to trial under the *Lex Iulia de vi privata*.
6 Lanfranchi, p. 477 n. 4 thinks this last law quite genuine, and says of the Senecan version ' è conforme ai concetti romani.' In the exercise, exile is imposed, not voluntary, but this does not affect the argument.
7 Thonissen, p. 244.
8 cf. Bornecque, vol. I, n. 313, *Déclam.* pp. 67, 71-2.
9 cf. e.g. xxxIx, 41, 5; xL, 37, 4; cf. Dar.-Sag. s.v. *veneficium*.
10 As Bornecque says, *loc. cit.* On the Greek law, cf. Thonissen, pp. 248-9.
11 cf. III, 9, 2 and VII, 3, 4 with Cic., *Pro Cluent.* 54, 148, Paul, *Coll.* 1, 2, 1, Marcianus, *Dig.* xLvIII, 8, 1, 1 and 8, 3, *pr.* Mommsen, *Straf.* p. 636, Sprenger, p. 248.

occasion invoke it[1]. The exercises concerned are both possible court-cases, and the frequency of such cases is clear to the reader of the *Pro Cluentio* of Cicero ; and the numerous references in the literature of the Empire have been convincingly shown to prove that the declaimers were drawing not so much on their imagination as on the criminal records of their own time[2].

VENEFICA TORQVEATVR DONEC CONSCIOS INDICET
(*Contr.* IX, 6, cf. 'Quint.', *Decl. min.* 381; Calp. Flacc., *Decl.* 12).

This exercise involves a step-mother who, after torture, confesses to the poisoning of her step-son, but accuses her own daughter of complicity. It is clear that any accomplice in poisoning would be liable under the *Lex Cornelia*, but the validity of the law is called into question by its conflict with the statute forbidding the torture of a free citizen[3], and Bornecque therefore classes it as Greek[4]. Exceptions, however, to this rule were made very frequently under the Empire in cases of *maiestas* and *perduellio*, and in the later Empire torture even of free persons for practising magical arts[5], (included under *venenum* in Quintilian's time[6], and probably long before) is prescribed. Ammianus Marcellinus, indeed, says (XIX, 12, 17) that torture of free persons for *maiestas* was prescribed in the *leges Corneliae*, though his evidence is not accepted by Mommsen[7]. Despite Mommsen's assertion[8] that such torture was not consecrated by legislative prescription, but merely the practice of the imperial tribunals, the following passage of Paul (*Sent.* V, 14, 1) would seem to give strong support to the declamatory law: ' In criminibus eruendis quaestio quidem adhibetur; sed non statim a tormentis incipiendum est, ideoque prius argumentis quaerendum, et si suspicione aliqua reus urgeatur, *adhibitis tormentis de sociis et sceleribus suis confiteri compellitur*.' Even if such a provision did not actually occur in the Sullan legislation, it may well have the practice of the *quaestio de veneficis* under the Empire to resort to torture.

---

[1] *Contr.* III, 9, 1, ' Lex Cornelia, te appello.'
[2] Morawski, *Wien. Stud.* IV (1882) pp. 166-7 ; cf. Simonds pp. 89-92. See also Lanfranchi, pp. 483-8, and above, p. 35.
[3] ' Liberum hominem torqueri ne liceat,' as ' Quint.', *Decl. maior.* VII has it.
[4] *Déclam.* p. 65 and vol. II, n. 226, comparing Cic., *Part. Or.* 34, 118 (Rhodes).
[5] *Cod. Theod.* IX, 16, 6 ; cf. Strachan-Davidson, *Problems of the Roman Criminal Law*, II, 172.
[6] VII, 3, 7.
[7] *Straf.*, p. 407, n. 1; cf. Ehrhardt in *P.-W.* s.v. *Tormenta*, Lécrivain in Dar. Sag. s.v. *quaestio per tormenta*.
[8] *Straf.*, p. 406. W. Rein, in the original edition of Pauly's *Real Encyclopädie* considered this law genuine (VI, 2032, s.v. *Tormenta*; but in Pauly-Wissowa s.v. there is no mention of it. Lanfranchi, pp. 551-2, omits to consider Seneca.

QVI COETVM ET CONCVRSVM FECERIT CAPITAL SIT
(*Contr.* III, 8).

That the law of the Twelve Tables made provision against nocturnal disturbances in the city is asserted in a declamation *in Catilinam*, doubtfully ascribed to Latro (c. 19): 'XII Tabulis cautum esse cognoscimus ne quis in urbe coetus nocturnos agitaret.' The penalty is not stated, but, according to the same source, the *Lex Gabinia* (of 139 B.C.), contained the clause : ' qui conciones ullas clandestinas in urbe conflavisset, *more maiorum* capitali supplicio multaretur.'[1] Incitement to seditious acts was punishable in the late Republic under the *Lex Iulia de vi*, which contained the actual expression ' coetum concursum '[2]; but it has been observed that the penalty under that law was banishment, except in the case of persons of low condition, who could be put to death[3]. On the other hand, even free persons convicted of causing sedition perhaps incurred death if the seditious rising resulted in loss of life[4]. The senate's apprehension of *coetus* is often mentioned in Livy[5] and the evidence would seem to suggest that this law, although no longer applicable in its present form, may well have existed at Rome in the earlier period of the Republic, and was possibly, indeed probably, thus expressed in the XII Tables.

QVI VIM IN IVDICIO FECERIT, CAPITE PVNIATVR
(*Contr.* VI, 5 cf. ' Quint.', *Decl. Min.* 386).

Bornecque[6] appears to misunderstand the point of this law, which concerns *not* injuries inflicted on a magistrate, but the intimidation of the jury by armed intervention. This was a crime punishable under the *Lex Plotia de vi*[7], and subsequently the *Lex Iulia de vi publica*[8]. It was certainly regarded as a grave offence at Rome, but the penalty under the latter law was banishment,

---

[1] cf. Rein, *op. cit.*, p. 473, 520-1; Simonds, p. 85. Mommsen (*Straf.* p. 564, n. 2) is not disposed to accept this evidence, which is admittedly declamatory, but (p. 563 n. 1) does not pronounce on our law. Sprenger, p. 250, makes some good points in its favour, and cites evidence of capital punishment for *seditio* under the Empire.

[2] Paul, *Sent.* V, 26, 3, *Dig.* XLVIII, 7, 4, pr. Lanfranchi, p. 431, notes that *coetus conventusve* appear as *maiestas* in *Dig.* 48, 4, 1, 1.

[3] Paul, *Sent.* V, 22, 1 = *Dig.* XLVIII, 19, 38, 2 ; cf. Bornecque, *Déclam.* p. 64, Sprenger, *loc. cit.*

[4] *Dig.* XLVIII, 6, 10, 1, cf. Mommsen, *Straf.* p. 659 n. 5 ; but Dr. Daube notes that Mommsen speaks only of an ' indication,' and he (D.) considers the passage weak evidence.

[5] II, 28, 1, 32, 1; III, 48, 1 ; xxx, 15; xxxix, 15. cf. Suet., *J.C.* c. 75.

[6] *Déclam.* p. 65, and vol. I, n. 317.

[7] Cic., *Pro Cael.* 1, 1, cf. Mommsen, *Straf.* pp. 655 ff. and 657 n. 2.

[8] See esp. Ulp., *Dig.* XLVIII, 6, 10.

not death, except for *humiliores*. The setting of the exercise is purely Greek, but a similar case could certainly have been made the subject of criminal proceedings at Rome ; and even though the Roman penalty was banishment under the *Lex Iulia*, there is no proof that it could not have been a capital offence at an earlier stage. In one passage of the Digest[1], there is a reference to the imposition of the death penalty on turbulent and seditious youths (under the Empire), though the circumstances are not clearly defined ; but it is not until the time of Constantine that clear evidence for the death penalty is available[2].

PER VIM METVMQVE GESTA NE SINT RATA
(*Contr.* ix, 3 ; IRRITA SINT iv, 8).

This is generally agreed to be a clause (put into statute-form) of a genuine praetorian edict of a certain C. Octavius (c. 80 B.C. ?) and may be referred to the *in integrum restitutio propter metum*, which nullified the effects of violence or intimidation[3]. The mention of *vis* was, according to Ulpian[4], later dropped. *Vis* primarily meant physical violence, but was evidently also interpreted as constraint of a person's judgment without the threat of violence[5].; and the Senecan exercises faithfully reproduce situations in which the word *vis* in the edict bears Ulpian's interpretation. In *Contr.* iv, 8, a *patronus*, being proscribed, fled to his *libertus*, who demanded freedom from services as the price of protection ; this the *patronus* agreed to by signed document, which he later repudiated on the strength of this edict. ix, 3 is more complicated, for three laws are involved ; a man who had brought up two exposed children promised to reveal their whereabouts to their natural father on condition that he retained one of the two. A pact was made, but

---

1 xlviii, 19, 28, 3.

2 *Cod. Theod.* ix, 10, 1 = *Cod. Iust.* ix, 12, 6 ; Mommsen, p. 659 ; Sprenger, p. 250 ; cf. Lanfranchi, pp. 468-9. Dr. Daube points out that *capite* here may as often, bear the meaning 'loss of civic status,' which would be in closer accord with the legal sources ; it appears to be generally taken as referring to the death-penalty here, but the exercise concerned does not prove it one way or the other.

3 cf. Lenel, *Ed. Perp.* (French trans., Paris, 1901) i, p. 127; F. Schulz in *Z.S.S.* xliii (1922) pp. 220-225.

4 Ulp., *Dig.*, iv, 2, 1, 'Ait praetor : quod metus causa gestum erit, ratum non habebo.' Olim ita edicebatur, ' quod vi metusve causa '; cf. Bornecque vol. i, n. 268, (his reference to a Greek parallel, *Déclam.* p. 63, being apparently dropped) ; Sprenger, pp. 250-1 ; Lanfranchi, pp. 157-8, who well compares *Consultatio* i, 6 ' Ea, quae per vim et metum gesta sunt, etiam citra principale auxilium irrita esse debere iam pridem constitutum est.'

5 Ulp., *Dig. ib.* 'vis enim fiebat mentio propter necessitatem impositam contrariam voluntati'; in doubting the genuineness of this, Schulz, *op. cit.* p, 133, does not consider the evidence of the elder Seneca.

the natural father sought later to repudiate it.[1] Here we have an exercise in conflict of statutes (*ex contrariis legibus*, as *Ad Herennium*[2] says) ; is the pact, which has the force of law, to override the claim of constraint of judgment, also the law permitting a natural father to redeem his exposed children by payment, or are the latter considerations to override the pact ? Latro claims (§8) that there is no case of *vis*, but his opponent argues, in words which agree well with those of Ulpian, ' vis est et necessitas, ubi, velim nolim, succumbendum est mihi.'

DE VI SIT ACTIO
(*Contr.* IX, 5, cf. V, 6).

Prosecutions for violence were made at Rome under the *Lex Plotia de vi*, and subsequently under the *Lex Iulia de vi*. This criminal legislation could not, as Bornecque observes[3] give rise to an *actio* ; but both the cases are agreed to be possible ones[4]. In V, 6, it seems fairly certain that such assaults were punished under the *Lex Iulia*[5], but in IX, 5, the prosecution would have had a harder task, for ' rapere ' in the *Lex Iulia* would have to be strained very considerably to be held to apply to a grandfather rescuing his grandson from the clutches of a *noverca*, who may well have been a poisoner ; and the law also appears to have included the saving clause *dolo malo*[6]—this, then, is why Latro is at pains to show (§8) that the defendant acted *bono animo*. It is an exercise demanding a careful interpretation of the spirit as well as the letter of the law. ' Is the use of force,' it asks, ' *with a good motive*, punishable as *vis* ? And what exactly constitutes *vis*?'

INIVRIARVM SIT ACTIO
(*Contr.* X, 1, and 6, cf. IV, 1, V, 6).

This is a genuine praetorian action, and although there are Greek parallels, which may, indeed, have influenced its character, there would seem to be no point in arguing that the declaimers had Greek Law in mind if their exercises are in conformity with the Roman conception of *iniuria*. This conception was not limited to cases of physical assault, with which the XII Tables had been mainly concerned, but extended to defamation, and to attacks on a man's honour or dignity. It is the last-named which form the

---

[1] This would fall under the praetorian clause ' Pacta conventa quae neque vi neque dolo malo ... facta erunt, servabo,' which Schulz, *op. cit.* p. 222 deduces from Cicero, *De Officiis* III, 24, 92 and I, 10, 32. cf. below p. 125 s.v. pacta conventa, and on the law regarding exposure.
[2] I, 11, 20 ; cf. above, p. 24.
[3] Vol. II, n. 219, cf. *Déclam.* p. 67.
[4] Bornecque, *Déclam.* pp. 73-4, Sprenger, p. 249.
[5] *Dig.* XLVIII, 6, 3, 4 Mommsen, *Straf.* p. 664. cf. Lanfranchi, pp. 467-8.
[6] *Dig.* XLVIII, 6, 5, pr.

subject of the exercises concerned. In x, 1, a poor man whose father had been murdered is accused of *iniuriarum* for merely dressing in mourning apparel and following his father's rich enemy with intent to suggest that the latter had been responsible, and with the result that he was excluded from public office. An *actio* on these grounds would undoubtedly have lain in the Roman courts[1], though, originally, it would have been brought under the more specific edict *ne quid infamandi causa fiat*[2]. Similarly, x, 6, and v, 6, which involve the unwarranted deprivation of civil rights are rightly brought as *actiones iniuriarum*,[3] though it is doubtful whether a magistrate could have been made accountable under them for decisions made in the course of his official duty[4].

DAMNI INIVRIA DATI ACTIO SIT
(*Contr.* III, 6, cf. 'Quint.', *Decl. maior.* XIII ; *Decl. min.* 385).

This is clearly the Roman enactment regarding unlawful damage to property. The words 'damni iniuriae actio' occur in Gaius III, §217, and we commonly meet *damnum iniuria* (Cic., *Pro Q. Rosc.* 11, 32 ; 18, 54, etc.), or *damnum iniuriae* (Gaius, III § 210 ; IV, 9, 171, etc.)[5] It was a provision of the *Lex Aquilia* (? 287 B.C.), which remained the standing source of law on the subject[6]. The exercise concerned involves a man who chased a tyrant into a private house, and set it alight in order to destroy him ; he succeeded

---

[1] Ulp. *Dig.* XLVII, 10, 15, 27; Sprenger, p. 225, Lanfranchi, pp. 342-4. See now Dr. Daube's full discussion, 'Ne quid infamandi causa fiat,' in *Atti del Congresso Internazionale di Diritto Romano e Storia del Diritto*, Verona, September, 1948, which shows that this exercise is concerned with a very practical, important legal development, the question whether, in the case of acts *infamandi causa*, the *actio iniuriarum* should lie. Labeo expressed himself in favour.

[2] See the very interesting article by Dr. Daube on *Collatio* 2, 6, 5 (*Essays Presented to J. H. Hertz* [1942] pp. 111-129) esp. pp. 124-5. I owe this reference to the kindness of the author, who has shown that this exercise is precisely analogous to the pattern formula proposed by the praetor for action on the ground of defamation, in which he put the case of a person wearing dishevelled hair with intent to bring *infamia* on another.

[3] cf. Cicero's definition, *Pro Caec.* 12, 35, 'actio iniuriarum . . . dolorem imminutae libertatis iudicio poenaque mitigat.'

[4] Bornecque, vol. 1, n. 292 ; Sprenger, *loc. cit.* W. W. Buckland in *J.R.S.* (1937) pp. 37 ff. argues that no civil action was possible for acts committed under cover of *imperium*, but admits (p. 47, n. 16) that *Dig.* XLVII, 10, 32, which allows the *actio iniuriarum*, is against this view. *Dig.* XLVII, 10, 13, 6, definitely disallows the action.

[5] cf. Mommsen, *Straf.* 829-30.

[6] See *Dig.* IX, 2, *passim*; cf. Buckland, *Textbook* pp. 585 ff., Grueber. *The Roman Law of Damage to Property* (*Lex Aquilia*), Oxford, 1886, *passim*. See further Daube in *L.Q.R.* LII (1936) pp. 253 ff., and his brochure 'On the Use of the Term *Damnum*' (Naples, 1948) (Estratto da 'Studi in onore di S. Solazzi').

and was rewarded, but the owner claimed damages. This is evidently a Greek setting, and the Greeks also had a parallel enactment (δίκη βλάβης) ; but the law concerned is Roman[1], for the expression 'damnum sarcire' in §2 is in close accord with Roman legal phraseology[2]. The exercise, though in itself fanciful, basically involves a consideration of the applicability of the law under circumstances in which the defendant has strong moral justification ; and it should be observed that cases of arson were subsumed under the *Lex Aquilia*[3] in Seneca's day.

QVI SCIENS DAMNVM DEDERIT QVADRVPLVM SOLVAT, QVI INSCIVS SIMPLVM
(*Contr.* v, 5).

This exercise concerns a man who refused to sell his rich neighbour a tree which interfered with the latter's view ; thereupon the neighbour set fire to the tree ; the fire spread to the man's house, and, being summoned, the rich man offered four times the value of the tree, and the simple value of the house. (Evidently the owner demanded four times the value of both).

Bornecque[4] considers that the rich man could have filed a legal complaint in the first instance, without taking matters into his own hands ; such a complaint would, he says, have been accepted ; therefore the law quoted must be Greek. But the evidence cited does not warrant this interpretation, for the rich man would only have had a legal case if a servitude existed[5]. If it did not exist, he could have taken action himself, provided his neighbour did not yield to persuasion, and such action could not have been *forcibly* prevented[6], though it did not preclude a claim for damages. So the situation in the exercise is given a Roman legal background by the evidence of a praetorian interdict. Sprenger[7] also considers that the law is Greek, though on better

---

[1] cf. Bornecque, *Déclam.* p. 71 and vol. I, notes 218 ff.

[2] Paul, *Coll.* 12, 2, 2 ; 3, 1, cited by Bornecque ; cf. 'noxiam sarcire' in Tab. VII, 14 (Gaius, *Dig.* XLVII, 9, 9).

[3] Ulp. *Dig.* IX, 2, 27, 5 ' si quis alteri damnum faxit, quod *usserit*, fregerit, ruperit iniuria.' Strongly in favour of the genuine juridical value of this type of declamatory exercise is Lanfranchi's excellent comparison of 'Quintilian,' *Decl. maior.* XIII (the poor man's bees which fly into his rich neighbour's garden) with *Dig.* IX, 2, 27, 12 and *Coll.* XII, 7, 10 (*op. cit.* pp. 324 ff.)

[4] *Déclam.* p. 64 ; cf. his edition, vol. I, notes 284, 285, 286, 289.

[5] Ulp. *Dig.* VIII, 2, 17, cited by B., presupposes a servitude, as Prof. Jolowicz points out to me.

[6] *Dig.* XLIII, 27, 1, 1, 2 (Labeo) and 6, concerns a praetorian interdict forbidding forcible prevention of a neighbour who removes, or restricts the growth of, an overhanging tree. But Labeo says he must *cut* it,

[7] p 222.

grounds ; he argues that whereas in the δίκη βλάβης of Greek Law[1] deliberate damage was punishable by payment of double the value (not four times the value, be it noted), and unintentional damage by payment of the simple value, this kind of distinction of penalty does not occur in Roman Law.

The latter statement appears to be inaccurate, for as early as the XII Tables distinction was made between deliberate and unintentional arson[2]. Moreover, the type of case in which deliberate arson led to further unintentional damage must have much exercised the Roman jurists, for several examples are given in the Digest[3], under the *Lex Aquilia*. If, for instance, a person sets a detached building on fire, and the fire spreads to a neighbouring house, the question arises whether he is directly subject to the *actio legis Aquiliae*, or whether he is merely *causa incendii*, in respect of the further damage. The jurist decides in this case that he is bound by the *Lex Aquilia* in respect of the entire result. But in other examples the opposite decision is given. The *Lex Aquilia* punished both intentional damage (*dolus*) and culpable negligence (*culpa*).[4]

There does not, however, appear to be a close parallel in Roman Law to the distinction between fourfold and simple damages on these grounds. Under the *Lex Aquilia* the damages awarded were the highest value of the property in the preceding month[5]. Fourfold damages are normal in cases of manifest theft, and a good example[6] has been cited of fourfold damage being payable for theft of or damage to articles exposed by fire, shipwreck, etc., provided the claim is laid within a year, and simple damages after that time ; these latter provisions agree with those of the praetorian *actio vi bonorum raptorum*.

The Senecan law, clearly, could not have formed part of the *Lex Aquilia*—even though the case itself was of a type dealt with under that statute. But it seems possible to regard it as an obsolete praetorian edict, dating from the period before 287 B.C., for the following reason. Manifest theft was originally a capital offence ;

---

[1] Dem. XXI, 43, ἂν μὲν ἑκὼν βλάψῃ, διπλοῦν, ἂν δ' ἄκων, ἁπλοῦν τὸ βλάβος κελεύουσιν ἐκτίνειν. Dinarchus I, 60 ; Meier-Schömann-Lipsius, *Att. Proc.* pp. 651 ff.

[2] *Tab.* VII, 14 qui aedes acervomve frumenti iuxta tugurium posita combusserit, vinctus verberatus igni necator, si *sciens dolo malo* incensit ; ast *casu*, noxiam sarcito. cf. Jolowicz, *op. cit.* p. 174.

[3] IX, 2, 27, 8 ; IX, 2, 27, 10 ; IX, 2, 30, 3 ; *Coll.* XII, 7 ; cf. Grueber, *Lex Aquilia*, pp. 85-6.

[4] Buckland, *op. cit.* p. 586. I do not, therefore, agree here with Lanfranchi, p. 334 ' la controversia ci sembra una delle meno rilevanti dal punto di vista giuridico.'

[5] Daube, however, has argued that *proximus* in the *Lex Aquilia* originally meant 'next following.' (*L.Q.R.*, LII, 1936, pp. 253 ff)

[6] Ulp. *Dig.* XLVII, 9, 1 pr ; Sprenger, p. 223.

by the praetorian edict it was subsequently reduced to four-fold damages. So deliberate damage to property was capital in the XII Tables; by the time of the *Lex Aquilia* it has been reduced as far as simple damages. What more likely, therefore, than that the intermediate stage was represented by the law which the elder Seneca has preserved for us?[1] It is certainly difficult to relate the declamatory law to *contemporary* legislation, but the fact remains that the conditions envisaged in the exercise are remarkably appropriate to Augustan Rome.

SEPVLCHRI VIOLATI SIT ACTIO
(*Contr.* IV, 4, cf. 'Quint.', *Decl. min.* 299, 369, 373).

Violation of sepulchre could give rise at Rome to a private action before the praetor, and therefore the terms of this law are quite genuine[2]. The penalty was a fine, varying according to the gravity of the offence[3]. Under the Empire the offence became a *crimen extraordinarium*. The exercise concerned involves a *vir fortis* who, losing his weapons in battle, borrowed, and subsequently replaced, those from the tomb of another *vir fortis*. This is again a rather absurd theme, but the principle involved is sound; for the praetorian edict contains the proviso *dolo malo*[4], and the hero concerned could not be charged with malice prepense. In addition, he has a strong moral case.

Therefore, there could be some value in a case of this kind, for it involves a consideration of circumstances which at their face value appear to constitute violation of sepulchre, but which do not fall quite strictly within the letter of the law, and certainly conflict with its spirit.

ADVLTERVM CVM ADVLTERA QVI DEPREHENDERIT DVM VTRVMQVE CORPVS INTERFICIAT, SINE FRAVDE SIT
(*Contr.* I, 4; IX, 1, cf. 'Quint.', *Decl. min.* 244, 284, 347 etc.)

As it stands this law would seem to grant permission to any person to slay an adulterous couple *in flagranti delicto*, but in the exercises concerned it is the husband who either takes action or requires it to be taken, under the law. The husband had from

---

[1] In drawing this conclusion, I have been much indebted to the acute criticisms of Mr. W. Geddes and Dr. David Daube.
[2] Ulp., *Dig.* XLVII, 12, 3 cf. Bornecque, *Déclam.* p. 71, Lanfranchi, p. 419, Düll, p. 74.
[3] Ulp., *Dig.* XLVIII, 12, 3, 8, Mommsen, *Straf.* p. 813.
[4] Praetor ait ' cuius dolo malo sepulchrum violatum esse dicetur, in eum in factum iudicium dabo' Lenel, *Ed. Perp.* (French trans, Paris, 1901) I, p. 263

early times the right to kill the wife taken in adultery—a 'survival of primitive vengeance,' as Greenidge calls it—cf. Cato apud Gell. x, 23, 5 'in adulterio uxorem si prehendisses, sine iudicio impune necares,' and also the right to beat, mutilate, or kill the adulterer without fear of consequences[1]. The same power appears to have survived until the late Republic[2]. But the *Lex Iulia de Adulteriis* (c. 17 B.C.) abolished the husband's power to kill the wife, and limited his power to kill the paramour to cases where the latter was *infamis* or *inhonestus*.[3] On the other hand, the father of a married woman possessed, in certain circumstances, under that law, the *ius necandi* over his daughter and her paramour, whatever his status, provided that he killed both together—'in continenti, prope uno ictu et uno impetu.'[4] Quintilian speaks as though the law giving the power to slay an adulterer with impunity was an accepted one,[5] but does not say who possessed that power; he also refers to a law forbidding the killing of the woman unless the man also were slain, but although his assertion is very definite,[6] it is possible from the context that he had the law of the schools in mind. The evidence of Roman Law is against the supposition that, after the *Lex Iulia*, a man might slay his adulterous wife with impunity, though it was customary to impose a milder penalty when such an act was committed in spontaneous anger[7]. The solution seems to be that the declaimers refer to a legal position which existed before the *Lex Iulia* was passed[8]. There is no conclusive evidence, but the Roman origin of the law is strongly favoured by the fact that Greek Law[9], unlike Roman, appears to have made no disposition whatever for the simultaneous killing of both delinquents. We know that the *Lex Iulia* superseded several earlier adultery statutes,[10] and we are therefore enabled to trace an interesting historical development. In the earlier Republic, either or both delinquents could be killed,

---

[1] cf. P. E. Corbett, *The Roman Law of Marriage* (Oxford, 1930) p. 128. Lanfranchi, pp. 439 ff. and authorities there cited.

[2] Horace, *Sat.* I, 2, 41 ff. (cf. Lejay on 46) and II, 7, 61, 'estne marito/matronae peccantis *in ambo* iusta potestas.' Schol. Cruq. has a muddled note.

[3] Paul, *Sent.* 2, 26, 4; *Coll.* IV, 10, 1; Corbett, *op. cit.* p. 135; Esmein, *Mélanges d'histoire du droit* (Paris, 1886) pp. 71 ff., fully discusses the *Lex Iulia*.

[4] *Dig.* XLVIII, 5, 24, 4; *Coll.* IV, 2, 3; Paul, *Sent.* II, 26, 1 = *Coll.* IV, 12, 1; Corbett, p. 137. Esmein, pp. 88 ff.

[5] III, 6, 17, 'nempe legem esse certum est' cf. V, 10, 39, 88.

[6] VII, 1, 7 'adulterum, inquit, cum adultera occidere licet. Legem esse certum est.' cf. V, 10, 104; Corbett, p. 128, n. 2; Simonds, p. 83, uses these passages as evidence.

[7] Paul, *Sent.* II, 26, 5; Pap., *Dig.* XLVIII, 5, 39, 8; *Coll.* IV, 10, 1.

[8] So Lanfranchi, p. 439, says 'Nelle numerosissime controversie che ci restano in tema di adulterio, vediamo conservato per lo più uno stato di diritto anteriore al momento in cui essi sono state redatte.'

[9] Thonissen, pp. 312-319; Beauchet, I, pp. 234-244.

[10] *Coll.* IV, 2, 2; cf. Rein, pp. 835-9.

without further proviso (so far as we know); in the later Republic both had to be killed simultaneously; under the Empire the husband was deprived even of this right, which remained only with the woman's father under certain defined conditions, and he (the husband) was only permitted to kill the paramour if he was of low status.

LICEAT ADVLTERIVM IN MATRE ET FILIO VINDICARE
(*Contr.* I. 4, Calp. Flacc., *Decl.* 23, 31).

This law is taken by Bornecque[1] to mean that 'It shall be permissible to punish adultery committed by one's mother *and by one's son*'; but the subject-matter of the exercise shows that it is the son who is required to kill his mother and her paramour, at his father's order, and it seems likely, therefore, that we should translate: 'It shall be permissible for the son also (i.e., as well as his father) to punish his mother's adultery.' That is, *filio* is Dative, not Ablative, and the point of *et* is that normally the responsibility would lie with his father. The law, as it stands, need not mean that the son may kill his mother, but merely that he may kill her paramour when his father cannot act for himself; but the juxtaposition of the previous adultery law creates a situation in which the son cannot do this without at the same time killing his own mother.

In Greece, several members of the family appear to have had the right to kill an adulterer taken in the act, and the son could certainly avenge his mother in this way[2]. The declamatory law has therefore commonly been regarded as Greek, or as a fiction based on the *cause célèbre* of Orestes and Clytaemnestra, much discussed in the Roman schools of rhetoric[3]. But the following passage, from the section of the Justinian Code dealing with the *Lex Iulia de Adulteriis* clearly shows that the Roman father could delegate to the son the power of killing the mother's paramour, provided that the status of the paramour was *inhonestus* or *infamis*.

Cod. Iust. IX, 9, 4 'Gracchus, quem Numerius in adulterio noctu deprehensum interfecerit, si eius condicionis fuit, ut per legem Iuliam impune occidi potuerit, quod legitime factum est, nullam poenam meretur: *idemque filiis eius qui patri paruerunt praestandum est.*'

---

[1] Edn. *ad loc.*; cf. *Déclam.* p. 61. But '*etiam* filio' is the reading of some MSS.
[2] Demosth. XXIII, 53 'ἐάν τις ἀποκτείνῃ .... ἢ ἐπὶ δάμαρτι ἢ ἐπὶ μητρὶ ἢ ἐπ' ἀδελφῇ ἢ ἐπὶ θυγατρὶ .... τούτων ἕνεκα μὴ φεύγειν κτείναντα.' (The reference to a sister suggests that the law of Calp. Flacc., *Decl.* 31 may possibly represent a Greek addition). cf. Plut., *Solon* c. 23, Beauchet, *op. cit.* vol. I, pp. 84 and 234; Sprenger, p. 201; Bonner and Smith, II, p. 203.
[3] Simonds, *op. cit.*, p. 64; cf. above, p. 15. Even Lanfranchi (p. 445) refers it to Greek law. Bornecque considers it imaginary.

Such a concession would be entirely in the spirit of Roman
Law, in which illegal acts committed under a binding order were
blameless[1], unless they were *atrocia*[2]. Matricide would certainly be
atrox, and the declaimers therefore, by juxtaposing the other
adultery-law, create a most neatly balanced case. If, indeed,
the first adultery law represents the genuine legal position prior
to the *Lex Iulia*, there is no reason why the second one should
not be equally old (always with a proviso that the son acts
under orders); in which case we have a possibility of conflict
within the provisions of an adultery-statute some time before
17 B.C., creating the outrageous position in which a son *may* (or
even *must*—the declaimers differ) kill his own mother. That adultery
statute may be even earlier than 43 B.C., since Cicero declaimed
a very similar exercise[3]. The only flaw in the declamatory argument
seems to be that the first adultery-law, though justifying the husband,
was never intended to apply to the son.

INTRA QVINQVENNIVM NON PARIENTEM REPVDIARE LICEAT
(*Contr.* II, 5).

This law is not quoted in so many words by the elder Seneca,
but is given by 'Quintilian' *Decl. min.* 251, and is clearly implicit
in the phrase ' illam sterilitatis nomine dimisit intra quinquennium
non parientem,' given in the Senecan argument. The exercise
concerns a wife who rendered signal service to her husband by
refusing, under torture, to divulge his plans for slaying a tyrant,
and who subsequently, after his murder of the tyrant, brings an
action for ingratitude against him when he divorces her for not
bearing children within five years of their marriage. Bornecque[4]
says : ' A repudiation of this kind would have been badly received
at Rome (Val. Max. II, 1, 4); but the husband, to divorce his wife,
did not have to invoke any special reason. An analogous disposition must have existed at Athens, though no specific mention
of a term of five years is given. (Plato *Laws*, 794 B fixes
the term at 10 years)'. This interpretation, though true in itself,
seems to ignore the fact that one of the most famous divorce cases
in Roman legal history, that of Spurius Carvilius Ruga, was made
on the ground of sterility[5]. Carvilius justified himself by arguing

---

[1] *Dig.* IX, 2, 37 pr.; III, 2, 11, 4 (son at father's order). Mommsen, *Straf.*, pp. 77-8.
[2] *Dig.* XLIII, 24, 11, 7 ; XLIV, 7, 20.
[3] *Contr.* I, 4, 7 cf. above, p. 30.
[4] *Declam.* p. 66.
[5] Gellius, IV, 3, 2 ; XVII, 21, 44 ; Dion. Hal., II, 25 ; Val. Max., II, 1, 4 ; Plut., *Quaest. rom.* 14 ; comp. *Thes. et. Rom.* 6 ; comp. *Lyc. et. Num.* 3 ; *P.-W.* V, 1, 1241, s.v. *divortium* and s.v. *Carvilius* (III, 2); Marquardt, *Privatleben*, I, 71; Karlowa, *Röm. Rechtsgeschichte* II, 188-9.

that he had given an oath to the censors that he married 'liberum quaerundum gratia[1],' and the case seems to have attracted particular attention, not necessarily as the earliest Roman divorce, but as the first in which a wife was repudiated, without restitution of the *dos*, for reasons not involving any delinquency on her part[2]. Divorce for sterility was considered without any disapproval by Roman lawyers[3], as it was for reasons of priestly duties, or ill-health, or prolonged absence of the husband on military service. The term of five years is not specifically mentioned in connection with sterility, but it is mentioned as the period accepted for the wife's remarriage, in presumption of her husband's death in captivity owing to lack of news of him[4]. Now it is well known that the problem of childless marriages much exercised Augustus and his ministers and led to the promulgation of the *Lex Papia Poppaea* in 9 A.D. Since we know that Augustus revived a number of obsolete laws[5], particularly on family questions, it does not seem an unwarrantable deduction, although the evidence is not conclusive, that this law may have been a genuine enactment, subject, no doubt, to certain provisos, and not merely a rhetorical invention[6]. The Augustan marriage-legislation was indeed badly received[7], and the present provision would have excellently served the purpose of putting pressure on the Roman wives. Moreover, such time-limits were actually imposed in this legislation, for Augustus limited the time of pre-nuptial engagements to three, and later to two, years[8]. The treatment of the subject by the declaimers (esp. Latro §14) is of genuine legal value; in the first place, he argues, permanent sterility cannot be proved, and secondly, there are numerous cases in which

---

[1] There is probably an allusion to this legal phraseology in Plautus, *Captivi* 889 and *Aulularia* 148 ; cf. O. Fredershausen, 'Studien über das Recht bei Plautus und Terenz,' *Hermes* XLVII (1912) p. 202.

[2] cf. Corbett, *op. cit.* pp. 218 ff., and see C. W. Westrup, *Introduction to Early Roman Law, The Patriarchal Joint Family*, vol. I (London-Copenhagen, 1944), pp. 83 ff.

[3] Hermog., *Dig.* XXIV, 1, 60, and Gaius, *Dig.* XXIV, 1, 61 ' saepe enim evenit uti propter sacerdotium vel etiam sterilitatem . . . . satis commode retineri matrimonium non possit.' cf. *Laudatio Turiae* (Girard, *Textes*, p. 780)

[4] Iulianus, *Dig.* XXIV, 2, 6 ; cf. Sprenger, p. 196. But the passage may be interpolated, cf. *Index Interp.* The Code of Manu (IX, 81) allows the wife to be superseded after eight years.

[5] *Mon. Anc.* II, 12 ' legibus novis latis complura exempla maiorum exolescentia iam ex nostro usu reduxi ' ; cf. also Dio Cassius, LVI, 6, 4 'καὶ γὰρ ἀπ' ἀρχῆς εὐθὺς ἅμα τῇ πρώτῃ τῆς πολιτείας καταστάσει ἀκριβῶς περὶ αὐτῶν (SC. παιδοποιίας καὶ γάμων) ἐνομοθετήθη, καὶ μετὰ τοῦτο πολλὰ καὶ τῇ βουλῇ καὶ τῷ δήμῳ ἔδοξεν.'

[6] Lanfranchi, in a brief discussion (pp. 233-4) also comes to this conclusion, but suspects some Greek element; for Greece, cf. Beauchet, I, 379.

[7] Suet *Aug.* c. 34.

[8] *ib.* ' tempus sponsas habendi coartavit'; cf. Dio, LVI, 7, 2-3.

childlessness may not be due to the wife, but to the husband's absence or illness or impotence. In the present case therefore, we have again a delicately-balanced position; there must be exceptions to the applicability of the law, and here we have the greatest services on the wife's part, and circumstances strongly militating against childbearing, on the one hand, and the explicit wording of the law on the other. Clearly it is not only a case of interpretation of *ius*, but of balancing *ius* against *aequitas*. The law quoted does not conflict with the freedom to divorce for any reason, but means that if it takes place on the ground of infertility, the husband need not restore the dowry or a large part of it. It may perhaps have been originally a censorian edict giving one of the grounds on which a man might divorce his wife without risk of moral stigma, and adopted in Augustan legislation to suit contemporary social conditions[1].

DE MORIBVS SIT ACTIO
(*Contr.* VII, 2).

There was undoubtedly a genuine Roman *actio de moribus*, but the instances in which it appears all concern cases of divorce. It was an action brought by the husband, as a counter-claim to the *actio rei uxoriae*, for retention of part of the wife's dowry, on the ground of her culpability—e.g., by misconduct[2]. But the Senecan exercise has nothing whatever to do with divorce, as it concerns an imaginary action brought against Popillius for the murder of Cicero, his former *patronus*. This is clearly a genuinely Roman subject, and Bornecque's suggestion[3] that the law may represent a Greek process περὶ τὰ ἤθη is therefore hardly acceptable. His alternative suggestion, that the rhetors are using or inventing an extension of the existing *actio de moribus* would be more likely, except that no evidence is quoted of such an extension. It is noticeable that no specific individual is represented as bringing the action, and the position envisaged may be that of the summoning of Popillius by the censors, who were the traditional guardians of Roman *mores*, and who in a *iudicium de moribus* would have been competent to stigmatise his action with the *nota censoria*[4]. Once more, the term *actio* is strictly

---

[1] On this legislation, see further V. Gardthausen, *Augustus und seine Zeit* (Leipzig, 1891), I, pp. 901 ff. and II, 1, pp. 523 ff., H. Last in *C.A.H.* x, c. 14.

[2] Ulp., *Reg.* VI, 9, 12, Gaius IV, 102; cf. Girard, *Manuel* (4th edn.) pp. 957-8, Buckland, *Text Book*, p. 109; Corbett, *op. cit.* pp. 130 ff.; Sprenger, pp. 194 ff.

[3] *Declam.* p. 70; cf. edn., vol. II, n. 59; Lécrivain, *op. cit.*, p. 686, citing Philostratus, *Vit. Apoll.* IV. 32.

[4] cf. Greenidge, *Roman Public Life* (rpd. London, 1930) p. 226; *Infamia in Roman Law* (Oxford, 1894) pp. 51, 67. On *iudicium de moribus*, see Livy XXIII, 23 4; Cic., *in Pis.*, 4, 10, *Pro Sest.* 25, 55; cf. *P.-W.* and Dar.-Sag. s.v. *mores*.

inapplicable, for the summons of the censors to a man to defend himself could not constitute an *actio*, unless the word is very loosely used.

PACTA CONVENTA LEGIBVS FACTA RATA SINT
(*Contr.* IX, 3).

This is very close in both letter and spirit to a praetorian edict quoted by Ulpian[1], which appears, perhaps in an earlier form, in Cicero[2]. Although a similar enactment existed in Greece[3], there is every reason to believe that the Roman edict is in the minds of the declaimers, for Cicero tells us that *pacta conventa* formed one of the chief subjects of Roman litigation[4].

EXPOSITVM QVI AGNOVERIT, SOLVTIS ALIMENTIS RECIPIAT
(*Contr.* IX, 3 ; cf. Quint., VII, 1, 14, IX, 2, 89 ; 'Quint.', *Decl. min.* 278 Sulp. Vict., *R.L.M.* p. 343).

Exposure of infants was a more common feature of Greek than of Roman life[5], and the theme was a frequent source of plots in New Comedy. At Rome, exposure was legally forbidden in early times[6], except in the case of deformed children[7], but it became increasingly common in the late Republic and early Empire[8], and was repressed by measures of increasing severity up to the time of Justinian[9]. The Senecan exercise concerns the conflicting claims of the natural parent, who desires to recover his child, when grown-up, and the foster-parent (*nutritor, educator*), who desires to retain him. According to Attic Law[10], the rights remained with the natural parent, who could at any time reclaim the child, without legal obligation to defray the cost of aliments (τροφεῖα) ; and the declamatory

---

[1] *Dig.* II, 14, 7, 7 'Pacta conventa, quae neque dolo malo neque adversus leges plebis scita senatus consulta edicta decreta principum neque quo fraus cui eorum fiat facta erunt servabo.' Lenel, *Ed. Perp.* (French trans.) I, p. 73.
[2] *De Off.* III, 24, 92. See Schulz's reconstruction, referred to above, p. 115.
[3] Beauchet, *op. cit.*, vol. IV, pp. 40-41.
[4] *De Orat.* II, 24, 100. See further Lanfranchi, pp. 316 ff. Düll, p. 74, accepts.
[5] See the articles *Expositio*, by Glotz and Humbert, in Dar.-Sag. and *Kinderaussetzung* in *P.-W.* by Weiss.
[6] Dion. Hal., *Ant. Rom.* IX, 22 'ὁ γὰρ ἀρχαῖος αὐτῶν νόμος γαμεῖν τ' ἠνάγκαζε τοὺς ἐν ἡλικίᾳ, καὶ τὰ γεννώμενα ἅπαντα ἐπάναγκες τρέφειν.'
[7] Dion. Hal., *Ant. Rom.* II, 15 ; cf. Cic., *De Leg.* III, 8, 19 (XII Tables) ; Sen., *De Ira* I, 15.
[8] Suet., *De gramm.* cc. 7 and 21 ; *Aug.* 65 ; Pliny, *Epp.* X, 65-6 ; Dio Cassius, XLV, 1; Carcopino, *op. cit.*, p. 77; Max Radin. 'The Exposure of Infants in Roman Law and Practice' (*C.J.* XX [1925] pp. 337-343).
[9] Paul, *Dig.* XXV, 3, 4 (? interpolated) ; *Cod. Iust.* IX, 16, 7, VIII, 51, 2 (both 374 A.D.) ; *Cod. Theod.* V, 7, 1 ; *Nov.* 153 ; cf. Tertullian, *Apol.* 9 ; Minucius Felix, *Oct.* c. 30 ; Lactantius, *Div. Inst.* V, 9, VI, 20.
[10] Beauchet, *op. cit.*, II, pp. 88-9 ; Taubenschlag in *Z.S.S.* 46 (1926) p. 71.

law, therefore, is not fully in accord with the law of Athens.¹ Indeed, τροφεῖα generally seems to refer to the repayment made by the child for his keep, not to the payment made by the original parents.²

In Roman Law, according to Mommsen³ and others, the natural father had no further claim on an exposed child, who could be either adopted, or manumitted, or treated as a slave by his foster-parent. But the first definite evidence for complete sacrifice of *potestas* is late,⁴ and it appears to be characteristic of an era when exposure was strictly repressed. The commoner view now is that in classical law exposure did not involve forfeiture of *potestas* ;⁵ and, in any case, it is noteworthy that the legal sources lay special emphasis on deliberate exposure⁶, as opposed to that done without the father's knowledge and consent, in penalising it so severely.

It may be argued, however, that if *potestas* in classical Roman Law remained with the natural parent, there would be no legal case for the claim to repayment of *alimenta*. Such a claim cannot, indeed, be proved for classical law, though it would be a natural concession to ensure an equitable settlement ; but it is clearly referred to in a constitution of Alexander Severus, dated 224 A.D., in *Cod. Iust.* VIII, 51, 1 ' Si invito vel ignorante te partus ancillae vel adscripticiae tuae expositus sit, repetere eum non prohiberis. *Sed restitutio eius* (si non a fure vindicaveris) *ita fiet ut si qua in alendo eo*, vel forte ad discendum artificium *iuste consumpta fuerint restituas.*' This admittedly refers to sons of slave-girls, not directly to free-born sons, but it should be noticed that in *Cod. Iust.* VIII, 51, 3 Justinian makes no distinction between such categories,⁷ which involve a similar idea of *potestas*. Finally, a rescript of Diocletian in *Cod. Iust.* V, 4, 16 shows that the repayment of aliments in the

---

¹ Pliny, *Epp.* x, 66 (referring to Bithynia, a region of Greek Law) is cited as evidence on this point by Weiss in *P.-W.*, but, as was shown by Cornil, ' Contribution à l' Etude de la patria potestas ' (*N.R.H.* XXI, 1897, pp. 430-1), Pliny's case refers to the child's own claim to liberty (*vindicatio in libertatem*), not to that of the natural parent (*vindicatio in potestatem*). Glotz in Dar. Sag. (p. 936) also misunderstands this passage. Bornecque, *Déclam.*, p. 62, is right.

² cf. Eur. *Ion*, 783-4.

³ *Ges. Schrift.* III, p. 11 and n. 2 ; Cornil, *l.c.* ; Sprenger, *op. cit.*, p. 188.

⁴ *Cod.Theod.* V, 7, 1 ; Suet., *De gramm.* c. 7, ' ab nutritore manumissus', does not necessarily imply loss of *potestas* by the absent parent.

⁵ Scaevola, *Dig.* XL, 4, 29; Buckland, *Text-Book*, p. 103, n. 12, Lanfranchi, 268-70.

⁶ *Cod. Theod.* V, 7, 1, 'scientes propria voluntate' ; *Cod. Iust.* VIII, 51, 2 'ab ipsis.'

⁷ ' sive ab ingenuis genitoribus puer parvulus procreatus, sive a libertina progenie sive servili condicione.'

recovery of an exposed daughter was, at any rate on one occasion, enforced : ' patrem, qui filiam exposuit, at nunc adultam sumptibus et labore tuo factam matrimonio coniungi filio desiderantis favere voto convenit, qui si renitatur, *alimentorum solutioni* in hoc solummodo casu parere debet.'

When the evidence, therefore, is considered, there seems to be on the whole a much better case for claiming that the declamatory law reflects Roman practice than for assuming it to be a fictitious concoction from Greek sources.[1]

LICEAT FILIVM EX ANCILLA TOLLERE LEGITIMVM
(*Contr.* VI, 3, cf. Sulp. Vict., *R.L.M.*, p. 336; Cyrus, in Walz, *Rhet. Graec.* VIII, 388 cf. IV, 169).

This law is taken to mean that children born of a free citizen and a slavewoman (presumably of his own household) may, if recognised by the father, have the same claim to inheritance as legitimate children ; Bornecque[2] comments that this rule is not Greek, and does not belong to the Roman law of Seneca's day, ' for which the axiom *partus sequitur matrem* is always valid.' This axiom refers to the freedom of such children, and so affects their right to inherit. Certainly the rule was that, except in special circumstances, the son of a citizen by a slave-woman was born a slave,[3] though this does not immediately imply that he could not be recognised by the father and subsequently instituted heir, subject to the claims of legitimate children, if any. The position which Bornecque envisages is evidently similar to that set out in the Code of Hammurabi, §170 : ' If a man's wife bear him children and his maidservant bear him children, and the father during his lifetime say to the children which the maidservant bore him : " My children," and reckon them with the children of his wife, after the father dies the children of the wife and the children of the maidservant shall divide the father's house equally. The children of the wife shall have the right of choice at the division.'[4]

In Augustan Rome concubinage was ' a recognised connection short of marriage,'[5] and although it is denied that the child of a *concubina* was related legally to the father, and had the *right* to claim inheritance, he could, if a slave, be legally manumitted

---

[1] As do Lécrivain, p. 682, Sprenger, p. 188, Weiss in *P.-W.*, and Glotz in Dar.-Sag. Contrast Rein, *op. cit.*, p. 444 note, Lanfranchi *l.c.*, Cousin, I, p. 691. Quint., VII, 1, 14 should not be adduced against it, for Q. is merely noting the inter-relationship of declamatory laws for purposes of debate.
[2] vol. I, n. 308, cf. Déclam. pp. 61-2, Beauchet, I, 497 ff., Dar.-Sag. s.v. concub.
[3] cf. Buckland, *Text-Book*, p. 68.
[4] Trans. R. F. Harper (Chicago, 1904).
[5] Buckland, *Text-Book*, pp. 128-9. See also p. 291.

by a public declaration, and given the full benefit of inheritance, *if the father so desired*.¹ It was not until the time of Constantine that his capacity to inherit was expressly forbidden, and even then, such a restriction applied only to senators and other distinguished persons, cf. *Cod. Theod.* IV, 6, 3 (= *Cod. Iust.* V, 27, 1): ' Senatores ... placet maculam subire infamiae ... si *ex ancilla ... susceptos filios in numero legitimorum habere* voluerint aut *proprio iudicio* aut nostri praerogativa rescripti.' This implies that it was open to other classes to do so, and agrees with St. Jerome, *Ep.* 69 *ad Oceanum*: ' multos videmus ... ancillas suas habere pro uxoribus, susceptosque ex his liberos colere ut proprios.'² This phraseology is very similar to that of Seneca, though he appears to use ' tollere legitimum ' loosely for ' in numero legitimorum habere,' and clearly refers to the institution of such children, not to their legal right of succession. In the exercise concerned, two brothers, one born in *iustum matrimonium*, the other, later, of a slave *concubina*, are both instituted heirs (§ I,'coheredem '), and there is, therefore, nothing in the case itself which runs contrary to Roman Law. But at what period and for what purpose would an enactment be necessary to authorise a man to manumit and institute (i.e. ' treat as legitimate ') his son by a slave-woman, when normally he might do the same for any slave ? Clearly, after the *Lex Aelia Sentia* of 4 A.D., which imposed severe restrictions on manumission, but made a special exception of natural children (Gaius, I, 19). As the question of the legal effects of concubinage³ is particularly connected with the early Empire, Seneca's law is possibly a fragment of Augustan legislation, emanating perhaps from the *Lex Papia Poppaea* of 9 A.D., to which the studies of ancient jurisconsults and modern scholars alike, on the question of the legal validity of *concubinatus*, so often find themselves directed.

MAIOR FRATER DIVIDAT PATRIMONIVM, MINOR ELIGAT

(*Contr.* VI, 3, cf. Sulp. Vict. p. 336; Cyrus, in Walz, *Rhet. Graec.* VIII, 388, 7).

This law, which occurs in the same exercise, represents a very ingenious, yet simple, method of ensuring a fair division of patrimony between two brothers. It is sometimes considered

---

[1] So Paul Gide (otherwise the most uncompromising opponent of the rights of natural children) ' De la condition de l'enfant naturel et de la concubine dans la législation romaine ' II (*N.R.H.* IV [1880] pp. 410-412). He cites, *inter alia*, Gaius, I, 19 (manumission), *Dig.* XXVIII, 6, 45 (institution as heir).
[2] Quoted by Gide, p. 411.
[3] See J. Plassard, *Le Concubinat Romain sous le Haut Empire* (Paris-Toulouse, 1921) on this much-debated question. Quint, (III, 6, 96; VII, 7, 10) has, indeed, a ' law ' granting legitimacy to the ' nothus ' if born *before* a legitimate son. cf. Cousin, I, p. 692.

fictitious,[1] but Sprenger[2] has pointed out that St. Augustine[3] quotes it as a custom. Düll[4] takes the matter a stage further by observing that the same disposition occurs in the mediæval collection of German folk-law known as *Sachsenspiegel*[5], composed by Eyke von Repgow (13th century). There is evidence of a Greek action arising out of division of patrimony, the δίκη εἰς δατητῶν αἵρεσιν, in which arbitrators were employed, and the practice was for one or more claimants to divide the lots, and the other, or others, to have prior selection[6]. It may have been customary for the elder son to have the privilege of division, but the evidence is not sufficient to prove his right to do so, unless authorised by will[7]. Greece, therefore, provides a close parallel for this procedure. But as yet there seems to have been no attempt to relate it to classical Roman Law. Now the 10th Book of the *Digest* consists of three so-called 'divisory actions[8],' one of which, the *actio familiae erciscundae*, deals specifically with questions of division of patrimony. From it, it is quite clear not only that the Romans made a point of securing equality of division, but that the son or daughter who had been unfairly treated might have redress by bringing the *actio familiae erciscundae* against the other. So in *Dig.* x, 2, 38, we read ' cum Lucius frater eius non amplius sua portione, immo *minus quam dimidiam consecutus sit*, quaero an Titiae competat adversus fratrem actio.' (She claimed that he had, in fact, received more than his due). Such cases were settled by the appointment of an arbitrator; so Cicero (*Pro Caec.* 7, 19) speaks of an ' arbitrum familiae erciscundae,' as does Paul, *Sent.* I, 18, 1. His formula, as we know from Gaius *Inst.* IV, 42, was ' quantum adiudicari oportet, iudex Titio (? tantum) adiudicato,' whereby he had a fairly free hand in deciding between rival claims. At the end of the chapter in the *Digest* on this action (x, 2, 57) occurs the following statement from Papinian: ' Arbitro quoque accepto fratres communem hereditatem *consensu* dividentes pietatis officio funguntur, quam revocari non oportet '; so here the case was settled by agreement. It was therefore not unusual for

[1] Lécrivain, p. 681, Bornecque vol. I, n. 307.
[2] *op. cit.* p. 187.
[3] *De Civitate Dei* XVI, 20 ' hinc fortassis effecta est inter homines pacifica consuetudo, ut quando terrenorum aliquid partiendum est maior dividat, minor eligat.'
[4] *Z.S.S.* LXIII (1943), p. 74, n. 30.
[5] III, 29, 2 ' swar zwene man eyn erbe nemen solen, die eldere sol teilen und die jungere sol kiesen ' (= ' when two men are to take an inheritance, the elder shall divide and the younger shall choose.') H. C. Hirsch in his edn. (Berlin-Leipzig, 1936) *ad. loc.* describes it as ' Berühmtes Rechtsprichwort.'
[6] Dem. XXXVI, 11, XLVIII, 13; cf. Beauchet, III, pp. 638-653.
[7] Beauchet, III, pp. 454 and 653; Meier-Schömann-Lipsius, p. 575, n. 257.
[8] Buckland, *Text Book*, pp. 252, 315.

two brothers to call in an arbitrator, to supervise the division. It seems likely that the initial procedure which the arbitrator suggested as a simple solution, (failing which he would himself assess), was 'maior dividat, minor eligat.' This has a striking modern parallel from the 16th century, where this very principle is used by the arbitrator. It is taken from F. von Weech's *Badische Geschichte* (Karlsruhe, 1890), p. 134, and reads as follows :

'In 1533, the margrave of Baden died, leaving two sons, Bernhard and Ernst. They decided to govern together and had a coin made ' Dedicated to brotherly harmony' ; the coin showed them both together. But by 1534 they quarrelled, and decided to divide. *They appealed to Kurfurst Friedrich of the Pfalz to arbitrate, and he suggested that they should follow the old custom, and that Bernhard the elder, should divide, and that Ernst, the younger, should choose.* But they did not like this proposal, and they preferred to decide by lot which of the two should divide. Bernhard after all had to divide. He expected his brother to prefer a part which was close to some land that was in Ernst's sole ownership. So he made that part rather small. But Ernst disappointed him, and chose the bigger part, even though it was remote from his private possessions[1].'

The deduction is clear—that this 'law' formed part of the procedure of *actio familiae erciscundae*. What is more, that action, we are told, was based on the XII Tables[2], and this procedure was certainly known then, for Plutarch records it as used centuries earlier in the very dawn of Roman history[3]. To quote a leading modern authority[4] on early Roman Law: ' By the introduction of *actio familiae erciscundae* in the XII Tables, a right had been given to the sons to demand partition of the family property (*familia*) upon the death of the house-father, and so the dissolution of the community (*consortium, societas*). By this partition of the property the sons (the brothers, *fratres consortes*) had each received his equal share to the *heredium*.' We know also that arbitrators existed at the time of the XII Tables[5]. So this so-called ' declamatory fiction ' may even be a fragment of the XII Tables of 449 B.C., passed on in the *actio familiae erciscundae*, known to the declaimers and St. Augustine, surviving in mediaeval Germany, forming the basis

---

[1] I owe this very valuable reference to Dr. Daube.
[2] *Dig.* x, 2, 1, *Tab.* v, 10.
[3] *Romulus* c. 3; Amulius (younger) divides, Numitor (elder) chooses (Daube).
[4] C. W. Westrup, *Introduction to Early Roman Law* (Comparative Sociological Studies), *The Patriarchal Joint Family*, II, Joint Family and Family Property (London-Copenhagen, 1934) p. 82 (cf. pp. 64-5).
[5] *Tab.* XII, 3; Jolowicz, p. 180, n. 2.

of an arbitration in the 16th century, and still in popular use today in the form, ' I cut, you choose.' The declaimers used laws of the XII Tables in Cicero's youth (*Ad Herenn.* I, 13, 23)—may they not have continued to do so occasionally in the Augustan Age ?[1]

FINAL CONCLUSIONS

From this re-examination of the laws of the Senecan *controversiae* the following conclusions may be drawn, though they may not necessarily apply to the later declamations of Quintilian and Calpurnius Flaccus.

Very few indeed of the fifty laws are clearly fictitious; nor indeed does it make sense that men who were living and debating in the greatest law-giving centre of the world should have needed to use their imaginations to conjure up imaginary statutes. Indeed, in the age of Sulla, when Roman declamation began, we know that they sometimes used laws from the XII Tables. Some of the ' laws ' used by the Senecan declaimers may well have been obsolete in their day, and revived merely for academic interest and learned dispute; but against this must be set a number of contemporary parallels, and the fact that our knowledge of the legislation of the early Empire is not great ; we have no Cicero to supply us with evidence, and the sorting out of the earlier from the later legislation in the *Digest* and the *Institutes* and *Code* of Justinian may well baffle the most learned. Admittedly, the ' laws ' may sometimes be little more than customs, but such cases form a small minority. Some are unquestionably based on the praetorian edict. The problem of their relationship to Greek sources is one of primary importance, and it must not be forgotten that these exercises were an inheritance from Greece, and that they frequently recur in the later Greek rhetoricians. But when Roman evidence exists, it seems misguided to stress the Greek parallels, for quite apart from the fact that in legislation, as in everything else, the Romans owed a debt to their Greek predecessors, the evidence of general thinking in these exercises seems predominantly Roman, for Quintilian's extremely important evidence tells us that the arguments used were often parallel to those of advocates in the Roman courts. A minority of the laws must, however, be regarded as Greek, in default of further evidence. But the majority are, if often not demonstrably Roman as they stand, far closer to Roman Law than has been generally supposed; the old tradition, started by the 17th century scholars, such as Meursius in his *Themis Attica*, of using them as

[1] It should also be noted that the exercise concerned mentions an *actio circumscriptionis*, which is in accord with the *Lex Plaetoria* (c. 200 B.C.) on that subject.

evidence for Attic Law, is only partly true, and many laws which may long ago have been transcribed in the praetors' and censors' offices of Rome, are perhaps gradually being restored to their rightful place in our heritage from the ancient world[1].

---

[1] I am glad to find myself, after much deliberation and independent investigation, in agreement with Lanfranchi, *Il diritto nei retori romani*, who has paid very great attention to the general legal background of all the declamatory exercises ; cf. p. 463 ' I casi di norme create di pura fantasia dei retori sono rarissimi, e crediamo di averlo dimostrato ad usura nel corso di nostro studio, contro l'esagerazione della dottrina comune. Essi si riportano per lo piu a norme di diritto romano, meno frequentemente a principi greci.' This does not, of course, mean, as Lanfranchi himself repeatedly stresses, that the declaimers are to be regarded as jurists. They are by no means free from legal errors, and their terminology is not always exact ; but some of the alleged errors (as instanced e.g. by Bornecque) require to be reconsidered, and even the terminology has sometimes been used by Lanfranchi as genuine contemporary evidence, against the excesses of interpolationist criticism.

CHAPTER VII

LITERARY CRITICISM, QUOTATION, AND ALLUSION IN THE SENECAN DECLAMATIONS.

One of the chief features of the Senecan declamations, which makes them so superior to those attributed to Quintilian and those of Calpurnius Flaccus, is the lively interest shown not only by Seneca himself, but by the declaimers whom he quotes, in the literature of the late Republic and early Empire. This interest was no doubt partly due to the established practice of the schools of rhetoric, where the paraphrase of poetry, the learning by heart of celebrated passages, of both poets and orators, and the investigation of difficulties and obscurities under the supervision of the *grammaticus*, formed the most important part of the education of the Roman boy. The interest and the love of literature and reading there gained often lasted, as Quintilian says,[1] throughout life, and it is not surprising that the declaimers in Seneca, many of whom had schools of their own, readily take up questions of literary interest. Seneca himself is a literary critic of considerable taste and ability, and stands high in the exercise of a calling in which the Roman genius is not, on the whole, seen at its best. But apart from their professional interest in literature, the declaimers must have found the atmosphere of Rome itself, in the Augustan Age at least, inspiring and exhilarating. Augustus and his ministers gathered round themselves in the city which ' drew to herself the gaze of all men '[2] as brilliant a society of men of letters as was ever destined to grace its precincts. As the city was gradually transformed from brick to marble, the new libraries accumulated the scattered learning of the ages, and scholars whose early studies had been pursued in centres as diverse as Athens and Rhodes, Alexandria, Pergamum, Halicarnassus, Corduba, and Marseilles, passed the years of their maturity in the peace of Augustan Rome.

Virgil, though his presence at a declamation is not recorded, they respected, the brilliant and sociable Ovid they welcomed to their declamations, and it is possible that even the industrious and indefatigable Livy found time to join them.[3] Pollio's criticisms they learnt to respect, and Messala was sometimes amongst them.[4] Horace, curiously enough, is never mentioned; while his friend

---

[1] I, 8, 12, ' cum grammatices amor et usus lectionis non scholarum temporibus, sed vitae spatio terminentur.'
[2] Dionysius of Halicarnassus, *De Ant. Orat.*, *Praef.*, c. 3.
[3] *Contr.* IX, 2, 26.
[4] *Contr.* II, 4, 8 and 10.

Maximus Lollius declaimed at Rome, he preferred to re-read Homer up at Praeneste ;[1] and while the rhetoricians enjoyed the luxury of a private declamation at the house of Pollio or Cestius, Horace was perhaps taking a quiet evening stroll around the Forum, chatting with less distinguished citizens, whose views on world affairs he may have found more stimulating, before betaking himself home to a modest supper. Horace likewise rarely attended the ' recitations ' of the poets (said to have been introduced by Pollio), which were social occasions similar to the declamations (' nec recito cuiquam nisi amicis idque coactus ' *Sat.* I, 4, 73 ; cf. *Contr.* III, *Praef.* 7, of Cassius Severus, 'raro declamabat et non nisi ab amicis coactus'). On the other hand, some of the poets, like Ovid and Alfius Flavus, were themselves declaimers, and it is highly probable that many who frequented the declaimers also frequented the poets and thereby increased the close association existing between them. But although we miss Horace, we sometimes find Maecenas[2] present, and on one occasion (*Suas.* I, 7) Dellius, the ' moriture Delli ' of *Odes* II, 3, though not present, is quoted by Seneca. Gargonius,[3] whose less attractive features are known to readers of the *Satires*, was evidently no more delectable as a declaimer.

References to Greek Literature in the declaimers are disappointingly few. Homer, as might be expected, is often quoted ; (*Contr.* I, 7, 14—*Iliad* XXIV, 478-9 ; *Contr.* I, 8, 15—*Iliad* VI, 407 ; *Contr.* VII, 7, 19—*Iliad* IX, 97 ; *Contr.* IX, 3, 14—*Iliad* V, 85 ; *Contr.* X, 2, 18—*Od.* XXIV, 514-5 and *Iliad* VI, 479 ; *Suas.* I, 5—*Iliad* V, 340 ; VII, 14—*Iliad* IV, 405). But nowhere is there any criticism; the quotations generally give the impression of having been dragged in and are not particularly apposite to the subject in hand. Plato has only a passing reference (*Contr.* III, *Praef.* 8)—a rhetorical criticism of his *Apology* as an unsatisfactory forensic speech (cf. Dion., *De Dem. c.* 23). Herodotus and Thucydides are each quoted once; but it is odd that the passages do not occur in our texts. They are generally assumed to be erroneous ascriptions. Certainly, the words of Leonidas to the Spartans ' ἀριστοποιεῖσθε ὡς ἐν Ἅιδου δειπνησόμενοι' (*Suas.* II, 11) are well known from other classical sources[4], but are nowhere else ascribed to Herodotus;

---

[1] *Epp.* I, 2, 1-2.

[2] *Contr.* II, 4, 13 ; IX, 3, 14; cf. *Suas.* I, 12. Gruppe, *Quaestiones Annaeanae* (Sedini, 1873) p. 30 is in error in arguing that here is no mention or evidence of Maecenas' presence at declamations.

[3] *Suas.* II, 16; VII, 14; *Contr.* I, 7, 18; IX, 1, 15; X, 5, 25. Remarkably similar language is used of a C. Gargonius in Cic., *Brut.* 48, 180.

[4] Diodorus, XI, 9, 4 ; Plutarch, *Apophth. Lac.* 225 D, 13 ; Val. Max., III, 2, *Ext.* 3, cited by Edward *ad loc.* Cic., *Tusc. Disp.* I, 42, 101, Sen., *Epp.* 82, 21, Stobaeus III, 7, 65 may be added.

and this may be a lapse of Seneca's otherwise remarkable memory. But the other quotation raises a more serious difficulty. 'δειναὶ γὰρ αἱ εὐπραξίαι συγκρύψαι καὶ συσκιάσαι τὰ ἑκάστων ἁμαρτήματα', attributed to Thucydides (*Contr.* IX, 1, 13), appears in almost the same form in [Demosthenes] XI, 13, and in very similar words in the second *Olynthiac* (II, 20), and is ascribed to Demosthenes by Theon (*Rhet. Graec.* II, 92, 14 Sp.). Isocrates VI, §102 has a similar idea, but the reflection does not appear in Thucydides, though it would not be out of place in one of his speeches. Sallust is said to have rendered it 'Res secundae mire sunt vitiis obtentui' (*Orat. Lepidi*, §24). Arellius Fuscus, in quoting these passages, observes that whereas either συγκρύψαι or συσκιάσαι, and ἑκάστων, could be deleted from the Greek without spoiling the sense, nothing can be removed from Sallust without detriment. Sallust himself, however, was criticised by Livy for aping *Thucydides* ineffectually in this sentence (ib. §14) ; and at first sight it would seem hardly satisfactory to ascribe to an 'error of attribution'[1] a sentence which Livy, Seneca, and Arellius Fuscus all believed to be genuinely Thucydidean. But it must be admitted that the balance of evidence suggests that they were mistaken ; for although εὐπραξία, or rather the Attic form εὐπραγία, is found several times in Thucydides,[2] the doublet συγκρύψαι καὶ συσκιάσαι is much more reminiscent of the Orators. This, together with the similarity of the passage of Demosthenes makes it probable that one of the three Romans was wrong and misled the other two. The error would be all the easier in that Sallust was a known imitator of Thucydides. The comparison of Sallust with Thucydides is again made by Velleius Paterculus (II, 36) and Quintilian (X, 1, 101), and was evidently a commonplace of literary criticism.[3] No other criticisms of Thucydides appear, except for a passing reference to the Funeral Oration (*Suas.* VI, 21). The famous 'Marathon Oath' of Demosthenes is once mentioned (*Suas.* II, 14) and in *Contr.* VII, 4, 8 Seneca, comparing the *compositio* of Calvus with that of Demosthenes, says 'ad exemplum Demosthenis viget : nihil in illa placidum, nihil lene est, omnia excitata et fluctuantia '—a criticism which, so far as Demosthenes is concerned, should be compared with the analysis of the orator's composition made by Dionysius (*De Dem.* cc. 43 ff.), who was himself writing in Rome while these exercises were being practised and whose often admirable criticism

---

1 cf. Bornecque, *ad loc.*, and Edward on *Suas.* II, 11.

2 I, 33 ; III, 39 ; V, 46 ; VII, 46 ; the plural in I, 84. All these, except VII, 46 are in speeches.

3 See now, P. Perrochat, 'Salluste et Thucydide,' in *Revue des Études Latines* XXV (1947), pp. 90-121.

of Greek Literature more than atones for the omissions of the declaimers.

Of Latin Literature, particularly the poets, the criticisms and discussions are far more frequent and interesting. Of prose writers, Cicero is most often quoted, and it is clear that the declaimers were particularly familiar with the *Philippics*, especially the second (quotations in *Suas.* vi, 3, 5, 7, 12 ; vii, 2, 5 ; *Contr.* vii, 2, 10; several allusions are also made in *Suas.* vi and vii)[1], the *Pro Milone* (*Suas.* vi, 2, vii, 3), and the *Catilinarians* (*Suas.* vii, 14; *Contr.* vii, 2, 10, may be either *Phil.* ii, 46, 119, or *In Cat.* iv, 2, 3; the same quotation is found in *Suas.* vi, 12).[2] The *Verrines*, Seneca complains, were not well known any longer, though he probably exaggerates in saying anyone could declaim a Verrine oration as his own (*Suas.* ii, 19). The *Pro Sext. Rosc. Am.* (*Contr.* vii, 2, 3) and the *Pro Archia* (*Suas.* vi, 26) are each quoted once, and allusions are made to the *Pro Marcello* (*Suas.* vi, 14) and the *Pro Ligario* (*Contr.* x, 3, 3); there are also several mere passing references. Allusions to passages of the letters *Ad Fam.* are made in *Suas.* vi, 1 and 8. The practice of declaiming a speech against Milo in refutation of Cicero, was a favourite one of Cestius (*Contr.* iii, *Praef.* §16 cf, Quint., x, 5, 20). Cicero's poetry was not, at least by Cassius Severus (*Contr.* iii, *Praef.* 8), highly rated.[3] The declaimers profess the same kind of general admiration for Cicero's works as does their contemporary Velleius Paterculus (ii, 66), and they would probably have agreed with the author of the *Dialogus* (*c.* 37) that 'nec Ciceronem magnum oratorem P. Quinctius defensus aut Licinius Archias faciunt ; Catilina et Milo et Verres et Antonius hanc illi famam circumdederunt'; even Asinius Pollio, who 'infestissimus famae Ciceronis permansit' (*Suas.* vi, 14) spoke of his works, in a remarkable prophecy, as 'destined to live for ever' (ib. 24).

Calvus is said by Seneca to have long fought a losing battle against Cicero for supremacy in oratory (*Contr.* vii, 4, 6)—a criticism which is supported by Quintilian's remark (x, 1, 115) that some judges still awarded him the palm. Calvus' composition, Seneca adds in the quotation already given, was normally full of vigour, though in the epilogue to the *Pro Messio* he adopted a calmer tone. His delivery was so violent that he would dash right across to his opponents' benches. These criticisms show that although generally classed as the leader of the ultra-Atticist group, who modelled

---

[1] See the notes of Bornecque and Edward on these *suasoriae*.

[2] The famous ' O tempora, o mores ' (*Suas.* vi, 3) may similarly be referred to any of the following: *In Verrem* iv, 25, 56; *In Cat.* i, 1, 2; *De domo sua* §137; §137 ; *Pro rege Deiotaro* §31.

[3] This was evidently the *communis opinio*; cf. Quint., xi, 1, 24, and Mayor on Juv., x, 122 ff.

themselves mainly on Lysias, Calvus had certain characteristics which ill befitted the plain style. He himself criticised Cicero as 'solutus et enervis' in *compositio* (Tac., *Dial. c.* 18, cf. Quint., xii, 1, 22), and we should not perhaps be too much influenced by Cicero's statement that he lacked *vis* (*Ad Fam.* xv, 21, 4, cf. *Brutus*, §§ 273 ff.), for Quintilian says (x, 1, 115) that he was also 'frequenter vehemens' (cf. Pliny, *Epp.* I, 2, 2).[1]

The histories of Sallust were evidently held in great esteem, though his speeches were, according to Cassius Severus (*Contr.* III, *Praef.* 8) only read in acknowledgment of his merits as a historian; 'orationes Sallustii in honorem historiarum leguntur.' His relation to Thucydides has already been mentioned, and in *Suas.* VI, 21 Seneca observes that he also copied Thucydides in occasionally making an encomium or 'funeral oration' after mentioning the death of a famous man, a practice which became especially common in Livy, who was 'benignus omnibus magnis viris,' and subsequent historians. These references, few as they are, make one regret the more the disappearance of most of Sallust's *Histories*, one of the greater losses in Latin Literature.

Livy, whom Seneca almost certainly had met (cf. *Contr.* IX, 2, 26 Livius . . . *aiebat*) is highly praised as 'candidissimus omnium magnorum ingeniorum aestimator,' and his 'plenissimum testimonium' to the dead Cicero, taken from one of the lost books, probably cxx, is quoted with great approval (*Suas.* VI, 22). Livy himself seems to have been something of a literary critic, for, apart from his above-mentioned criticism of Sallust, he is reported to have commented on the use of antiquated or sordid diction, by some contemporary orators, who mistook obscurity for dignity, in the words of the rhetorician Miltiades 'They err on the right side' (ἐπὶ τὸ δεξιόν[2] μαίνονται, *Contr.* IX, 2, 26). By this criticism, which was evidently applied to the archaising school, Livy must have meant that such stylists, despite their misguided obscurity, which as an admirer of Cicero he disliked (cf. Quint., II, 5, 20; VIII, 2, 18), did make some attempt at restraint and conscious artistry, as opposed to the complete Asianists. But Seneca adds that their style is more difficult to correct than the redundancy of Asianism, which can at any rate be pruned and chastened (cf. Cic., *De Orat.* II, 21, 88; *Brut.* 91, 316; Quint., II, 4, 4 ff.).

In exercises which must have owed something to New Comedy for their stock characters and romantic situations, it is rather surprising to find no reference to either Plautus or Terence; but

---

[1] See further, Sandys' *Orator*, Introd. xlvi-xlvii; Hendrickson, *A.J.P.* XLVII, 234 ff.

[2] So Bornecque; ἐπὶ τὸ λεξικόν was the previous reading.

there is a reference to Laberius (*Contr.* VII, 3, 9),[1] and the mimes of Publilius Syrus were well known to the declaimers, and had considerable influence on their style. Seneca thrice refers to the use of a 'Publiliana sententia' (*Contr.* VII, 2, 14 ; VII, 3, 8, and VII, 4, 8), and adds that the more far-fetched and boldly expressed *sententiae* in Publilius were eagerly imitated by the younger and less judicious declaimers. Such expressions, so bold as to become almost ludicrous, as 'mortem meam effudit,' meaning 'he poured away the draught that was to be my death' are said to have come from Publilius ; and we may compare the equally stupid expression of Gargonius in *Suas.* VII, 14 'Juba et Petreius mutuis vulneribus concucurrerunt et *mortes feneraverunt.*" On the other hand, Cassius Severus (*Contr.* VII, 3, 8), a great admirer of Publilius, observed that such imitations reflected only his worst side, and expressed the liveliest approval of such *sententiae* as 'tam dest avaro quod habet quam quod non habet' and 'desunt luxuriae multa, avaritiae omnia,' and 'o vita misero longa, felici brevis' (*fragg.* 628, 236, 438, Meyer). It is possible that a number of allusions to Publilius exist in the declamations, and some profit might be yielded by a careful comparison with the fragments of his works.

Reminiscences of, or allusions to, Catullus and Lucretius are rare ; but it seems possible to view Seneca's humorous instruction to his sons in *Suas.* VI, 16 'decipere vos cogar, velut salutarem daturus pueris potionem. Sumite pocula,' as a reminiscence of the famous passage in Lucretius, Book I, 936 ff. ;[2] and in *Contr.* VII, 4, 7, he quotes the celebrated description by Catullus (LIII, 5) of Calvus as 'salaputium disertum.' It is interesting to note Seneca's appreciation not only of Calvus' oratory (he tells the famous story of Vatinius' exasperation on being prosecuted by Calvus—'num, si iste disertus est, ideo me damnari oportet ? ') but also of his poetry, which he describes as 'quamvis iocosa . . . plena . . . ingentis animi,' a criticism which probably does Calvus more justice than Horace's sarcastic 'nil praeter Calvum et doctus cantare Catullum' (*Sat.* I, 10, 19).[3]

Of the Augustans, Horace is never quoted by the elder Seneca, but he could hardly have failed to have read him. Reminiscences

---

[1] An interesting historical sketch of the development of *double entendre* from Pomponius through Laberius to Cicero; cf. the example from Publilius in *Contr.* VII, 4, 8.

[2] cf. Munro *ad loc.*, who wrongly gives the reference as *Suas.* VII ; Edward *op. cit.*, p. 141, considers it ' a distinct allusion.' Others may regard it as merely a traditional simile, but cf. Quint., III, 1, 3-4.

[3] This much-discussed reference is sometimes held to imply no disparagement of these poets; cf. Rand in *Harvard Studies in Class. Phil.* XVII (1906), p. 29; see further, B. L. Ullman in *C.P.* X (1915), pp. 270 ff.

do seem to occur, as, for instance (*Contr.* IV, *Praef*, 11) when speaking of Haterius (the voluble declaimer of whom Augustus said 'Haterius noster sufflaminandus est') he says 'multa erant quae reprehenderes, multa quae suspiceres, cum, torrentis modo, magnus quidem sed turbidus flueret '—a criticism which immediately, if not intentionally, recalls, the censure of Lucilius by Horace (*Sat.* I, 4, 11) ' cum flueret lutulentus, erat quod tollere velles.' Direct allusions are hard to determine with certainty, but there are a number of *loci communes* common to Horace and the declaimers which raise interesting problems of relationship. Thus the *locus de varietate morum* is expressed by the rhetorician Musa as follows (*Contr.* VII, 1, 14): 'alii vivere sine reipublicae administratione non possunt, aliis in privato lare et extra omnem invidiam secessisse praecipua tranquillitas est ; aliis non potest persuaderi ut matrimonio obligentur, aliis ut careant : *sunt qui castra timent*, sunt qui cicatricibus suis gaudent,' a reflection which Horace has so admirably expressed in his first Ode (cf. *Epp.* I, 1, 77 ff.; Sen., *Dial.* X, 2, 1-2). Diatribes against the worship of money and the craze for luxurious display are common enough in the Roman satirists and elsewhere ; Horace's first satire, his sixth Epistle of Book I, Juvenal's ' inter nos sanctissima divitiarum maiestas ' (I, 112), moralisings in Grattius (vv. 312 ff.) and Manilius (IV, init.) are all developments of the *locus communis de divitiis* so familiar in the declamations. So in *Contr.* II, 1, 17, ' census senatorium gradum ascendit, census equitem Romanum a plebe secernit, census in castris ordinem promovet, census iudices in foro legit,' Fabianus expresses in the measured τετράκωλον of declamatory prose a reflection to which Horace or Juvenal would have given the sting of satirical *indignatio*. The sixth Satire of Horace's first book has been shown by Hendrickson[1] to be rhetorical in structure; its opening passage likewise contains a rhetorical theme—'that even before the reign of Servius, that king of lowly birth, many a man sprung from insignificant ancestry, lived a noble life and rose to high honour '—which has become familiar to us in the declamations[2]. Horace is generally supposed to have drawn these reflections largely from the mass of current popular philosophy[3]; he may, also, have declaimed some of them as ' theses ' or ' loci ' at school in Rome, even though his teachers themselves

---

[1] *A.J.P.* XXIII (1902) pp. 388-399.

[2] cf. above p. 62. This theme is fully developed in Juvenal, *Sat.* VIII, 1-20, and other indications of it appear in Sallust, *Jug.* c. 85, Vell. Pat., II, 128, Val. Max., IV, 4, 11, Sen., *De Ben.* IV, 30 ; cf. Casimir Morawski, *De rhetoribus latinis observationes* (Cracow, 1892) pp. 17-18, and S. Rossi in *Rivista Indo-Greco-Italica di Filologia* III, (1919) pp. 18-20.

[3] cf. G. C. Fiske, *Lucilius and Horace* (Madison, Wisconsin, 1920).

perhaps owed them to their philosophical contemporaries and predecessors.

Virgil is treated on the whole with respect by the declaimers, and some of the most interesting literary criticism in the elder Seneca concerns quotations from him. Arellius Fuscus, who was accustomed to quote frequently from him in order to please Maecenas (*Suas.* III, 5), who was sometimes present at the declamations, tended to introduce paraphrases and reminiscences of Virgil even though the subject matter of the declamation did not require it, and even militated against it (*Suas.* III, 4 ' valde autem longe petiit et paene repugnante materia, certe non desiderante, inseruit'). In this *suasoria*, in which Agamemnon deliberates whether to sacrifice Iphigeneia, Calchas having declared that he may not otherwise sail, Fuscus introduced a paraphrase of the passage in the first *Georgic* (427 ff.), in which Virgil describes the moon at the period when rain is imminent; after quoting his paraphrase Seneca merely gives Virgil's lines with the comment : ' Vergilius haec quanto et simplicius et beatius dixit : Luna, revertentes ... ' On the same occasion (*Suas.* III, 5-7) Fuscus sought to imitate the expression ' plena deo.' (which, though ascribed to Virgil, does not occur in our texts)[1] and thereby occasioned some pleasantry, for Gallio, with a sense of humour worthy of the elder Seneca, borrowed the phrase and applied it to the more impassioned of the declaimers themselves. So when Messala asked his opinion of the rhetor Nicetes he replied ' plena deo ' (' inspired ! ') a comment which subsequently delighted the Emperor Tiberius, who disliked Nicetes' exuberant style. Tiberius on a later occasion had asked Gallio his opinion of Haterius, to which without thinking, Gallio made his customary reply, and had to explain himself to the emperor by telling the whole story. Ovid, too, comes into this story, for we are told that he, also, in order to compliment Virgil by openly borrowing from him, introduced the line ' feror huc illuc, vae, plena deo ' into his tragedy—probably the *Medea*. This single anecdote of Seneca, therefore, shows how closely interested in declamation and its literary quotations and allusions were poets, orators, and statesmen alike, and may well have supplied us with a tiny fragment (wherever in the mosaic it belongs) of Virgil's original text.

Another interesting criticism which involves both Virgil and Ovid is that made in *Controversiae* VII, 1, 27. There we read that

[1] See Edward's notes on *Suas.* III, 5-7, and Bornecque, vol. II, n. 344. It immediately suggests the raving of the Sibyl, but I do not think Edward's attempt to fit it into the text of *Aeneid* VI, 51 or 77 quite convincing. Servius' words on line 50 ' nondum deo plena ' may provide a key for the solution of this puzzle.

Cestius, in his bombastic 'nox erat concubia et omnia, iudices, canentia sub sideribus muta erant' wished to be recognised as imitating Virgil's beautiful lines in *Aen.* VIII, 26 ff. 'nox erat et terras animalia fessa per omnes alituum pecudumque genus sopor altus habebat.' The declaimer's efforts at imitation do not concern us greatly; but it is with interest that we learn that, according to Julius Montanus, himself a poet and friend of Virgil,[1] Virgil himself in these lines imitated and improved upon two lines of Varro of Atax. 'Desierant latrare canes urbesque silebant; omnia noctis erant placida composta quiete.' Ovid's comment on these lines of Varro was that the last line would have been much better expressed if simply reduced to 'omnia noctis erant,' a criticism in which Seneca himself did not concur, but which is characteristic of the growing desire for brevity and point.

A similar example of pruning is found in *Suas.* II, 20. The expression 'belli mora' had been coined by Latro, and was introduced in a poem by Arbronius Silo in the line 'ite triumphantes; belli mora concidit Hector,' the point being that Hector alone had delayed the conclusion of the war. Seneca observes that this idea finds more appropriate expression in Virgil, *Aen.* XI, 288 ff. 'Quidquid ad adversae[2] cessatum est moenia Troiae Hectoris Aeneaeque manu victoria Graium haesit et in decimum vestigia rettulit annum,' but adds that Messala considered[3] that Virgil should have stopped at 'haesit' as the rest was merely 'explementum'; Maecenas however, defended Virgil, and the line would certainly be abrupt and the sense inadequately expressed if the words 'et in decimum vestigia rettulit annum' were deleted. Seneca appears to have forgotten that Virgil in *Aen.* X, 428 had described Abas as 'pugnae nodumque moramque,' but whether Latro or Virgil first invented this sententious expression it retained its popularity and re-appears in the younger Seneca and Lucan[4]. An interesting point here is that these criticisms of Virgil must have been made within a decade of the poet's death, and are therefore some of the earliest we possess, since Maecenas died in 8 B.C.

Maecenas again appears as a staunch defender of Virgil in *Suas.* I, 12. A Greek declaimer of very poor taste, Dorion, had, in a paraphrase of Homer (*Od.* IX, 481 ἧκε δ' ἀπορρήξας κορυφὴν ὄρεος μεγάλοιο) used the extravagant and bombastic expression

---

[1] Donatus, *Vita Vergilii* (cited by Bornecque). On Montanus, who was also a friend of Ovid (*Ex Ponto* IV, 16, 11) cf. Teuffel, II, § 252, 13.

[2] apud durae, MSS of Virgil.

[3] Heyne agrees.

[4] *Agam.* 211, *Phoen.* 458, cf. *Tro.* 124; Lucan I, 100; cf. below, p. 161. Page on *Aen.* X, 428 wrongly quotes it as occurring in *Aen.* XI, 290.

ὄρους ὄρος ἀποσπᾶται καὶ χειρία βάλλεται νῆσσος.' (' A mountain is torn from the mountain and an island seized in his hand is hurled '). Maecenas observed how effectively and naturally Virgil had employed a similar hyperbole when he wrote (*Aen.* x, 128) ' fert ingens toto conixus corpore saxum, *haud partem exiguam montis* ' ; and likewise, in describing Antony's ships at Actium, he tones down the hyperbole by saying (*Aen.* VIII, 691) ' *credas* innare revulsas Cycladas.' So Quintilian (who quotes this is as an example of hyperbole in VIII, 6, 68) gives an instance of toning down from Virgil, *Ecl.* III, 103 (ib. 73). The Homeric line quoted above is also imitated by Ovid (*Met.* XIII, 882), and defended by Hermogenes (p. 203, Rabe); and it is interesting to compare the discussion recorded by Seneca of Virgil's borrowings from Homer with the detailed study of Macrobius, which itself probably reflects in part the criticisms of the *obtrectatores Vergilii*.

Apt quotations from Virgil were certain to win applause ; so Fuscus on one occasion quoted *Aen.* IV, 379 ff. 'scilicet is superis labor est, ea cura quietos sollicitat' (*Suas.* IV, 4), though one of his pupils attempted so clumsily to apply the quotation in the *suasoria* in which Alexander is deterred by the soothsayers from entering Babylon, that his master wittily reminded him that Virgil also wrote a line ' capulo tenus abdidit ensem ' (*Aen.* II, 553) ! Seneca himself in *Contr.* VII, 5, 10 quotes Virgil's ' primus ibi ante omnes' (*Aen.* II, 40), and it is possible that Latro in *Contr.* II, 7, 7 ('o nos nimium felici et aureo, quod aiunt, saeculo natos') is alluding to the fourth Eclogue. References to prose works of Virgil are very rare, and it is interesting to note that in *Contr.* III, *Praef.* 8, Cassius Severus says that Virgil's happy genius deserted him in prose. In the absence of any further knowledge of Virgil's prose-writings, we must assume this to be a reference to his published correspondence with the Emperor Augustus.[1]

But although the declaimers are so familiar with and fond of quoting Virgil, the poet does not seem to have returned the compliment. ' Ite hinc, inanes, ite, rhetorum ampullae, inflata † rhoso non Achaico verba, et vos, Selique Tarquitique Varroque, scholasticorum natio madens pingui, ite hinc, inanis cymbalon iuventutis,' he exclaims in the *Catalepton* (v), abandoning declamatory rhetoric at an early age for the happier haven of philosophy. Although Virgil was familiar with rhetorical devices, he is not at all a good example of the influence of declamation. He can, to be sure, express a neat *sententia*—' una salus victis nullam sperare salutem ' (*Aen.* II,

---

[1] cf. Tac., *Dial.* c. 13, Donatus, *Vita Verg.* 31, Macrobius I, 24, 11 ; Teuffel, II, § 229, 4 ; T. R. Glover, *Virgil* (6th edn. London, 1930) p. 156, n. 3.

354)—or make a pretty repetition[1]—'servataque serves, Troia fidem' (*Aen.* II, 160). His speeches may sometimes show a general rhetorical cast,[2] and Servius sometimes pauses to note 'rhetoricus locus.'[3] Norden[4] sees rhetorical influence in parallelism of phrase, and generations of rhetoricians went to Virgil for illustrations for their figures. But in Virgil rhetoric is never obtrusive, and it is with truth that Teuffel[5] remarks that the first Latin poet to show clear indications of declamatory influence is Ovid.

The elder Seneca's criticisms of Ovid are most instructive, and merit the careful consideration of all who would understand the mind and art of that brilliant writer. In the latter half of *Contr.* II, 2 (§§8-14) Seneca informs us that he heard Ovid as a youth declaim the exercise in question. Elegance, neatness, and general amiability were his characteristics ('habebat ille comptum et decens et amabile ingenium'), and his prose style was really poetry without the metre ('solutum carmen', cf, Ovid's 'et quod temptabam dicere versus erat' *Trist.* IV, 10, 26). Destined for a legal career, he was the pupil of Arellius Fuscus, and a great admirer of Latro, many of whose *sententiae* he introduced in his verses. An example given by Seneca is *Met.* XIII, 121-2, 'arma viri fortis medios mittantur in hostes ; inde iubete peti,' borrowed from Latro's expression in the *suasoria* known as 'Armorum iudicium,' 'mittamus arma in hostes et petamus.' Similarly, in *Am.* I, 2, 11-12 'vidi ego iactatas mota face crescere flammas, et rursus nullo concutiente mori,' Ovid is said to have adapted Latro's, 'non vides ut immota fax torpeat, ut exagitata reddat ignes?' As a declaimer he bade fair to surpass his master, except that his treatment of rhetorical commonplaces was too desultory and unsystematic, and his dislike of argumentation led him to avoid *controversiae* in favour of *suasoriae*. His diction was restrained in declamation, but less so in his poems 'in quibus non ignoravit vitia sua sed amavit.' Seneca tells an interesting anecdote in this connection. Some of Ovid's friends one day asked to be allowed to write down three of his verses which they would rather see deleted from his work ; he agreed, on condition that he should himself write down three lines he would particularly like to

---

[1] cf. Morawski, *Ovidiana*, (Cracow, 1903), p. 15, who compares *Contr.* IV, 2, 2; VII, 1, 26 ; Ovid, *Met.* VIII, 459.
[2] R. Heinze, *Vergils epische Technik*, (3rd edn. Leipzig, 1915), pp. 422 ff.
[3] e.g. on *Aen.* VI, 847 ff.; H. Nettleship, *The Ancient Commentators on Virgil* (Introd. to the 4th revised edn. of Conington, London, 1881) pp. CVI-CVII, gives further citations. See also *Thesaurus Linguae Latinae* s.v. declamo.
[4] *P. Vergilius Maro, Aeneis Buch* VI (Leipzig, 1926) pp. 376 ff. ; but see also D'Alton, *op. cit.*, p. 456.
[5] II, § 247, 7 'Er (Ovid) ist der erste römische Dichter, von dem man sagen kann, dass er sich der Rhetorik verschrieben und die Kunstgriffe der Deklamatoren in die Poesie eingeführt hat '; cf. below, pp. 149 ff.

retain. When the papers were opened, the verses selected were found to be identical, one being 'semibovemque virum semivirumque bovem' (*A.A.* II, 24) and the second 'et gelidum Borean egelidumque Notum' (*Am.* II, 11, 10). The third is lost owing to a lacuna in the MSS of Seneca. The critic's final opinion is that Ovid did not lack the judgment so much as the will to restrain his fancies,[1] and the poet's own comment is characteristically drawn from that feminine society which he found so peculiarly congenial —'he said that a pretty face was sometimes the prettier for a beauty-spot.'[2]

Ovid's inability to let well alone was realised by his contemporaries ; so Scaurus (*Contr.* IX, 5, 17) called the declaimer Votienus Montanus 'the Ovid among orators,' for Ovid 'nescit quod bene cessit relinquere.' In a neat critical dictum, Scaurus observed that 'it is a greater virtue to know how to finish than how to speak,' and quoted as an example of Ovid's fault in this respect *Met.* XIII, 503 ff. (Hecuba on the sacrifice of Polyxena at the tomb of Achilles) 'cinis ipse sepulti in genus hoc pugnat' ('saevit' MSS of Ovid) for he proceeds to add 'tumulo quoque sensimus hostem,' and not content with repeating the point, must then explain 'Aeacidae fecunda fui.'

Not all declaimers, however, were as punctilious as Scaurus, and Seneca informs us that Cestius referred to Ovid as 'the man who filled our age not only with amatory arts, but with amatory maxims as well' (*Contr.* III, 7, 2), and censured his pupil Alfius Flavus for using, in the declamation in which a mad son gashed his own limbs and was poisoned by his father, the expression 'ipse sui et alimentum erat et damnum', a ludicrous reminiscence of Ovid, *Met.* VIII, 877-8 (of Erysichthon) 'ipse suos artus lacero morsu coepit et infelix minuendo corpus alebat.' Scaurus also quotes 'inepta loci', from *Priapea*, III, 8, in *Contr.* I, 2, 22. So again P. Vicinius (*Contr.* X, 4, 25), a great admirer of Ovid, declared that the poet's verses should be memorised to provide useful *sententiae*, and quoted *Met.* XII, 607-8 as an example. These comments of Seneca show how closely related declamation and poetry were under the early Empire ; and when it is remembered that the poets themselves influenced one another, as when for example, it is said of Ovid (*Suas.* III, 7) that he frequently borrowed from Virgil, not in order to plagiarise but quite openly in order to win approval, it may be seen that the credit for originality of thought and expression is often very difficult to assign.

---

[1] Exactly as Quint., X, 1, 88, 'nimium amator ingenii sui,' and 98, 'si ingenio suo imperare quam indulgere maluisset'; cf. Sen., *N.Q.* III, 27, 13.

[2] To which his critics might now reply by quoting *Tristia*, V, 13, 13-14.

At this point, it may be worthy of note, although the subject belongs strictly to literary theory rather than literary criticism, that the elder Seneca's works contain a number of interesting comments on questions of plagiarism. Such a topic was bound to arise for discussion in an exercise in which credit for originality played so large a part. Seneca tells us (*Suas.* II, 19—à propos of 'belli mora') that in his earlier days the ears of the critics were so keen that scarcely a word could be safely purloined. The Roman declaimers were particularly liable to be charged with plagiarism from the Greeks. In *Contr.* x, 4, 18 we learn that such borrowings often brought as much ill as good, and in §21, Latro is defended against suspicion of plagiarism because he both despised and ignored the Greeks. On the other hand, Triarius (*Contr.* x, 5, 20) made capital out of a Greek *sententia* by making a slight alteration in wording, a practice which Cassius Severus compared with that of thieves who stole cups and puts new handles on them. Arellius Fuscus went so far as to defend translating from Greek (*Contr.* IX, 1, 13) on the ground that he did so 'for exercise, not for theft.' But the commonest resort was to express someone else's ideas in one's own words (*Contr.* x, *Praef.* 11), and improve on them if possible (cf. *Contr.* VII, 1, 27, of Virgil, 'expressisset in melius'). These views are of interest when compared with the classical theory of imitation[1] which we find outlined, for instance, in the *Ars Poetica* of Horace (131 ff.).

Students of Latin Literature also owe to the elder Seneca a stirring passage of 25 lines on the death of Cicero by the poet Cornelius Severus (*Suas.* VI, 26), lines which are worthy of Lucan at his best, as well as passages on the same subject from the historians Aufidius Bassus, Cremutius Cordus, Bruttedius Niger, and, most valuable, Asinius Pollio, from whom a citation is given which Seneca declares to be as eloquent as anything in his *Histories* and worthy of the master-orator himself. In addition to these quotations, 23 lines of the poem on the expedition of Germanicus to the North Sea by Albinovanus Pedo, whom Quintilian (x, 1, 90) thought worth reading, owe their preservation to the elder Seneca (*Suas.* I, 15).[2]

The literary criticism and reminiscence in Seneca's work so far collected has been mainly that concerning the major authors, but a fair impression of Seneca's ability as a critic cannot be gained without consideration of his accounts of the declaimers themselves which occur mainly in the excellent prefaces to the books of *Con-*

---

[1] On the subject generally, see E. Stemplinger, *Das Plagiat in der griechischen Literatur* (Leipzig-Berlin, 1912), and G. C. Fiske, *Lucilius and Horace* (Madison 1920) c. 1 ; J. F. D'Alton, pp. 428 ff.

[2] On Pedo, cf. Teuffel, II, §252, 6, and Edward's note on this passage.

troversiae. A high opinion of him is expressed by a modern authority[1]: 'Amongst the Roman critics, I would consider the Elder Seneca as occupying a place of distinction . . . he has given us a striking analysis of the psychology of the declaimers . . . Seneca evidently tried to get into close contact with the personalities of the men whom he was portraying, and sought to throw some light on the working of their minds.' He sets forth his own impressions of their style in simple and unstudied language, and is not endeavouring to frame his criticism in conformity with any stereotyped scheme. . . . His prefaces alone would win for him a high rank among Roman critics.' Seneca's prefaces provide us with sketches of Latro (I), Fabianus (II), Cassius Severus (III), Pollio and Haterius (IV), Albucius (VII), Scaurus, Labienus, Moschus and others (X). They are replete with anecdotes, and their criticisms are expressed in brief sententious fashion, often with antithesis and neat point, as might be expected from the author of the *Controversiae*. The following may be taken as typical examples: III *Praef.* 2 (of Cassius Severus)— 'His oratorical style was vigorous, elegant, full of clever[2] point; no one was less tolerant of any superfluity in his speeches than he was; there was no part that could not stand on its own, nothing which the hearer could afford to miss without loss; everything was directed to an end, had some object in view; no one ever exercised greater control over the emotions of his audience.' IV, *Praef.* 7-8 (of Haterius)—'He had an abundance not merely of words but of ideas, he would discourse on the same subject as often as you liked and as long as you liked, frequently varying his figures and developments, and was incapable of being either exhausted or restrained.'[3] VII, *Praef.* 1 (of Albucius)—'That unseasonable philosophy of his found unlimited and endless scope in his declamations; he rarely developed a declamation in full; you could not call it an outline, you could not call it a declamation; there was far too little in it for a declamation, far too much for an outline. When he spoke in public he summoned up all his resources, and then there was no stopping him; often, while he declaimed, the trumpet thrice sounded (i.e., he spoke for nine hours), so anxious was he to say not merely everything that ought to be said but everything that could possibly be said in the exercise. He argued awkwardly rather than precisely: he would pile argument on argument and, as if nothing was sufficiently established, he would confirm all his proofs by fresh

---

[1] J. F. D'Alton, *op. cit.*, pp. 545-6. cf. Saintsbury's *History of Criticism* (Edinburgh and London, 1900), vol. I, pp. 230-240.

[2] ingeniosis, Bornecque; ingentibus, mss. cf. the criticisms of Tac,, *Dial.* c. 26, and Quint., x, 1, 116-7.

[3] cf. Sen., *Epp.* 40, 10; Tac., *Ann.* IV, 61.

proofs.'[1] x, *Praef.* 2 (of Aemilius Scaurus)—'He was a careless speaker. He would often learn up his case in the courtroom itself, often while he dressed; then, like a litigant rather than a pleader, he would try to provoke some reply from his opponents and quarrel with it; he knew his own powers. Nothing could be imagined more elegant, nothing more alert; his style was rather old-fashioned, his diction had the dignity that derives from the avoidance of vulgarities, his expression and demeanour were wonderfully adapted to the authority of the orator. Yet all this only serves to show, not how great an orator the lazy Scaurus was, but how great an orator he might have been.' *Ib.* 9 (of Musa)—'Who could endure a fellow who said of water-pipes "they rain back up to the sky," or who called the sprinkling of perfumes, "scented showers," a cultivated garden "engraved forests," and the picture of a tree "groves that arise from the canvas"? Or that remark about sudden deaths which he made when you took me to hear him: "All the birds that fly, all the fishes than swim, all the beasts that run find their graves in our bellies. You ask why we die suddenly; by deaths we live."[2] Don't you think we ought to have taken it out of his hide for that, even though he had been recently manumitted?'

The incidental criticisms, which Seneca expresses throughout his work are equally sensible and just; he is ready to applaud a good *sententia* or an ingenious *color*, but he frequently condemns them as far-fetched (*longe arcessitus*, *Contr.* I, 6, 9), puerile (*puerilis*, *Suas.* II, 16, Dionysius' μειρακιώδης, *De Isoc.* c. 12, *De Dem.* cc. 5, 20, 21), in bad taste (*cacozelia*[3], *cacozelos*, *Contr.* IX, 1, 15, IX, 2, 28, *Suas.* II, 16, VII, 11) or stupid (*Contr.* I, 3, 11; I, 4, 12) or inept (*Contr.* I, 4, 7). His ideal of style is not that of the strict Atticist, who sees no virtue but plainness;[4] but on the other hand he is outspoken against the wild excesses of Asianism.[5] Of the Greek declaimers, poor specimens of a master-race, he has a low opinion; he relegates them to the end of each exercise (perhaps because they declaimed after the Romans?) and frequently criticises them adversely; yet he is not too prejudiced to give a word of approval for their better efforts. He is fully aware of the art that conceals art,[6] and his critical dicta are sometimes admirably expressed, as in *Contr.* VII, *Praef.* 3. 'Nothing is more damaging than obvious preparation; for it is obvious that there is some mischief afoot.' His tolerance and balance are nowhere better exemplified than in his remark in *Contr.* X, *Praef.* 10: 'I am

---

1 On Albucius, cf. Suet., *De Rhet.* c. 6.
2 For a similar *Gorgiasm*, and its influence, see below p. 155.
3 cf. Bardon, p. 17, and above, p. 69, n. 6.
4 *Contr.* II, 1, 24.
5 *Contr.* II, 1, 25; X, 5, 21; *Suas.* I, 12 etc. D'Alton, p. 212.
6 *Contr.* I, *Praef.* 21; X, *Praef.* 14.

not one of those very exacting critics, who judge everything by a precise measure ; I think many concessions must be made to genius ; but the concessions must be of faults, not of prodigies,' an outlook which is exactly that of Horace, *A.P.* 351 ff. ' verum ubi plura nitent in carmine, non ego paucis offendar maculis, quas aut incuria fudit aut humana parum cavit natura ' ; nor indeed would it be unfair to regard the elder Seneca as the Horace of Augustan prose criticism.

CHAPTER VIII

SOME INDICATIONS OF DECLAMATORY INFLUENCE
ON THE LITERATURE OF THE EARLY EMPIRE

From the Augustan Age onwards, as might be expected from the growing popularity of the practice of declamation, the influence of *suasoriae* and *controversiae* on Latin Literature becomes ever more marked.[1] To trace its operation in any detail is clearly beyond the scope of the present work, and separate monographs have been devoted to this aspect of the work of individual authors. Of Ovid alone, Norden[2] goes so far as to say : ' We need a commentary on Ovid, in which his material is compared with the declamations known to us, and his verses analysed from this point of view.' This is perhaps an over-statement, inasmuch as the declamations represent a specialised and heightened form of rhetoric, and the demonstrable parallels do not seem to be as frequent as Norden would suggest ; a great deal of Ovid can be shown to be generally ' rhetorical ' in form or style, but not specifically 'declamatory.'[3] In the following pages, only those examples will be selected which seem to have a sharply-defined relationship with the Senecan declamations. Selected works of contemporary writers will mainly be considered here, namely, the early poems of Ovid, whom Seneca

1 An excellent general account is given by Norden, *A.K.* I, pp. 300 ff. Of particular value for their acumen and subtle detail are all the publications on the subject of Casimir Morawski, of which *De Rhetoribus Latinis Observationes* (Cracow, 1892), *De sermone scriptorum latinorum aetatis quae dicitur argentea observationes* (Lwow, 1895) [= *Eos* II (1895), pp. 1-12], *Observationum de rhetoribus latinis auctarium* (Lwow, 1899) [= *Eos* v, (1899) pp. 1-6], *Rhetorum Romanorum Ampullae* (Cracow, 1901), *Parallelismoi* (Cracow, 1902), and *Ovidiana* (Cracow, 1903) deserve special mention. Examples given below are from my own reading, but I have noted where I am anticipated.
2 *op. cit.* II, p. 892. Teuffel, *Gesch. d. röm. Lit.* II, § 247, 7 does not go quite so far as this.
3 See R. Ehwald, *Ad historiam carminum Ovidianorum recensionemque symbolae* (Progr. Gotha, 1892), *Exeg. Kommentar zur* XIV. *Heroide Ovids* (Gotha, 1900) ; (these are known to me only by subsequent references and summaries); Morawski, *Ovidiana* (Cracow, 1903) ; H. de la Ville de Mirmont, *La Jeunesse d' Ovide* (Paris, 1905) chapters II, and III (pp. 67 ff.) ; C. Brück, *De Ovidio Scholasticarum Declamationum Imitatore* (Diss., Giessen, 1909) ; F. Eggerding, *De Heroidum Ovidianarum Epistulis Quae Vocantur Commentationes* (Diss., Halle, 1908). N. Deratani, *Artis rhetoricae in Ovidii carminibus, praecipue amatoriis, perspicuae capita quaedam* (Moscow, 1916) is unfortunately inaccessible to me. Cazzaniga, *Elementi retorici nella composizione delle Lettere dal Ponto di Ovidio* (Varese, 1937) is rather too general for the present purpose. Recent scholars have tended to be more sceptical regarding Ovid's indebtedness to rhetoric, and admittedly some of the evidence which has been presented is based on a very wide interpretation of the word rhetoric, which can be applied to almost every turn of thought and expression of which the human mind is capable. cf. Brookes Otis in *T.A.Ph.A.* LXIX (1938), p. 216, and H. Fränkel's *Ovid—a Poet between Two Worlds* (California, 1945), pp. 169 ff.

heard declaim,[1] the *Epitome* of Velleius Paterculus, who may be regarded as the earliest extant ' rhetorical ' Roman historian, and the *Tragedies* of the younger Seneca, to whom, with his brothers Mela and Novatus, the *Controversiae* were dedicated.

We have already seen how closely in touch with the schools of declamation Ovid was, and how he studied under Arellius Fuscus and imitated Latro. He was also a friend of the declaimer Gallio (*Suas.* III, 7). It is not surprising, therefore, that his earliest poems reveal evidence of the influence of his declamatory exercises. The *Heroidum Epistulae* of Ovid, says Purser[2] are ' derived from the *suasoriae* of the schools . . . little else than *suasoriae*.' If the word *suasoria* be taken in its broadest sense, this is true ; but the *Heroides* would be more accurately described as *prosopopoeiae*,[3] or *ethopoeiae*[4] or 'imaginary monologues',[5] for they are not all of a type in which advice is given to another person. The letter of Dido to Aeneas is partly advisory, but others are merely plaintive monodies (e.g. Penelope-Ulixi), or gentle or passionate rebukes (Briseis-Achilli, Medea-Iasoni, etc.). The type of exercise is that which the later Greek progymnasmatists introduce with the words τίνας ἂν εἴποι λόγους . . . what kind of a speech would, e.g. Andromache make over Hector's body?[6] or Niobe lamenting her children, or Achilles deploring the death of Patroclus?[7] So, in *Heroides* XIV, 53-66, we have a dramatic soliloquy of Hypermnestra deliberating whether or not to murder Lynceus. But that Ovid did not enter fully into the spirit of these exercises is clear from his naive admission in *Heroides* X, 79-80 :

' nunc ego non tantum quae sum passura recordor,
sed quaecumque potest ulla relicta pati.

He does not throw himself with sufficient zest into the characterisation for which they afforded so excellent an opportunity, and many of his lines are commonplaces which any heroine might have been expected to utter on such an occasion.[8]

---

[1] *Contr.* II, 2, 8.

[2] Introduction to Palmer's edition (Oxford, 1898), p. XIII. Only the first 14 poems are used as evidence here, as the authenticity of the rest is less certain.

[3] cf. Quint., III, 8, 49, 52 ; cf. Martini, *Einleitung zu Ovid* (Prague, 1933) p. 17 ; Teuffel, *op. cit.*, II, § 248, 3.

[4] Hermog., *Progymn.* c. 9 (p. 20, Rabe).

[5] Seneca's third *suasoria* contains elements of this type. cf. above, p. 53.

[6] Hermog., *Progymn.* p. 21.

[7] Aphthonius, *Progymn.* c. 11 = *Rhet. Graec.* II, 45 (Spengel).

[8] Readers who find this judgment a little harsh will find a sensitive appreciaton, by Lucille Haley. ' The Feminine Complex in the *Heroides* ' in *C.J.* XX (1924) pp. 15-25.

An interesting example of the influence of the *suasoria* is seen in *Amores* II, 11, where Ovid advises his wife against taking a journey by sea. This reminds the reader of the θέσις on that subject 'an navigandum?'[1]; and the first *suasoria* of Seneca in which Alexander deliberates *an Oceanum naviget*. Then again, a more fully developed *suasoria* in verse is seen in Book XIII of the *Metamorphoses*, where we have speeches of Ajax and Ulysses in support of their claim to the arms of Achilles. The *Armorum Iudicium* was, we know from the elder Seneca,[2] a stock *suasoria* of the schools. The second book of the *Tristia* has also been claimed to be an extended *suasoria*,[3] and has been analysed rhetorically,[4] though the influence is not so marked here as in Book XIII of the *Metamorphoses*. It is particularly noteworthy that the influence is, in all these examples, that of the *suasoria* rather than the *controversia*, for the elder Seneca tells us that *suasoriae* were a predilection of Ovid.[5]

Most interesting and important are the traces in Ovid's work of *sententiae*; not so much the mere γνῶμαι which any poet might have created or transmitted, but the heightened, pointed, apt 'comment' that might equally well be transplanted to the pages of the elder Seneca. 'Res est sollicti plena timoris amor,' says Penelope (*Heroides* I, 12), an obvious enough remark, one of the many 'amatory maxims'[6] coined by Ovid, and developed at rather wearisome length throughout the poem[7]. But this is not specifically declamatory. On the other hand, when Ovid says in *Amores* I, 8, 43 'casta est quam nemo rogavit,' 'chaste is she whom no one has tempted,' we immediately recollect the *controversia* (I, 2) of the girl in the hands of the *leno*, who tried to preserve her purity and subsequently applied for the priesthood. 'When,' ask the declaimers (§13) 'does a girl cease to be *casta*?' 'Nulla satis pudica est, de qua quaeritur' says Asprenas (§10). 'Casta est quam nemo rogavit,' we may imagine Ovid replying.

Amores III, 3 opens in very rhetorical fashion with the exclamation: '*Esse deos, i, crede. Fidem iurata fefellit.*' The existence of the gods was a favourite *quaestio* to which the declaimers loved to allude. '*Liquet nobis deos esse*; qui non aluit eget, qui in domum suam fratrem non recepit in publico manet' says Vallius Syriacus

---

1 cf. above p. 4, and below p. 163.
2 *Contr.* II, 2, 8. Two 'declamations' of Antisthenes survive, on this subject.
3 cf. S. G. Owen's edition (Oxford, 1889), Introduction to Book II.
4 By Ehwald, in his Gotha programme (1892); cf. Mirmont, pp. 117 ff.
5 *Contr.* II, 2, 12 'libentius dicebat suasorias'; Brück, pp. 21-2, gives good examples of the rhetorical *deliberatio* (e.g. *Met.* VIII, 44 ff.), but his attempt to apply to Ovid the detailed rhetorical rules of the *suasoria*, pp. 60-70, seems to me far-fetched.
6 *Contr.* III, 7, 2 'amatoriis... sententiis'.
7 cf. Eggerding, *op. cit.*, pp. 232-3.

(*Contr.* I, 1, 11). '' Ergo tu, cum tam innocens quam dicis vixeris, ista passa, *credis deos esse*?' asks Cestius (*Contr.* I, 2, 8) and 'Interrogo te hoc loco, mulier; responde mihi; *sunt dii*?' (*Contr.* I, 3, 2). Clearly the brief, pointed, emphatic, ironical opening of Ovid's poem is indebted to the declaimers.

A famous poem in the *Amores* (I, 13) is that in which Ovid upbraids the goddess of dawn for compelling him to leave his mistress. His reproaches, cast in a conventional mould, end with a briillant point—" Iurgia finieram. *Scires audisse*; *rubebat*.' This is a good example of Ovid's humour, says a German editor;[1] yes, but it is a particular kind of humour—the wit of the declamatory schools, and that particular point (three words, be it noted) is just the kind of *sententia* that the elder Seneca's contemporaries would have delighted in introducing.

Not all of Ovid's efforts are so successful. The *Ariadne-Theseo* letter in the *Heroïdes* (x) offers an example of bathos. The heroine has exhausted herself with lamentation, with running to and fro on the shores of Naxos, and climbing rocky vantage-points. Seeing the fast-receding ship, she summons up her remaining energy for a short speech, of precisely two lines (ll. 35-36) : 'Whither dost thou flee? come back, wicked Theseus ! turn back thy ship—*it has not its full complement* ! (*numerum non habet illa suum*). Editors soberly quote parallels for this use of *numerus*, but surely the elder Seneca would have drily added ' inepte ' or ' pueriliter Ovidius ' to that observation, which might well have stood in a collection of ' Points from the Declamations.' Not content with this *tour de force*, Ovid must needs follow it up with a frigid antithesis 'haec ego ; quod voci deerat, plangore replebam ' (cf. *Contr.* II, 5, 9 ' deerat iam sanguis, supererat fides ') and a play on words ' verbera cum verbis mixta fuere meis '—both favourite devices of the declaimers. The *Heroides* are, in fact, as Martini[2] has truly remarked, the most rhetorical of all Ovid's works. Oenone, upbraiding Paris, and scorning Helen's passion for him (v, 105) says, pithily ' ardet amore tui ? *sic et Menelaon amavit* '—a neat ' hit,' which is similar in form to a *sententia* made by Ovid himself in the declamation quoted by the elder Seneca (*Contr.* II, 2, 10), where, after a similar rhetorical question, he adds ' *senes sic amant*.' And, in that context, we may note a *sententia* which would have been equally appropriate in his poems, ' Facilius in amore finem impetres quam modum.'

[1] P. Brandt, *P. Ovidii Nasonis Amorum Libri Tres* (Leipzig, 1911), *Einleitung*, p. 34 ; so H. Fränkel, *op. cit.* p. 15.

[2] *Einleitung zu Ovid*, p. 17. ' Keinen seinen Werke zeigt so enge Beziehungen zur Rhetorik wie die Heroides.'

Then again, Hypsipyle, attacking Jason and speaking of her twin children by him, has a cutting remark, which is again characterised by brevity and pungency (VI, 123-4) :

si quaeris, cui sint similes, cognosceris illis :
fallere non norunt : cetera patris habent.

Less sharply-pointed, and therefore less influenced by declamation, are such *sententiae* as ' tarde, quae credita laedunt, credimus ' (II, 9-10) ; 'quaecumque ex merito spes venit, aequa venit' (ib. 62) ; ' peius adulterio turpis adulter obest ' (IV, 34); ' nitimur in vetitum semper, cupimusque negata ' (*Am.* III, 4, 17); ' quidquid servatur, cupimus magis ' (ib., 25). It is mainly by the innuendo or the sting that we recognise the declamatory touch[1].

Rhetorical figures, some of them perhaps hitherto unnoticed, abound in the *Heroides*. It is noticeable that again and again the heroines introduce an appeal, in which each line begins with *per* ' in the name of . . .'. Natural enough, perhaps, for any deserted and disconsolate lover, but so frequently does it appear that it is clearly a convention (*Heroides*, II, 35 ff. III, 103 ff. IV, 167, VII, 157, VIII, 117 ff., X, 73-4, XII, 77 ff. 191-2, XIII, 159 ff.). It is the *figura iurisiurandi* of which the declaimers were so fond.[2] So Ovid's teacher, Arellius Fuscus, in *Contr.* IX, 4, 4 says ' rogo vos *per* securitatem publicam, *per* modo restitutae libertatis laetitiam, *per* coniuges liberosque vestros ' : Latro, in *Contr.* X, I, 7 ' *per* has lacrimas, *per* hunc squalorem, *per* haec necessaria omnibus,' etc. Fuscus again in *Suas.* VII, 9 ' *per* te, M. Tulli, *per* quattuor et sexaginta annos pulchre actos, *per* salutarem reipublicae consulatum, *per* aeternam . . . ingenii tui memoriam, *per* rempublicam, etc.' In *Contr.* VII, *Praef.* 7, the elder Seneca tells an amusing story of the declaimer Albucius, who said to an opponent in court, ' Swear by your father's unburied ashes, swear by your father's memory' and followed out the theme. His opponent's counsel sprang up and said ' We accept the challenge ; my client will swear.' ' I wasn't making a challenge,' complained the nonplussed Albucius, ' I was using a figure of speech. If you act like that, we must do away with all such figures.' ' Do away with them, then,' retorted the opponent—' we can live without them ! ' The figure appears to be known as *figura iurisiurandi* to the declaimers.[3] Julius

---

[1] *Sententiae* recur in Ovid's later works, and Quint., IV, 1, 77 says that in the *Metamorphoses* the poet uses them as a means of transition from one story to another. *Met.* I, 162, ' scires e sanguine natos,' a neat conclusion, is similar.

[2] cf. *Suas.* VII, 14 ' cum coepisset scholasticorum frequentissimo iam more a jurejurando.' A variant of the form with *per* is that with *sic* or *ita* and a subjunctive (' so may this or that blessing befall you ') cf. *Heroides*, IV, 168 ff., VII, 159 ; *Tristia*, IV, 5, 25-34.

[3] cf. Bardon, *op. cit.* p. 95.

Rufinus, however, (*R.L.M.* p. 43) calls it *obsecratio* or *obtestatio*, and quotes the famous example in Virgil, *Aeneid* IV, 314 ff.; in Virgil the use is a natural one, but, no doubt, the figure dates back to imitations of the famous Marathon oath of Demosthenes.[1] Quintilian hits the mark admirably when he says (IX, 2, 98) ' nec meretur fidem qui sententiolae gratia iurat, nisi si potest tam bene quam Demosthenes '—a criticism which might justly be applied to the *Heroides* of Ovid. Other rhetorical figures in the *Heroides* may be briefly sketched. Antithesis, is, of course, extremely common throughout Ovid, but *Heroides* XII, 163-174 is noteworthy as containing seven antitheses in 12 lines. *Anaphora* may be illustrated by II, 49 ff. (*credidimus* four times in five lines), and *ib.* 99-101. *Occultatio*, or the introduction of an idea by alleging that there is no need to mention it, occurs in I, 91 ff. and VIII, 67 ff. *Aposiopesis* is seen in XII, 207, XIII, 164, *zeugma* in VI, 55 and VII, 7-8, *paronomasia* in IX, 31 (honor)(onus) and X, 38, and the figure ἐκ τοῦ ἀδυνάτου in V, 29 ff.

A most interesting account of Ovid's use of the figure ἀντιμεταβολή, popular with the declaimers, is given by Morawski.[2] This figure is a special form of antithesis, in which the contrast is effected by an inversion of the same words in the same case.[3] The two examples which he quotes are (i) *Heroides* XIV, 106 ' tu mihi *dux comiti*, tu *comes* ipsa *duci*,' and (ii) *Met.* XIII, 97 ' atque *Aiax armis*, non *Aiaci arma* petuntur.' Of the four parallels from the elder Seneca which Morawski cites (*Contr.* I, 3, 2; IV, 4, 1; IX, 5, 16; X, 5, 11) the second is perhaps the neatest: ' uterque quod alteri deerat commodavimus; ille *viro arma*, ego *armis virum*.' He proceeds to give a number of examples from Silver Latin authors. Such subtle points as this might well escape the student who is on the alert for rhetorical touches, not merely the casual reader.

A quite deliberate use of the figure *adnominatio*,[4] in which a noun is repeated in different cases (cf. *Ad Herennium*, IV, 22, 31) is the following couplet (VI, 127-8):—

'*Medeam* timui ; plus est *Medea* noverca ;
Medeae faciunt ad scelus omne manus.'

---

[1] cf. [Longinus] π. ὕψ. c. XVI, 2 who calls it σχῆμα ὁμοτικόν, and Tiberius, π. σχημ. (*Rhet. Graec.* III, 69 Sp.). who calls it τὸ ὅρκου σχῆμα. This consensus is held to point to a common source in the περὶ σχημάτων of Caecilius of Calacte, friend of Dionysius of Halicarnassus in Rome, and contemporary of Ovid; cf. Ofenloch, *Caecilius Calactinus* (Leipzig, 1907) p. 73.

[2] *Ovidiana*, pp. 7-8, following Ehwald's commentary on the *Metamorphoses* (1898) II, 227 ff. and his tract on *Heroides* XIV (Gotha, 1900).

[3] See Volkmann, *Rhet.* p. 488.

[4] This figure is known to the Greeks as πολύπτωτον (Herodianus, π.σχημ. *Rhet. Graec.* III, p. 97, Spengel); cf. Volkmann, *op. cit.*, p. 470.

Equally rhetorical, as Morawski[1] has observed, is Hypsipyle's further bitter outburst (VI, 151) '*Medeae Medea* forem,' where the maximum of point is obtained by the minimum amount of repetition. He compares *Met.* XIII, 390 ' nec quisquam *Aiacem* possit superare nisi *Aiax*,' *Trist.* II, 230 ' bellaque pro magno *Caesare Caesar* aget,' and the following example from Sen., *Suas.* VII, 9 ' ille verus est *Cicero* quem proscribi Antonius non putat nisi a *Cicerone* posse,' but the poet is better than the declaimer at his own job.

Quite often these rhetorical tricks are missed by editors. So in x, 123-4, Ariadne laments :—
    Ossa superstabunt volucres inhumata marinae ?
    haec sunt officiis digna sepulchra meis ?
Palmer finds the expression odd, but regards it as ' grim realism ' ; it is nothing of the kind, but a variation of the old saying of Gorgias γῦπες ἔμψυχοι τάφοι (π. ὕψους c. III, 2) of which Norden[2] sees an imitation in *Met.* VI, 665, and for which he appositely refers the the reader to *Contr.* x, *Praef.* 9.

Finally, the declaimer in Ovid is clearly seen in his endeavour to vary the same theme again and again ;[3] examples are legion, and one must suffice. In *Heroides* x, 53-4 Ovid writes 'et tua, quae possum, pro te vestigia tango, Strataque, quae membris intepuere tuis.' ' Nesciens quod bene cessit relinquere,' he continues :—
    ' incumbo, lacrimisque toro manante profusis
    'pressimus,' exclamo, 'te duo : redde duos.'
and, still unsatisfied,
    ' venimus huc ambo, cur non discedimus ambo ?
    perfide, pars nostri, lectule, maior ubi est ? '
A hard-pressed declaimer, seeking anxiously ' aliquid novi dicere', could hardly have descended to greater depths of weak sentimentality.

It would, however, be a disservice to the poet to insist on the bad effects of declamation upon him. Declamatory rhetoric gave to Ovid virtue as well as vice ; without it he might never have attained to the cleverness and sparkle which we admire in him at his best, and even in his more mature works, particularly the *Metamorphoses*, some of his most charming descriptions are

---

[1] *op. cit.*, p. 8.

[2] *A.K.* I, 385, cf. II, 893 n. 1. On this stock theme, see also E. R. Bevan, ' Rhetoric in the Ancient World,' in *Essays in Honour of Gilbert Murray* (London, 1936) pp. 198-9. Morawski, *Parallelismoi* (Cracow, 1902), p. 4, well compares *Macbeth*, Act. III, Sc. 4, ' our monuments shall be the maw of kites.'

[3] I do not, of course, mean to imply that ' theme and variation ' is necessarily a rhetorical practice, but merely that in Ovid's case rhetoric exaggerated a natural tendency.

rhetorical ἐκφράσεις. The *Heroides* and *Amores* are the youthful works of one who, albeit dissolute, loved elegance, ingenuity, and wit, and they were written before the shadow of the imperial power fell across his life. In the poems of his exile, in which the endless plaints and self-pity have robbed him of much of the sympathy he deserved, the brilliant *lumina* of his early works rarely appear. To abandon for ever the intellectual life, the luxury, the sunshine and colour of Rome for the solitude and dreary barrenness of Tomi was to him, of all people, a most crushing blow; Morawski even goes so far as to say: 'urbe porro relicta etiam urbanitas deseruit Ovidium.' But he had in his day been a poet among declaimers and a declaimer among poets; they influenced him, and he influenced them in his turn,[1] and no other Augustan was quite so close to them in spirit.

That the practice of declamation had its effect on the writing of history is not surprising, for historians in both Greece and Rome had long delighted in giving their work a rhetorical flavour,[2] and the declamations of the early Empire merely served as an additional relish.[3] The declaimers themselves, as we have seen, frequently used historical themes, particularly in *suasoriae*, and prided themselves on decorating their speeches with historical examples and allusions, while taking full advantage of the traditional concession which permitted them to diverge at will from standards of strictest accuracy.[4] Several of the Augustan historians, including Pollio and Livy, frequented the declamatory schools, and few of their successors escaped the influence of an ever more prevalent practice. In subject-matter the declamations encouraged speeches, descriptions,[5] digressions, and exaggeration; in style they encouraged sententiousness, artificiality, and the introduction of fixed locutions popular in the schools.

It is difficult to assign a point at which the heightened declamatory rhetoric began to make its influence felt. Much of the brilliant epigrammatic brevity of Sallust would have satisfied an audience of declaimers, and it is noteworthy that the younger Seneca (*Epp.* 114, 17) says that it was in Sallust's day that 'amputatae sententiae et verba ante exspectatum cadentia et obscura brevitas' came into vogue. He proceeds to show how Sallust himself was moderate in

---

[1] cf. *Contr.* III, 7, 2; X, 4, 25.

[2] e.g. Theopompus, Clitarchus, and especially Timaeus; contrast the views of Polybius, collected by J. F. D'Alton, *op. cit.*, pp. 501-3.

[3] D'Alton, pp. 520-523.

[4] Cic., *Brut.* 11, 42 'concessum est rhetoribus ementiri in historiis.'

[5] cf. Cic., *Orat.* 20, 66; Quint., X, 1, 31; Pliny, *Epp.* II, 5, 5; VII, 9, 8; Lucian, *De conscr. hist.* §§ 15-16 and § 28.

such effects, which became very frequent in the *History of the Punic War* of his imitator, L. Arrunteius. In Livy, declamatory features, both of style and of subject-matter, occasionally appear, though even he is not throughout a good example of the influence. Despite his love of antithesis and chiasmus, rhetorical argument and rhetorical question, the 'lactea ubertas' of his rich periodic style is more reminiscent of the old Republic than the new Empire. In subject-matter, he is now and again close to the declamatory schools; as in Book IX, where he has a digression (cc. 17-19) on the question 'what would have happened to the Roman state if it had had to make war on Alexander?' It has been well argued[1] that this essay, on a character so popular with the declaimers, may be a rhetorical exercise composed earlier and inserted as a pleasant digression. Then, again, in Book XL, cc. 8-16, Livy's account of the quarrel between Perseus and Demetrius, sons of Philip of Macedon, has been excellently compared[2] with the declamations; for declaimers loved fabulous quarrels between brothers (cf. *Contr.* I, 1.) The picture of the wretched father deciding on the merits of the case, and the speeches of each brother, are such that 'the reader will think himself transported to the haunts of the declaimers, and will feel that a scene from the Senecan declamations has been inserted in the history of Livy.' In style, Livy's phraseology occasionally recalls the *Controversiae*, but the parallels offered[3] are not always convincing. An interesting example may be given from Book II, 45, 4, where Livy has the neat *sententia* 'novum seditionis genus silentium otiumque inter armatos.' Now Morawski[4] has shown, from numerous examples in the younger Seneca and elsewhere, that the expression 'genus est . . .' followed by a paradox, is a reminiscence of such phrases as 'genus est rogandi rogare non posse' in *Contr.* X, 4, 6. So Livy here offers contemporary evidence of this particular favourite locution. The *History* would repay a study comparing it with the declamations, but the influence is nothing like so obvious as it becomes in Livy's immediate successors[5], and even his many rhetorical speeches are not, like those of the declaimers, constantly in search of point.

[1] W. B. Anderson in *T.A.Ph.A.* XXXIX (1908), pp. 94 ff.; cf. his edn. (*Cambridge*, 1912), Appendix II.

[2] C. Morawski *Observationum de rhetoribus latinis auctorium* (Lwow, 1899) [= *Eos* V, pp. 1-6]. Professor Walbank, however, considers that Livy is here merely following Polybius (*J.H.S.* LVIII [1938], 62).

[3] e.g. by H. de la Ville de Mirmont in *Bulletin Hispanique* XV (1913) pp. 408-9.

[4] *De sermone scriptorum latinorum . . . observationes* (Lwow 1895) [= *Eos* II] pp. 5-6. His exx. are Sen. *de ira* I, 12, 6; I, 16, 3; II, 23, 4; II, 32, 3; *de clem.* I, 22, 1; *de ben.* IV, 40, 4; Pliny, *Paneg.* 70; 'Quint.,' *decl. maior.* II, 14, VII, 4, XI, 2; *decl. min.* 335 init.

[5] As Norden has truly remarked, *A.K.*, pp. 234-7.

An interesting contrast may be seen between Livy's account of the death of Cicero, as preserved by the elder Seneca,[1] and the account of Cremutius Cordus, which follows it[2]. Livy—'candidissimus omnium magnorum ingeniorum aestimator,' as Seneca styles him—pays an eloquent, but restrained, tribute to the dead orator. Cremutius Cordus writes : ' Proprias enim simultates deponendas interdum putabat, publicas numquam vi decernendas ; civis non solum magnitudine virtutum sed multitudine quoque conspiciendus'—where antithesis and *homoeoteleuton* though regarded as 'tolerable' by Seneca, betray the rhetorician, and are strongly reminiscent of the style of Velleius. So Quintilian (x, 1, 104) finds in the style of Cremutius Cordus ' audaces sententias,' a good example of which is his description of Cicero in *Suas.* VI, 19 as ' pretium interfectoris sui.' His contemporary Bruttedius Niger, says the elder Seneca[3], endeavoured to describe the dreadful spectacle of Cicero's head upon the *rostra*, but found the task beyond his powers—how typical of the declamatory historian that he should have been tempted to try ! Livy, quoting Cicero's last words to his assassin, makes him say simply 'Moriar in patria saepe servata,' and if Cicero did say anything, those may well have been his words. Aufidius Bassus makes the orator utter a stupid frigid *sententia*—' Quid si ad me primum venissetis ?' the point of which is obscure, but which apparently means 'You fear to slay me—you, an accomplished assassin—what if I had been your first victim?' We learn, too, that Aufidius Bassus represented Cicero as not merely offering himself up to be killed, but actually thrusting himself forward with eagerness—a typical example of declamatory exaggeration[4].

The influence of declamation on the style of historical writing, is perhaps best illustrated by examples from Velleius Paterculus[5], whose epitome of Greek and Roman History appeared about 28 A.D. Norden has observed that Velleius is 'the first to write history from a rhetorical standpoint,' and has noted some good indications of declamatory influence.

In style, though not in stupidity, Velleius Paterculus is a good successor to rhetorical historians of the Augustan Age, like Cremutius Cordus and Aufidius Bassus. Antithesis and chiasmus abound in his *History* ; characteristic sentences are II, 5, 3 ' quem moriturum

---

[1] *Suas.* VI, 17 and 22.
[2] *ib.* 19 and 23.
[3] *ib.* 20.
[4] *ib.* 18; cf. *Contr.* VII, 2, 14, quoted above, p. 50, n. 1.
[5] The text of Robinson Ellis (O.C.T., 1898), is followed throughout.

miserat militem victorem recepit'; II, 23, 5 'cum ab inimicis tenerentur, oppugnabantur ab amicis, et animos extra moenia, corpora necessitati servientes intra muros habebant'; II, 26, 2 'in qua civitate semper virtutibus certatum erat, certabatur sceleribus, optimusque sibi videbatur, qui fuerat pessimus'; II, 37, 4 'non esse turpe ab eo vinci quem vincere esset nefas, neque inhoneste aliquem summitti huic quem fortuna super omnis extulisset'; II, 53, 3 'ut cui modo ad victoriam terra defuerat, deesset ad sepulturam'; II, 60, 2 'sprevit itaque caelestis animus humana consilia et cum periculo potius summa quam tuto humilia proposuit sequi.' Parallelism of clauses is particularly common, e.g., II, 45, 3 'cuius domus quam infeste a Clodio disiecta erat, tam speciose a senatu restituta est,' and most interesting are examples of *tricolon*, which the declaimers so much favour : II, 1, 1 'in somnum a vigiliis, ab armis in voluptates, a negotiis in otium conversa civitas,' II, 2, 2 'vita innocentissimus, ingenio florentissimus, proposito sanctissimus' (with *homœoteleuton*); II, 10, 1 'adeo natura a rectis in vitia, a vitiis in prava, a pravis in praecipitia pervenitur' (*sententia*, plus alliteration). *Homœoteleuton* is often noticeable; cf. I, 15, 1 'cum esset in bello conquirendus potius miles quam dimittendus et post bellum vires refovendae magis quam spargendae.' Other characteristics already noticed in the declaimers are: play on words (II, 27, 5, 'si eundem et vincendi et vivendi finem habuisset'), apostrophe (II, 32, 1 'succlamavit universa contio *te*, Q. Catule'; II, 66, 3 'nihil tamen egisti, M. Antoni,' for despite the author's allegation of genuine feeling, this is probably rhetorical *indignatio*)[1], and rhetorical questions (e.g., II, 53, 2 and II, 75, 2 where the ideas are commonplace).

The *sententiae* of Velleius are generally quite successful; cf. II, 40, 4 'numquam eminentia invidia carent'; II, 57, 3 'sed profecto ineluctabilis fatorum vis, cuiuscumque fortunam mutare constituit, consilia corrumpit' (cf. the *locus communis de fortuna*); II, 67, 2 'adeo difficilis est hominibus utcumque conceptae spei mora'; II, 69, 6 'neque reperias quos aut pronior fortuna comitata sit, aut veluti fatigata maturius destituerit quam Brutum et Cassium.' The best example of an unsuccessful *sententia* has already been quoted by Norden;[2] it is II, 4, 6, where speaking of Cicero, Velleius says 'eiusque corpus velato *capite* elatum est, cuius opera super totum terrarum orbem Roma extulerat *caput*,' where the forced antithesis may be compared with Haterius' *sententia*

---

[1] The chapter is very rhetorical and is well compared with *Suasoria* VI of the elder Seneca. It is noteworthy that Ellis *ad. loc.* compares the expression 'vox publica' used by Cornelius Severus in *Suas.* VI, 26 with Velleius' words 'abscisaque scelere Antoni vox publica est.'

[2] *op. cit.*, I, p. 302.

on the same subject in *Contr.* VII, 2, 5 'qui modo Italiae umeris *relatus est*, nunc sic a Popillio *refertur*?'

Finally, the influence of rhetoric is seen in the brevity and point which marks the style throughout, and in the avoidance of the period. When, occasionally, Velleius attempts a period, his inexperienced hand leads him into long, unwieldy efforts which a stylist like Livy would hardly have countenanced, cf. II, 18,4-6; II, 41, 1-2. Norden also sees rhetorical influence in the many character-sketches which occur in Velleius, and Morawski has shown how such appreciations, introduced after mention of the death of a great man, and estimating the evils which he escaped by his death, reflect rhetorical practice. Both the style and the spirit of the declaimers had, by the time of Tiberius, begun to affect the writing of history, and the influence seen in Velleius may be further traced in the work of Valerius Maximus. Quintus Curtius, Tacitus, and Florus also offer evidence of another important feature, which Velleius' *Epitome* lacks—the declamatory speech.[1]

If we now turn from the time of Tiberius to that of Nero, we find ample opportunity for observing the influence of declamation in the works of the younger Seneca. It would, indeed, be surprising if such influence were *not* noticeable, for Seneca spent many days of his life with his father or his brothers listening to the declaimers[2] whose names appear in the *Controversiae* and *Suasoriae*. His prose style owes much to the declamations in its pointedness, condensation, and love of antithesis, parallelism, and word-play.[3] But even more instructive and interesting evidence of this influence is seen in his Tragedies, where it is noticeable not so much in direct reminiscences of the declaimers (though these occasionally occur) as in the cast of the speeches, the development of *loci communes*, especially in the Choruses, the superabundance of *sententiae*, the nature of the descriptions, and even the characterisation and subject-matter of the Tragedies themselves; not to

---

[1] See Norden, pp. 304-5, and 336 ff., and Morawski, in *Eos*, II, (1895) pp. 1-12. The latter (p. 8) quotes excellent examples of *tetracola* from Val. Max. III, 4, 2 ; III, 7, 1 ; v, 4, Ext. 3, and a good *epiphonema* on fortune from II, 7, 10 (= *Contr.* IX, 4, 5). Q. Curtius IX, 4, 18 echoes *Suas.* I, on Alexander and the Ocean (cf. also Edward's edn. *ad. loc.*). On Florus and declamation, see the Preface to Graevius' edn. (Amsterdam, 1702). Further works by Morawski are 'Zu lateinischen Schriftstellern' in *Wien. Stud.* IV (1882), pp. 166 ff., and 'Zur Rhetorik bei den römischen Schriftstellern' in *Philologus* LIV (1897), pp. 143-8, and *Zeitschrift für öst. Gymn.* XLIV (1893) p. 97.

[2] cf. *Contr.* I, *Praef.* 4 'quos ipsi audistis,' X, *Praef.* 2 'cum illum mecum audieritis,'; *ib.* 9 'quem interdum solebatis audire.'

[3] See the excellent introduction by W. C. Sumners to his *Select Letters of Seneca*, pp. 78, 82, 85, 89. The influence of the elder Seneca is directly traced by E. Rolland, *De l'influence de Sénèque le Père et des rhéteurs sur Sénèque le Philosophe* (Ghent, 1906), and (less convincingly on the whole) by C. Preisendanz, in *Philologus*, LXVII (1908) pp. 68-112.

speak of such smaller details as the abundance of antitheses and rhetorical figures, and numerous other *minutiae* of style[1].

Perhaps the most striking direct reminiscence of the Senecan declamations is *Agam.* 35-6 :

Avo parentem, pro nefas, patri virum,
natis nepotes miscui—*nocti diem,*

for this is a clear example of *tetracolon*, and recalls *Contr.* IX, 2, 27 ' serviebat forum cubiculo, praetor meretrici, carcer convivio, *dies nocti*[2].' The elder Seneca had criticised the last phrase; perhaps his son introduced it ' with his tongue in his cheek.' Similarly, the description of Hector by Arbronius Silo as ' belli mora ' (*Suas.* II, 19) a phrase previously used by Latro, finds a close parallel in Sen., *Agam.*, 211 ' non sola Danais Hector et bello mora[3] ' and Bornecque[4] has observed the similarity of *Agam.* 293 'si parum est, adde 'et nepos ' to *Contr.* I, 4, 12 ' adice et patrem.'

Reminiscences based on *sententiae* are not always certain, as the sentiments expressed are sometimes of so general a character that they are hardly safe evidence of direct borrowing. But the following examples, which show fairly close parallelism of phraseology, may be reminiscences[5]. *Agam.* 694 ' miseris colendos maxime superos putem,' cf. *Contr.* VIII, 1, 2 'magis deos miseri quam beati colunt[6].' *Agam.* 202 'mors misera non est commori cum quo velis,' cf. *Contr.* IX, 6, 2 ' morientibus gratissimum est commori[7].' *Oed.* 517 ' ubi turpis est medicina, sanari piget,' cf. *Contr.* VI, 7, 2 'mori potius debuit frater quam sanari turpiter[8].' *Medea,* 433 ' remedia quotiens invenit nobis deus periculis peiora ; cf. *Contr.* VI, 7, 2 ' quaedam remedia graviora ipsis periculis sunt[9].'

---

[1] The studies of F. Kunz, *Sentenzen in Senecas Tragödien,* (*Prog.,* Wiener-Neustadt, 1877) and R. M. Smith, *De arte rhetorica in L.A. Senecae tragoediis perspicua* (Diss. Leipzig, 1885) are superseded by the exhaustive work of H. V. Canter, *Rhetorical Elements in the Tragedies of Seneca* (Illinois Studies in Language, no. x, Illinois, 1925). A short sketch is also given by L. Hermann, *Théatre de Sénèque* (Paris, 1924) pp. 534 ff.; note also Morawski, *Parallelismoi,* pp. 21-3, H. E. Butler, *Post-Augustan Poetry from Seneca to Juvenal* (Oxford 1909), pp. 49-69, and J. F. D'Alton, *op. cit.,* pp. 459-61. The text of the *Tragedies* used is that of Peiper and Richter (Leipzig, Teubner, 1902).
[2] cf. above p. 68. I find myself anticipated here by Rolland, p. 63 ; cf. Hermann p. 525.
[3] cf. *Tro.* 124, *Phoen.* 458, Lucan I, 100 (cf. R. J. Getty's edition [Cambridge, 1940] *ad loc.*)—noted also by Morawski, *op. cit.* p. 5, and Rolland, p. 65.
[4] *Déclam.,* p. 123. The reference is wrongly given there as *Agam.* 273.
[5] See Canter, *op. cit.* p. 13, n. 26. Not all of his instances, however, appear to me convincing.
[6] *Déclam., loc. cit.*
[7] Leo (*Observationes criticae in Sen. Trag.,* Berlin 1878, p. 153) observed the parallel but doubted direct influence. Preisendanz, *Philologus,* 67 (1908) pp. 85-6 supports it; also Canter, p. 13, n. 25.
[8] Preisendanz, pp. 106-7.
[9] Leo, *loc. cit.* ; Preisendanz, p. 106.

But the influence of declamation is seen to greater advantage by a study of the general cast of Seneca's work than by attempts to provide parallels, which, though occasionally enlightening, are often insufficiently close to carry conviction. It has often been remarked that the subjects of Seneca's *Tragedies* are declamatory in character. They can hardly be said to be directly derived from the themes of the schools, for, although parricide and incest, tyranny and unnatural passion were common in rhetorical themes, the *Oedipus*, *Phaedra*, and *Thyestes* legends existed long before the days of declamation. But it is probably true to say that from the range of Greek and early Roman Tragedy open to him, Seneca selects the most sensational themes, and those which offer most scope for declamatory treatment. The subject of *Thyestes*—Seneca's most gruesome play—was popular with the declaimers whom the elder Seneca heard (*Contr.* I, 1, 21)[1]. We have the murder of children by a parent in *Hercules Furens* and *Medea*, the murder of a wife in *Hercules Furens*, the murder of children in *Thyestes* and *Troades* and of a husband in *Agamemnon*: all are subjects encouraging depiction of the more savage and unnatural emotions[2]; but we find no Alcestis, and Seneca's Antigone is a mouthpiece for rhetorical argument, not to be compared with the creation of Sophocles.

In characterisation, Seneca, like the declaimers, tends to depict types rather than individual characters[3]. Lycus in the *Hercules Furens* is a stock tyrant, Hercules himself the stock 'vir fortis'; Phaedra is the stock *noverca*; Medea is certainly *ferox invictaque*, and, if we may adapt Horace[4], Megara is *flebilis* and Ulysses *perfidus*, but they lack subtlety and individuality. Andromache in the *Troades* is perhaps the best exception, for in her love and fears for her child, her loyalty to Hector, and her resignation to tragic misfortune, her character shines through the rhetoric of her phraseology, and she stands out in the memory as Seneca's finest heroine.

The Chorus, from the days of Euripides and Agathon, had long ceased to take the active and appropriate part in the play

---

[1] Hermann, p. 526, rightly points out that the declaimers may therefore themselves have been influenced by earlier Roman tragedy, but has no doubt of their direct influence on Seneca.

[2] cf. *Contr.* I, 1, 21 'ut gravissimarum iniuriarum inexorabilia et ardentia induceremus odia Thyesteo more'; Canter pp. 22-3 ('His subjects are in fact the most sensational, and hence best adapted to rhetorical treatment, that he could find'), D'Alton, p. 460.

[3] cf. Canter, p. 14 and his quotation from Dimsdale, *Hist. of Lat. Lit.* (1915) p.402.

[4] *A.P.* 123-4.

which Aristotle[1] and Horace[2] considered desirable ; but rarely can Choruses have strayed so far from the path in quest of the flowers of rhetoric as some of those of Seneca. The first Chorus of the *Hercules Furens* is rightly praised for the beauty of its description of early morning, and the scene of Arcadian simplicity charmingly culminates with the fisherman perched on his wave-worn rocks. But its subsequent praises of the simple life, contrasted with the distractions and cares of the city, are, despite their pleasing reminiscences of Horace, merely an embroidered version of a *locus communis*[3] and a θέσις ' rusticane vita an urbana potior ?' (Quint., II, 4, 24). So in *Thyestes* (546-622) the Chorus begins by contrasting the lull in the struggle between Atreus and Thyestes with their previous violent strife and proceeds to a pleasing comparison with the sea after a storm, and a picture that recalls the Bay of Naples on a summer's day. Having wandered so far, it proceeds for the last 25 lines to moralise on the mutability of Fortune—the *locus communis de fortuna*, of which the declaimers were so fond (*Suas.* I, 9, etc., cf. *Agam.* 57-107). In the *Medea* (301 ff.), a lyric which has closer relationship with the subject of the tragedy, the Chorus elaborates a well-worn theme on the dangers of navigation[4], a theme which was the subject of a θέσις, and appears in the first *Suasoria* of Seneca ; in fact, the description of the bold navigator entrusting his life to a single plank ('potuit tenui fidere ligno inter vitae mortisque vias nimium gracili limite ducto') is quite reminiscent of Sen., *Contr.* VII, 1, 10 'parva materia seiungit fata.[5]'

It has often been remarked that Seneca revels in descriptive passages, and though these are not necessarily always rhetorical, their length, and the frequency of enumeration and repetitions sometimes betray rhetorical influence. Their subjects sometimes provide interesting parallels with the declamations. So in the *Agamemnon*, 421-578, we have an extended description of a storm— far more detailed than that of Aeschylus, *Agamemnon*, or Virgil, *Aeneid I*, and therefore probably influenced by the *descriptiones* of the declaimers on that subject.[6] The long passage in the *Hercules Furens* (662 ff.) in which Theseus describes the journey to the underworld is in many ways admirable, but the colours are not those of a Virgil—they are laid on with the rhetorician's brush. In the *Thyestes*, 909 ff., Atreus has a *descriptio* of the drunken orgy of his

---

[1] *Poetics*, c. 18, *sub fin.*
[2] *A.P.* 193 ff.
[3] ' de varietate morum '; cf. above, p. 139.
[4] cf. Morawski, *op. cit.*, p. 11.
[5] cf. Bornecque's note *ad loc.*
[6] cf. above, p. 59.

brother Thyestes, which reminds the reader of the similar descriptions in the declamations.[1] Finally, the descriptions of horror and swoons which Latro so enjoyed find frequent echoes in Seneca, and some of his passages are quite anatomical in their analysis of the emotions of terror.[2] These are but a few of many instances of the influence of the rhetorical *descriptio* on the Tragedies[3].

Particularly declamatory are some of the speeches. In the *Phoenissae*, for example (535 ff.), Jocasta's address to Polynices, dissuading him from continuing the war against his brother, is a perfect example of a *suasoria* in verse. She uses the *figura iurisiurandi*: 'Per decem mensum graves uteri labores perque pietatem inclitae precor sororis et per irati sibi genas parentis,' begs her son to withdraw, outlines the destruction already caused, repeats her prayers in the name of Oedipus, runs into a series of rhetorical questions, introduces a neat epigram or two ('ut fiat tua, vis esse nullam?' and 'nemo sic vastat sua') and ends with ten rhetorical questions in succession in the last 20 lines (565-85). Speeches in self-defence also exhibit rhetorical characteristics. So Lycus, in *H.F.*, 401 ff., defending his act in usurping the throne of Thebes, raises a series of imaginary objections, to which he provides his own epigrammatic replies ('cruento cecidit in bello pater? cecidere fratres? ... bella delectat cruor. sed ille regno pro suo, nos improba cupidine acti? quaeritur belli exitus, non causa'). Medea similarly defends herself in *Med.* 236-51 in rhetorical strain. Most characteristic of declamation, too, are the many soliloquies and self-exhortations in Seneca's plays.[4] Oedipus in *Phoen.*, 140 ff., after an unintentionally appropriate comment 'Quid perdis ultra verba?,' indulges for the next forty lines in a singularly ineffective, wordy, rhetorical self-exhortation to suicide—a windy piece of second-rate bluster of which a bad declaimer might have been proud. In *Tro.* 642 ff., Andromache has a *prosopopoeia* in which she debates with herself whether to surrender Astyanax and save Hector's tomb from being razed to the ground or permit both the child and the tomb to be destroyed. It is an agonising moment; but Andromache's carefully-balanced arguments, indicating her conflicting allegiances, are not redeemed from a certain intellectual coldness even by the many vigorous rhetorical questions which she projects at herself. ('Quid agimus? animum distrahit geminus timor: hinc natus, illinc coniugis sacri cinis, pars utra vincet'?) Finally numerous passages are in themselves 'forensic contests.' In *H.F.*, 448 ff., Amphitruo and Lycus argue, in smart *stichomythia*, the

---

[1] cf. above, pp. 59-60.
[2] cf. esp. *H.O.*, 706-9.
[3] cf. Canter, pp. 37 ff., 70 ff.
[4] cf. Canter, pp. 66 ff.

question : ' Is Hercules to be considered of divine origin or not ? ' In *Tro.* 203-352, we have 150 lines of argument between Pyrrhus and Agamemnon as to whether Polyxena should be slain or not (esp. 326-341).[1] Some speeches are more rhetorical than others; in the *Troades*, 888-902, Andromache's rejection of Helen's suggestion of marriage with Pyrrhus seems particularly coloured by rhetoric—a situation in which Helen, of all people, at such a time, counselled marriage with a Greek, offered great rhetorical, rather than truly dramatic, possibilities. And it was not really necessary in *Agamemnon* 545-552 for Ajax, having just escaped drowning, to fulminate from his rock.

Rhetorical exaggeration is another of Seneca's characteristics which probably owes much to the schools.[2] In *Tro.* 49-50 (cf. *Agam.*, 656-8) the sword of Pyrrhus, plunged into Priam's throat, comes out bloodless ! In 481-2, Andromache states that there is not enough left of Troy even to hide a child, and in 1160-61 the messenger declares that the Greeks bewailed the death of Polyxena even more loudly than the Trojans ! A stormy sea invariably hits the stars or clouds (*Phaed.* 1008, *Agam.* 471, *Med.* 345). The love of gruesome detail, in which Seneca is only equalled by his nephew Lucan, may perhaps be partly a Spanish characteristic, but probably owes something to the declaimers. The earth greedily drinks up Polyxena's blood (*Tro.* 1162-4) ; the effect of the crash of Astyanax from the tall tower is described with anatomical exactitude, (*ib.* 1110 ff.), the scattered remnants of Hippolytus' body are carefully put together (*Phaed.* 1256 ff.), and the messenger's description of Atreus cooking his young nephew's limbs (*Thy.* 760 ff.) is worthy of the *Mikado.*

In the style of the *Tragedies*, as in Seneca's prose style, many declamatory features are noticeable. There is a superabundance of *sententiae*, and whole passages of *stichomythia* occur in which each line is a *sententia* in itself.[4] The *sententiae* themselves are often not especially rhetorical, but merely represent common thoughts in a neat and pointed form. They are the Greek γνῶμαι, pithy reflections on various aspects of human life and conduct. In form they are often reminiscent of those of Publilius Syrus, who was, as we have seen,[5] also popular with the declaimers. A few of the scores of such examples are :—

' serum est cavendi tempus in mediis malis ' (*Thy.* 487)
' saepe in magistrum scelera redierunt sua ' (*Thy.* 311)
' fortuna belli semper ancipiti in loco est ' (*Phoen.* 629)

---

[1] cf. *Suas.* III (Iphigeneia).
[2] cf. Canter, pp. 138-9.
[3] cf. Canter, pp. 88 ff.
[4] cf. Canter, pp. 88 ff. ; J.W. Duff, *op. cit.* p. 264.
[5] cf. above, pp. 55 and 138.

'tacere multis discitur vitae malis' (*Thy.* 319)
'iuvenile vitium est regere non posse impetum' (*Tro.* 250).
But other *sententiae* are markedly rhetorical in form, deriving their effect from anaphora, antithesis, or paradox, such as 'optanda mors est sine metu mortis mori' (*Tro.* 869); 'quod non potest vult posse qui nimium potest' (*Phaed.* 215); 'fortuna fortes metuit, ignavos premit' (*Med.* 159); 'qui nil potest sperare, desperet nihil' (*ib.* 163). Condensation of thought is frequently noticeable and the search for point is unending; though sometimes neat, the results are also sometimes stupid or colourless. A typical example of unnecessary point is *Tro.* 55-6 'caret sepulchro Priamus et flamma indiget, ardente Troia'; of stupid point, *Thy.* 1050-1 may serve as an example; Thyestes, after realising that he has eaten his children, observes 'natos premo premorque natis,' a remark only surpassed by his 'parcamus umbris' a few lines before. In *H. F.* 1259-61, we have a typically condensed idea used as a climax 'cuncta iam amisi bona; mentem, arma, famam, coniugem, natos, manus, *etiam furorem*,' where the implication is that he was happier when mad.[1]

Only a few of the many rhetorical figures in Seneca's plays can be mentioned here. *Apostrophe* is particularly interesting, for so frequently do heroes and heroines appeal to their soul (*Tro.* 613, 662, *Med.* 41, 895, 937, *Oed.* 1024, *Ag.* 868, *Thy.* 283-4, 324, 423, *Phaed.* 592, etc.), or to their grief (*Tro.* 595, *Med.* 139), or wrath (*H. F.* 75), or virtue (*H. F.* 1315), that they are strongly reminiscent of the 'Dura, anime, dura' of *Contr.* II, 3, 6, and elsewhere[2], though perhaps even a declaimer would have hesitated before saying 'quid terga vertis, anime?' (*Ag.* 228). *Parallelism of clause*[3] is common, as in *H. F.* 463-4 ('Quemcumque miserum videris, hominem scias' capped by 'Quemcumque fortem videris, miserum neges'), *Tro.* 510-512 ('fata si miseros iuvant, habes salutem; fata si vitam negant, habes sepulchrum'), cf. *Med.* 140-1, *Thy.* 613 ff., etc. *Antithesis*, itself extremely common, often makes the parallel more pointed, e.g., 'si moreris, antecedo; si vivis, sequor' (*Phoen.* 76); 'si vivo, feci scelera; si morior, tuli' (*H. F.* 1278). Rhetorical questions (of which Canter[4] counts upwards of 400), exclamations, asyndeton, anaphora, climax, all appear; paronomasia, a frequent trait of Seneca's prose writings, may also be noticed in his plays (*H. F.* 581; 1184-5; *Tro.* 301-2, 1148, *Phoen.* 89-90, etc.), as may the σχῆμα ἐκ τοῦ ἀδυνάτου, of which *Contr.* I, 5, 2, is an example[5] (cf. *H. F.* 373 ff., *Thy.* 476-82), and the *figura iurisiurandi* (*Ag.* 929).

[1] cf. J. W. Duff, *op. cit.* p. 260.
[2] cf. above, p. 69.
[3] cf. Duff, p. 263.
[4] *op. cit.* p. 140.
[5] Canter has a good note on this figure, p. 60, n. 6.

A characteristic which owes much to the rhetorical schools is that in which a verb is repeated in a different form, particularly, in a change from active to passive, or vice versa,[1] as *H. F.* 726-7 ' cuius aspectus *timet* quidquid *timetur* ' ; *Tro.* 1099-1100 ' non flet e turba omnium qui *fletur* ' ; *Thy.* 416 ' cum quod *datur* spectabis et *dantem* aspice '; *Med.* 218-9 ' *petebant* tunc meos thalamos proci, qui nunc *petuntur*.' Bold expressions such as ' ubi hanc anilis *expuam leti moram* ?' (*Tro.* 1169), ' clusum nefas ' of the children of Thyestes (*Thy.* 1041), ' inhospitalem Caucasum mente indue ' (*Med.* 43), no doubt would hardly have been risked had not declamation paved the way. In these and other detailed characteristics of style Seneca cannot escape the influence of the declaimers whom he heard so often in his youth, and it may even be claimed that there is scarcely an aspect of declamatory rhetoric which could not be illustrated from his plays.

These are but a few indications, taken from selected works of selected authors whose lifetimes coincided with those of some of the declaimers mentioned by the elder Seneca ; but they are perhaps sufficient to show the kind of effect which those declaimers had on the literature of the early Empire. On the credit side, they gave the style point, neatness, and condensation, and also a means of expansion of ideas and literary embroidery : on the debit side, they were undoubtedly responsible for much rant and bombast, false effect, and artificial expression. Few now can spare time for the effusions of Latro, Cestius, Arellius Fuscus, Gallio and their lesser contemporaries, but we must nevertheless not underestimate their influence on the language and literature of imperial Rome.[2]

---

[1] cf. above, p. 70.
[2] As does, in my opinion, E. P. Parks, *op. cit.* pp. 108-111. It is true that technical writers such as Vitruvius, Mela, and others do not show declamatory characteristics to the same degree, but the influence may also be traced, apart from the works considered above, in prose in Valerius Maximus, the younger Seneca's prose works, Tacitus, Pliny's *Panegyricus*, and Florus, and in verse in Lucan, Juvenal, and Statius, to name only a few.

BIBLIOGRAPHY

A good bibliography up to 1901 is given by H. Bornecque in his *Les Déclamations et les Déclamateurs d'apres Sénèque le Père* (Lille, 1902). Its chief important omissions are listed below. The works mentioned in the 'General Literature' section, prior to and subsequent to that year, exclude those of a purely (or mainly) textual nature. The list is centred on the Senecan declamations and does not include studies on the authenticity of those ascribed to Quintilian. See also Bursian, *Jahresbericht für Alterthumswissenschaft* 183, pp. 204 ff. (literature from 1894-1914, report by Lehnert), and 248, pp. 106 ff. (also by Lehnert); Marouzeau, *Dix Années de Bibliographie Classique* and *L'Année Philologique*; Teuffel, *Gesch. d. röm. Lit.* (6th ed. by Kroll-Skutsch) vol. II, §§267 ff.; Schanz-Hosius, *Geschichte der römischen Literatur*, vol. II (Munich, 1935) pp. 343 ff.; and W. A. Edward's edition of the *Suasoriae* (as listed below) pp. XLV-XLVI.

I. EDITIONS

(a) THE ELDER SENECA

A. Kiessling, *Annaei Senecae Oratorum et Rhetorum Sententiae, Divisiones, Colores* (Leipzig, Teubner, 1872).

H. Bornecque, *Sénèque le Rhéteur, Controverses et Suasoires, nouvelle édition revue et corrigée avec Introduction et Notes* (Paris, 1932). Despite numerous misprints, this edition is a most valuable contribution by a master of the subject.

W. A. Edward, *The Suasoriae of Seneca the Elder* (Cambridge, 1928). (A useful edition, especially as it is the only work of its kind in English).

(b) OTHER RHETORICAL TREATISES

F. Marx, *Incerti Auctoris de Ratione Dicendi ad C. Herennium Libri IV* (Leipzig, 1894).

E. Stroebel, *M.T. Ciceronis ... rhetorici libri ... de inventione* (Leipzig, Teubner, 1925).

K. W. Piderit, *Cicero, De Oratore*, 6th edn. by O. Harnecker (Leipzig, 1886).

A. S. Wilkins, *M. T. Ciceronis De Oratore Libri tres*. 3 vols. (Oxford, 1882-92).

O. Jahn, *M.T. Ciceronis Brutus*, 5th edn. by W. Kroll (Berlin, 1908).

J. E. Sandys, *M. T. Ciceronis ad M. Brutum Orator* (Cambridge, 1885).

W. Kroll, *M. T. Ciceronis Orator* (Berlin, 1913).

A. S. Wilkins, *M. T. Ciceronis Rhetorica* (Oxford Classical Text, vol. II). (For the lesser rhetorical works of Cicero).

G. Lehnert, *Quintiliani quae feruntur Declamationes* XIX *Maiores* (Leipzig, Teubner, 1905).

C. Ritter, *M. Fabii Quintiliani Declamationes Quae Supersunt* CXLV (Leipzig, Teubner, 1884).

G. Lehnert, *Calpurni Flacci Declamationes* (Leipzig, Teubner, 1903).

H. E. Butler, *The Institutio Oratoria of Quintilian*, Text and Translation, 4 vols. (London, Loeb Classical Library, rpd. 1933-6).

F. H. Colson, *M. Fabii Quintiliani Institutionis Oratoriae Liber* I (Cambridge, 1924).

W. Peterson, *M. Fabi Quintiliani Institutionis Oratoriae Liber* X (Oxford, 1891).

R. G. Austin, *Quintiliani Institutionis Oratoriae Liber* XII (Oxford, 1948).

A. Gudeman, *P. Corneli Taciti Dialogus de Oratoribus* (Leipzig,² 1914).

W. Peterson, *Corneli Taciti Dialogus de Oratoribus* (Oxford, 1893).

R. P. Robinson, *C. Suetoni Tranquilli de Grammaticis et Rhetoribus* (Paris, 1925).

C. Halm, *Rhetores Latini Minores* (Leipzig, 1863).

H. Rabe, *Hermogenis Opera* (Leipzig, Teubner, 1913).

C. Walz, *Rhetores Graeci*, 9 vols. (Tübingen, 1832-6).

L. Spengel, *Rhetores Graeci*, 3 vols. (Leipzig, Teubner, 1853).

II. GENERAL LITERATURE

(a) WORKS PUBLISHED BEFORE 1902, BUT NOT INCLUDED IN BORNECQUE'S BIBLIOGRAPHY

E. Bonnell, *De mutata sub primis Caesaribus eloquentiae condicione, in primis de rhetorum scholis* (Berlin, 1836).

A. Wittich, *De rhetoribus latinis eorumque scholis* (Eisenach, 1853).

M. Sander, *Quaestiones in Senecam rhetorem syntacticae* (Diss., Greifswald, 1872).

G. H. Hulsebos, *De educatione et institutione apud Romanos* (Utrecht, 1875).

C. Morawski, ' Zu lateinischen Schriftstellern ' (*Wien. Stud.* IV, [1882] pp. 166-8).

A. Ahlheim, *De Senecae rhetoris usu dicendi quaestiones selectae* (Diss., Giessen, 1886).

C. Morawski, ' Zur Rhetorik bei den römischen Historikern ' (*Zeitschrift für die österreichische Gymnasien,* XLIV, [1893] pp. 97 ff.

F. Marx, *Prolegomena* to edn. of *Ad Herennium* (Leipzig, 1894).

O. Rossbach, Article ' Annaeus,' in *P.W.* (1894).

E. Wölfflin, ' Der Vorname des Rhetors Seneca ' (*Rh. M.*, L, [1895] p. 320).

T. S. Simonds, *The Themes treated by the elder Seneca* (Diss., Baltimore, 1896).

R. Hess, *Zur Deutung der Begriffe sententia, divisio, color bei Seneca* (Schneidemühl, 1900).

(b) WORKS PUBLISHED SINCE 1902

E. G. Sihler, ' θετικώτεον ' (*A.J.P.* XXIII, [1902] pp. 283-294).

C. Morawski, *Parallelismoi, sive de locutionum aliquot usu et fatis apud auctores graecos nec non latinos* (Cracow, 1902).

C. Morawski, *Ovidiana* (Cracow, 1903).

H. de la Ville de Mirmont, ' Le déclamateur Alfius Flavus ' *Révue de Philologie*, XXVIII (1904) p. 250).

G. Jaeneke, *De statuum doctrina ab Hermogene tradita* (Diss., Leipzig, 1904).

A. S. Wilkins, *Roman Education* (Cambridge University Press, 1905), pp. 79-88.

O. Leuze, ' Metellus caecatus ' (*Philologus* LXIV, [1905] pp. 95 ff.).

H. de la Ville de Mirmont, *La Jeunesse d'Ovide* (Paris, 1905) pp. 67 ff.

W. Pelta, ' Zu Aufidius Bassus ' (*Rh. M.* LXI [1906] pp. 620-4).

E. Rolland, *De l'influence de Sénèque le père et des rhéteurs sur Sénèque le philosophe* (Ghent, 1906).

G. Boissier, 'The Schools of Declamation at Rome' (originally published in *Révue des deux mondes*, XI, [1902] pp. 480-508 ; in *Tacitus and Other Roman Studies*, trans. W. G. Hutchison, (London, 1906), pp 163-194).

G. Boissier, Article 'Declamatio' in Daremberg et Saglio, *Dictionnaire des Antiquités grecques et latines*.

L. Lützen, *De priorum scriptorum argenteae latinatis studiis scholasticis* (Progr. Eschwege, 1907).

W. B. Anderson, 'Contributions to the Study of the Ninth Book of Livy' (*T.A. Ph. A.* XXXIX [1908], pp. 89-103).

C. Preisendanz, 'De Senecae rhetoris apud philosophum filium auctoritate' (*Philologus*, LXVII, 1908, pp. 68-112).

F. Eggerding, *De Heroidum Ovidianarum Epistulis Quae Vocantur Commentationes* (Diss., Halle, 1908).

M. Cerrati, *La grammatica di A. Seneca, il retore* (Turin, 1908).

L. Friedländer, *Roman Life and Manners* (Eng. trans., London, 1908-13, by Magnus and Frieze, of *Darstellungen aus der Sittengeschichte Roms*, 7th edn.)

J. de Decker, 'Les rhéteurs spirituels a Rome' (*Bulletin de la Societé pour le Progrès des études phil., et hist.* no. 1, [1909] pp. 55-79.

C. Brück, *De Ovidio Scholasticarum Declamationum Imitatore* (Diss., Giessen, 1909).

W. Hoffa, *De Seneca patre quaestiones selectae* (Diss., Göttingen, 1909).

H. E. Butler, *Post-Augustan Poetry from Seneca to Juvenal* (Oxford, 1909).

J. Aistermann, *De M. Valerio Probo Berytio capita quattuor* (Bonn, 1910).

H. de la Ville de Mirmont, 'Les déclamateurs espagnols aux temps d'Auguste et de Tibère' (*Bulletin Hispanique* XII (1910) pp. 1 ff.; XIV (1912) pp. 11 ff.; 229 ff.; 341 ff.; XV (1913) pp. 154 ff., 237 ff. 384 ff.).

W. C. Summers, *Select Letters of Seneca* (London 1910) (Introduction).

O. Seeck, *Untergang der antiken Welt* (Berlin, 1911), vol. IV, pp. 168-204.

A. Stock, *De prolaliarum usu rhetorico* (Diss., Königsberg, 1911).

J. de Decker, *Juvenalis Declamans* (Ghent, 1913).

W. C. Summers, ' Declamations under the Empire ' (*Proc. Class. Assoc.*, 1913, pp. 87-102).

W. Fleskes, *Vermischte Beiträge zum literarischen Porträt des Tyrannen im Anschluss an die Deklamationen* (Diss., Münster, 1914). (summarised by Lehnert in Bursian 248, pp. 107-8).

R. Kohl, *De scholasticarum declamationum argumentis ex historia petitis* (Paderborn, 1915) (=*Rhetorische Studien* IV).

M. Schamberger, *De declamationum Romanorum argumentis* (Diss., Halle, 1917).

J. Klek, *Symbuleutici qui dicitur sermonis historia critica* (Paderborn, 1919) (=*Rhetorische Studien* VIII).

S. Rossi, ' Vita e realtà nelle Controversie di Seneca il retore ' (*Rivista Indo-Graeco-Italica di Filologia* II (1918) pp. 203 ff., III (1919) pp. 13-28).

A. Krumbacher, *Die Stimmbildung der Redner in Alterthum bis auf die Zeit Quintilians* (Paderborn, 1920) (=*Rhetorische Studien* X).

W. C. Summers, *The Silver Age of Latin Literature* (London, 1920).

F. H. Colson, Declamare-κατηχεῖν (*C.R.* XXXVI [1922] pp. 116-7).

H. A. Ormerod, *Piracy in the Ancient World* (Liverpool, 1924).

H. V. Canter, *Rhetorical Elements in the Tragedies of Seneca* (Illinois Studies in Language, X, 1925).

N. Deratani, ' De poetarum vestigiis in declamationibus Romanorum conspicuis ' (*Philologus* LXXXV [1930] pp. 106-111).

A. Gwynn, *Roman Education from Cicero to Quintilian* (Oxford, 1926).

J. W. Duff, *Literary History of Rome in the Silver Age* (London, 1927) pp. 23-64.

N. Deratani, ' Le réalisme dans les Declamationes ' (*Revue de Philologie* LV [1929] pp. 184-9).

W. Morel, article ' suasoria ' in *P.-W.* (1931).

J. F. D'Alton, *Roman Literary Theory and Criticism* (London, 1931).

H. Throm, *Die Thesis—Ein Beitrag zu ihrer Entstehung und Geschichte* (Paderborn, 1932) (=*Rhetorische Studien* XVII).

H. Bornecque, ' Les sujets de *suasoria* chez les Romains ' (*Rev. d'hist. de la phil. et d'hist. gén. de la civilisation*, 15 janvier, 1934, pp. 1 ff.).

J. W. H. Atkins, *Literary Criticism in Antiquity* (2 vols, Cambridge, [1934], vol. II, pp. 143-155).

L. Bieler, ' Kritisch-exegetisches zur Suasória de Alexandro des Arellius Fuscus' (*Wien. Stud.* LIII [1935] pp. 84-94).

W. Hofrichter, *Studien zur Entwicklungsgesch. der Deklamation von der griech. Sophistik bis z. römischen Kaiserzeit* (Breslauer Diss., Ohlau, 1935). (summarised in *Phil. Woch.* 1936, 1223 ff.

J. Cousin, *Études sur Quintilien*, 2 vols. (Paris, 1936).

Nougaro, *L'éducation romaine au temps de Sénèque le père* (Mémoire de dipl. d'études supérieures, Fac. des Lettres de Paris, 1937).

A. M. Guillemin, *Le Public et la Vie littéraire a Rome* (Paris, 1937), pp. 55-63.

C. J. Fordyce, ' The Whole Truth in Roman Procedure ' (*C.R.* LII [1938] p. 59).

A. A. Day, *The Origins of Latin Love Elegy* (Oxford, 1938) pp. 59-75.

A. F. Sochatoff, ' The basic rhetorical theories of the elder Seneca ' (*C.J.* XXXIV [1939] pp. 345-354).

J. Carcopino, *Daily Life in Ancient Rome* (trans. E. O. Lorimer, London, 1941), pp. 114-121.

H. Bardon, *Le Vocabulaire de la Critique Littéraire chez Sénèque le Rhéteur* (Paris, 1940).

H. Bardon, ' Mécanisme et stéréotypie dans le style de Sénèque le Rhéteur ' (*L'Antiquité classique* XII [1943]).

E. Patrick Parks, *The Roman Rhetorical Schools as a Preparation for the Courts under the Early Empire* (Johns Hopkins University Studies in Historical and Political Science, Series lxiii, No. 2, Baltimore, 1945).

III SELECT LIST OF RELEVANT WORKS ON ROMAN LAW

The editions of standard works listed below are those consulted, and are not necessarily the latest revisions.

(a) TEXTS

C. G. Bruns, *Fontes Iuris Romani Antiqui* (6th edn. by T. Mommsen and O. Gradenwitz, Leipzig, 1893).

P. F. Girard, *Textes de Droit Romain* (Paris^3, 1903, and subsequent edns.).

E. Poste, *Gai Institutiones Iuris Civilis* (4th edn. by E. A. Whittuck, Oxford, 1894).

F. de Zulueta, *The Institutes of Gaius* (Part I, Oxford, 1946).

J. B. Moyle, *Imperatoris Iustiniani Institutionum Libri Quattuor* (Oxford⁵, 1912).

T. C. Sandars, *The Institutes of Justinian* (rpd. London, 1941).

P. Krüger and T. Mommsen, *Corpus Iuris Civilis* (6th stereotyped edn., Berlin 1893; containing Justinian's Institutes, Digest, Code, and Novels).

T. Mommsen, *Codex Theodosianus* (Berlin, 1905).

O. Lenel, *Das Edictum Perpetuum* (3rd edn. 1927; French trans., Paris, 1901).

(b) TEXTBOOKS

P. F. Girard, *Manuel élémentaire de Droit Romain* (Paris,⁴ 1910, and subsequent edns.).

W. W. Buckland, *Text-Book of Roman Law from Augustus to Justinian* (Cambridge², 1932).

W. W. Buckland, *Elementary Principles of the Roman Private Law* (Cambridge, 1912).

(c) HISTORIES

W. Rein, *Das Criminalrecht der Römer von Romulus bis auf Justinianus* (Leipzig, 1844).

A. W. Zumpt, *Das Criminalrecht der Römischen Republik* (2 vols. in 4, Berlin, 1865-9).

T. Mommsen, *Römisches Strafrecht* (Leipzig, 1899; French trans. in 3 vols. by J. Duquesne, Paris, 1907).

E. Westrup, *Introduction to Early Roman Law*, Comparative Sociological Studies, 3 vols. (London-Copenhagen, 1934-1944).

H. F. Jolowicz, *Historical Introduction to the Study of Roman Law* (Cambridge, 1932).

F. Schulz, *History of Roman Legal Science* (Oxford, 1946).

(d) RHETORIC AND LAW

J. Stroux, *Summum Ius Summa Iniuria* (Festschrift Paul Speiser-Sarasin, Leipzig, 1926).

S. Riccobono, in *Gnomon* v (1929), pp. 65-87 (review of Stroux).

H. F. Jolowicz ' Academic Elements in Roman Law ' (*L.Q.R.* XLVIII [1932] pp. 171-190).

J. Himmelschein, *Studien zu der antiken Hermeneutica Iuris* (Leipzig, 1935).

F. Blatt, 'Written and Unwritten Law in Ancient Rome' (*Classica et Mediaevalia*, v [1942] pp. 137-158).

E. Steinwenter, 'Rhetorik und römische Zivilprozess' (Z.S.S. LXV, 1947, pp. 69-120).

(e) DECLAMATORY LAWS

Ioannes Meursius, *Themis Attica* (ed. Graevius, Utrecht, 1685).

C. Lécrivain, 'Le droit grec et le droit romain dans les Controverses de Sénèque le Père et dans les Déclamations de Quintilien et de Calpurnius Flaccus' (*N.R.H.* XV (1891) pp. 680-691).

J. Sprenger, *Quaestiones in rhetorum Romanorum declamationes iuridicae* (Diss., Halle, 1911).

F. Lanfranchi, *Il Diritto nei Retori Romani* (Milan, 1938).

R. Düll, 'Iudicium domesticum, abdicatio und apokeryxis' (*Z.S.S.* LXIII, 1943, pp. 54-116).

(f) VARIOUS SPECIAL WORKS

P. M. Schisas, *Offences against the State in Roman Law* (London, 1926).

C. H. Brecht, *Zur Abgrenzung des Begriffes 'Perduellio'* etc. (Munich, 1938).

W. W. Buckland, *The Roman Law of Slavery* (Cambridge, 1908).

E. Levy, 'Captivus Redemptus' (*C.P.* XXXVIII, 1943, pp. 159-176).

W. W. Buckland, *Equity in Roman Law* (London, 1911).

J. L. Strachan Davidson, *Problems of the Roman Criminal Law* (2 vols. Oxford, 1912).

Max Radin, 'The Exposure of Infants in Roman Law and Practice' (*C.J.* XX, 1925, pp. 337-343).

E. Grueber, *The Roman Law of Damage to Property* (*Lex Aquilia*) (Oxford, 1886).

D. Daube, 'On the third chapter of the Lex Aquilia' (*L.Q.R.* LII, 1936, pp. 253-268).

D. Daube, 'Collatio II, 6, 5' (*Essays Presented to J. H. Hertz*, 1943, pp. 111-129).

D. Daube, *On the use of the term 'Damnum'* (Naples, 1948).

D. Daube, ' Ne quid infamandi causa fiat ' (*Atti del Congresso Internazionale di Diritto Romano e Storia del Diritto*, Verona, 1948).

P. E. Corbett, *The Roman Law of Marriage* (Oxford, 1930).

A. Esmein, ' Le Délit d' Adultère à Rome et la loi Iulia de Adulteriis ' (*Mélanges d'histoire du Droit*, Paris, 1886, pp. 71-169).

P. Gide, ' De la condition de l'enfant naturel et de la concubine dans la législation romaine ' (*N.R.H.* IV, 1880, pp. 377-99, 409-26).

J. Plassard, *Le Concubinat Romain sous le Haut Empire* (Paris-Toulouse, 1921).

A. H. J. Greenidge, *Infamia in Roman Law* (Oxford, 1894).

E. Albertario, ' Sul diritto agli alimenti ' (*Studi di diritto romano*, I, Milan, 1933, pp. 251 ff.).

O. Fredershausen, ' Studien über das Recht bei Plautus und Terenz ' (*Hermes*, XLVII, 1912 pp. 199 ff.).

Hugh Last, 'The Social Policy of Augustus' (*Cambridge Ancient History*, vol. X, ch. 14).

On the subject of Greek Law, the following may be consulted:—

J. J. Thonissen, *Le Droit Pénal de la République Athénienne* (Brussels-Paris, 1875).

M. H. E. Meier and G. F. Schömann, *Der Attische Process* (new edn. by J. H. Lipsius, Berlin 1883-7).

L. Beauchet, *Histoire du Droit Privé de la République Athénienne* (4 vols., Paris, 1897).

J. H. Lipsius, *Das attische Recht und Rechtsverfahren* (2 vols., Leipzig, 1905-12).

R. J. Bonner and G. Smith, *The Administration of Justice from Homer to Aristotle* (2 vols. Chicago, 1930 and 1938).

INDEX

A

ABDICATIO, 101-3, 107.
Academy, 3, 5.
Accius, 21.
Achilles, arms of, 79, 143, 151.
Actio, 85, 108, 111;
  circumscriptionis, 131 n. 1;
  damni iniuria dati, 116;
  dementiae, 73, 93-4, 107;
  de moribus, 124;
  de vi, 115;
  familiae erciscundae, 129-30;
  ingrati, 7, 79, 87-8, 107;
  inscripti maleficii, 86, 107;
  iniuriarum, 89, 115-6;
  maiestatis, 108-9;
  malae tractationis, 94-5, 107;
  proditionis, 109-10;
  reipublicae laesae, 97-8, 107;
  rei uxoriae, 88, 94, 124;
  sepulchri violati, 119;
  veneficii, 111-2;
  vi bonorum raptorum, 118.
Adnominatio, 154.
Adoption, 32, 58, 61.
Adultery, 25, 35, 36, 41, 119-122.
Advocacy, 44, 45, 48, 52, 80-83, 88, 95, 131.
Aelian, 101 n. 5.
Aequitas, 46-7, 57, 124.
Aeschines, 12 and n. 2, 68, 95 n. 3, 96 n.2, 103 n. 1, 104 n. 2, 105 n. 4.
Aeschylus, 163.
Agamemnon, 24, 76, 140;
  of Aesch., 163;
  of Seneca, 161, 162, 163, 165, 166.
Agamemnon (rhetor), 76, 80.
Agathon, 162.
Agrippa, 40.
Ajax, 15, 23, 25, 27, 151, 165.
Albinovanus Pedo, 60, 145.
Albucius, 8, 40, 42, 43, 51, 61, 63, 65, 66, 72, 146, 147 n. 1, 153.
Alexander the Great, 9, 34, 55, 79, 142, 151, 157.
Alexander of Pherae, 28.
Alfius Flavus, 40 n. 2, 134, 144.
Aliments, 95, 125-7.
Alliteration, 66, 159.
Ammianus Marcellinus, 90 n. 7, 112.
Amphitruo, 164.
Anaphora, 68, 154, 156, 166.
Anaximenes, 11 (see s.v. *Rhet. ad Alex*.)
Andocides, 105 n. 1.
Andromache, 162, 164, 165.
Anthypophora, 65.
Antigone, 162.
Antiphon, 12 n. 4.
Antisthenes, 15 n. 2, 151 n. 2.
Antithesis, 67, 75 n. 3, 152, 154, 158-9, 160, 166.
Antonius (orator), 16 n. 4, 21, 30, 109.
Antonius (triumvir), 18, 31 n. 2.
Aper, 42.
Aphthonius, 3 n. 2, 4, 10 n. 3, 11 n. 1, 150, n. 7.
Apollodorus, 51.
Aposiopesis, 154.
Apostrophe, 69, 159, 166
Appellatio, 19.
Appian, 104, 111 n. 4.
Apsines, 12, 103.
Aquae et ignis interdictio, 90, 106, 110-1
Arbitration, 129-130.
Arbronius Silo, 141, 161.
Arellius Fuscus, 58, 60, 64, 66, 135, 140, 142, 143, 145, 150, 153, 167.
Argentarius 65.

Aristotle, 2, 5, 6-7, 11, 12, 15 n. 5 47, 54 n. 1, 95 n. 1, 96 n. 2, 163.
Arrunteius, 157.
Arson, 117-9.
Asconius, 14 n. 2.
Asianism, 21, 63, 66, 76, 137, 147
Asprenas, 35, 65, 151.
Astyanax, 164, 165.
Atellane farces, 69.
Atreus, 163, 165.
Atticism 63, 136-7, 147.
Auctor ad Herennium, 2, 13, 15, 19, 20, 22, 23 24, 25 and n. 2, 26, 27, 28, 30, 33 n. 2, 35 n. 4, 39, 66, 68 n. 2, 70, 108, 109 n. 4, 115, 154.
Augustine, 4, 13, 129.
Augustus, 10 n. 1, 18, 35, 40, 42, 43 n. 5, 44, 111, 123-4, 133, 139, 142.
Aulus Gellius, 6 n. 5, 16 n. 3, 18 n. 3, 51 n. 9, 78, 88, 92 n. 1 104 and n. 2, 3; 122 n. 5.

B

BADEN, history of 130.
Blandus, 60, 62.
Blindness, 76, 79, 96, 107.
Bombast, 64, 70, 74 76, 77, 141, 147, 167.
Broccus, 32 n. 2.
Bruttedius Niger, 40, 145, 158
Brutus, 14.
Burial, 100-101, 107, 119.

C

CACOZELIA, 65, 69, 72 n. 3, 147
Caecilius of Calacte, 154 n. 1.
Caepio, 14.
Caesar (Julius), 9, 10, 34, 37, 97 n. 3, 104, 109 n. 6.
Calpurnius Flaccus, 27 n. 1, 88, 89, 91 and n. 5, 94, 97, 101 n.8, 103, 111 121, 133.
Calvus, 1, 26, 29, 72, 135, 136-7, 138.
Capito, 72, 78.
Carbo, 17.
Carthage, 23, 27.
Carvilius, 122.
Cassius (lawyer), 45.
Cassius Longinus, 108.
Cassius Severus, 21, 35, 40, 43, 70, 73, 134, 136, 137, 138, 142, 145, 146.
Catius Crispus, 32 n. 2.
Cato the elder, 16, 17 n. 1, 23, 35, 62, 71, 97 n. 3, 108, 120.
Cato the younger, 8-9, 43 n. 5, 62, 75.
Catullus, 138.
Causa, (t.t.) 1, 2, 22, 29, 30.
Causa Curiana, 46, 47, 48.
Censors, 18, 105, 123, 124.
Centumviri, 38, 45, 94.
Cestius, 40, 41 n. 3, 50 n. 1, 51 n. 1 55, 59, 73, 74, 136, 141, 144, 152, 167.
Character-sketches, 160.
Cicero, declamation practised by 29, 30 31;
  subjects declaimed by, 10, 30-31;
  evidence of on terminology of decl., 1-2, 17, 21, 22, 28-30;
  exx. of *theses* in, 2-5;
  exx. of *suasoriae* in, 23, 27;
  exx. of *controversiae* in, 15, 27-8;
  views of on decl. 29, 30;
  on early Roman orators, 17;
  on arguments from equity, 46-7
  quotations from in decl., 136;
  status in speeches of, 13-14;
  criticism of by Calvus, 137

Cicero (*continued*)
  poems of, 136;
  colloquialisms in *Letters* of, and in decl., 64;
  legislation on exile of, 111;
  historians on death of, 158, 159 and n. 1;
  Cornelius Severus on death of, 145;
  decl. on death of, 23, 31, 34.
Cicero (Quintus), 29.
Cimon, 34.
Clitarchus, 156 n. 2.
Clodius, 14.
Clytaemnestra, 15, 24, 121.
Coetus concursus, 34 n. 8, 113.
Colloquialism, 64.
Color, 55-6, 73, 74, 79 n. 7, 147.
Color insaniae, 55, 102 n. 7.
Commentari 17, 28.
Concubinage, 127-8.
Confession in law, 103, 107, 112.
Conflict of statutes, 48, 82, 115, 122.
Constantine, 90, 114, 128.
Constitutio, 13, 19, 20, 22, 25, 27, 41, 110. See further s.v. *status*.
Controversia, evidence on use of term, 1-2, 22, 25-6, 29, 30, 41;
  early Greek background of, 12;
  relation of to *thesis*, 6-8, 9-10;
  exx. of in *Ad Herenn*, 23-6;
  exx. of in Cicero, 27-8;
  exx. of in Seneca, 32-4, 84-132;
  exx. of in Suetonius, 18-19;
  criticisms of, 71-83.
Coponius, 46.
Cornelius Hispanus, 32 n. 2, 50 n. 3.
Cornelius Severus, 145.
Cornificius, see s.v. Auct. ad Herenn.
Crassus, 16 n. 6, 17, 18, 21, 29, 33, 38, 46, 62.
Craton, 63.
Cremutius Cordus, 145, 158.
Croesus, 62.
Curatio, 73, 86, 93-4.
Curtius, 9 n. 2, 160.
Customs officials, 19.
Cyrus (rhetor), 127, 128.

D

DAMAGE (private property), 116-9;
  (public property) 98-9, 107.
Declamation, Greek background of, 1-16;
  philosophical theses in, 4-8;
  early history of at Rome, 16-20;
  evidence of Suetonius on, 18-20;
  evidence of *Ad Herennium* on, 22-6;
  evidence of Cic., *De Inv.* on, 27-8;
  Cicero's practice in, 10, 29, 30-1;
  elder Seneca's evidence on, 1-2;
  elder Seneca's views on, 71-2;
  contemporary criticisms of, 73-4;
  Petronius on, 75-6;
  Dialogus on, 76-7;
  Pliny on, 78;
  Martial on, 78-9;
  Juvenal on, 79-80;
  Quintilian on, see s.v. Quintilian;
  procedure of, 51-3;
  speech-divisions of, 53-4;
  diction of, 63;
  composition of, 65,75;
  descriptions in, 58-60;
  social life in, 34-7;
  Greek influence on, 37-8;
  laws in, 84-132;
  literary criticism in, 133-148;
  influence of on literature, 149ff.
Declamare, earliest use of, 28;
  developed meaning of, 29;
  distinguished from *dicere* by Calvus, 1, 29

Declamatio, earliest use of, 20-1;
  original meaning of, 22, 25-6;
  developed meaning of, 41.
Declamator, 29, 30.
Declamatorius, 20 n. 3, 29.
Declamito, 17, 20 n. 3, 30.
Deliberatio, 22, 151 n. 5.
Dellius, 134.
Demetrius, 17.
Demetrius of Phalerum, 12.
Demetrius, on style, 65 n. 2, 69 n. 2.
Demosthenes, 9, 21, 62, 95, 98 n. 1, 99 n. 2, 103 n. 1, 105 n. 1, 4; 118 n. 1, 121 n. 2, 129 n. 6, 135, 154.
Depulsio, 13, 14.
Descriptions, 38, 58-60, 156, 160, 163-4.
Dinarchus, 89, 118 n. 1.
Dio Cassius, 10 n. 1, 34 n. 4, 43 n. 5, 44 n. 5, 7, 8; 92 n. 9, 106 n. 2, 111 n. 3, 123 n. 5, 8; 125 n. 8.
Dio Chrysostom, 22, 101 n. 5.
Diodorus, 134 n. 4.
Diogenes Laertius, 5 n. 1, 8; 15 n. 2; 95 n. 4.
Dionysius of Halicarnassus, 54 n. 1, 55 n. 4. 57 n. 4, 68, 69, 93 n. 2, 95 n. 1, 102 n. 4, 104 n. 2, 122 n. 5, 125 n. 6, 7; 133 n. 2, 134, 135, 147, 154 n.1.
Disinheritance, 6, 32, 35, 63, 101-3.
Divisio, 32, 39, 56, 74, 97.
Division of Patrimony, 106, 128-31.
Divorce, 34, 41, 88, 94-5, 122-4.
Dolabella, 31 n. 1.
Dorion, 141.
Dowry, 88, 89, 90, 94, 95, 123-4.
Draconian code, 98.
Dreams, 56, 61.
Drusus, 35.

E

ELECTION-LAW, 105-6.
Encolpius, 75-6.
Ennius, 17 and n. 1, 66.
Ennodius, 95.
Ephorus, 34.
Epicureans, 5, 8.
Epiphonema, 65, 160 n. 1.
Equity, 46, 47, 57, 124, 126.
Ethopoeia, 150.
Euripides, 126 n. 2. 162.
Exile, 99, 110-111, 156.
Exposure of infants, 114-5, 125-7.

F

FABIANUS, 58-9, 63, 66, 74, 139, 146.
Fabius Maximus, 40.
False witness, 92, 107.
Festus, 96 n. 3, 99 n. 4.
Flamininus, 33, 108.
Flaminius, 27.
Florus, 160 and n. 1, 167 n. 2.
Fortunatianus, 27 n. 1, 88, 95.
Fortune, *locus* on, 61, 62, 63, 78, 159, 163.
Freedmen, 87, 107-8, 114.
Frontinus, 97 n. 3, 101 n. 1.

G

GABINIUS, 109.
Gaius (lawyer), 19 n. 3, 92 n. 5, 105 n. 2, 107 n. 1, 116, 117 n. 2, 123 n. 3, 124 n. 2, 128, 129.
Gallio, 32 n. 2, 40, 56, 74, 140, 150, 167.
Gargonius, 65, 134, 138.
Gavius Silo, 32 n. 2.
Gesta Romanorum, 38.
Gnipho, 28.

Gorgias, 55, 147 n. 2, 155.
Gracchus (C.), 17.
Grattius, 139.
Greek history, 9, 23, 33 n. 1.
Greek law, 84, 92, 93-7, 98, 99, 100, 102, 103, 106, 107, 111, 112, 115, 117, 118, 120, 125, 127, 129.
Greek novels, 38.
Greek tragedy, 23, 24, 28.
Greek vocabulary, 65.

H

HAMMURABI, code of, 96, 97 n. 2, 127.
Hannibal, 9, 22, 27, 79.
Haterius, 40, 57, 59, 63, 74, 139, 140, 146, 159.
Heraclides Ponticus, 97.
Hermagoras, 3, 12-14, 15, 17, 47.
Hermogenes, 3 and n. 2, 4; 4, 10 n. 3, 12, 15 and n. 3, 5; 24 n. 2, 27, 89, 97, 103, 142, 150, and n. 4, 6.
Herodotus, 134.
Heroes, 33, 62, 88-9, 119.
Hirtius, 31 and n. 1.
Historiae, 18.
Historical examples, 62.
Homer, 134, 141.
Homicide, 98-101, 104, 107, 120-1.
Homoeoteleuton, 68, 159.
Horace, 5 n. 8, 34, 35 and n. 2, 5; 36 and n. 1, 4; 42 and n. 1, 59 n. 1, 64, 93 n. 5, 120 n. 2, 133, 134, 138-9, 145, 148, 162, 163.
Horatius, 27.
Hortensius, 56 n. 3.
Hyperbole, 70, 142, 165.
Hyperides, 98 n. 3.

I

IDIOTISMUS, 64, 65.
Illegitimacy, 127.
Ill-treatment, 94-5, 107.
Imitation, 145.
Impersonation, 21, 52.
Implere, 61.
Improvisation, 18, 49.
Incest, 41, 77, 92-3, 107, 162.
Infamia, 105, 116, 124.
Infanticide, 114-5, 125-7.
Ingratitude, 7, 79, 86, 87-8, 122.
Inheritance, 24, 127-8.
Injury, 25, 115-6.
Insanity, 25, 93-4, 107.
Intentio, 13, 14.
Intimidation, 113-5.
Intoxication, 56, 59-60.
Invectives, 31 n. 3.
Iophon, 94.
Iphicrates, 34.
Isaeus, 95 n. 3.
Isaeus (rhetor), 78, 79.
Isidore, 53.
Isocrates, 54 n. 1, 69, 135.
Iudicatio, 14.
Iudicium de moribus, 124 and n. 4.

J

JEROME, 5 n. 9, 26 n. 2, 30 n. 1, 128.
Julius Bassus, 59.
Julius Montanus, 141.
Julius Rufinus, 154.
Julius Victor, 88, 92.
Junius Otho, 56.
Justinian, 55 n. 6, 87 n. 2, 4; 90 and n. 1, 2;

Justianin (*continued*)
95 n. 7, 101, 102 n. 7, 106 n. 8, 114 n. 2, 121, 125 n. 9, 126 and n. 6, 7; 128, 131.
Juvenal, 22, 39 n. 4, 52 n. 4, 53 n. 1, 55 n. 5, 61 n. 3, 78-80, 88 n. 1, 136 n. 3, 139 and n. 2, 167 n. 2.

L

LABEO, 45, 98 n. 5, 104, 117 n. 6.
Laberius, 69, 138.
Labienus, 39, 40, 43, 146.
Lactantius, 125 n. 9.
Latro, 31, 35, 36, 39, 40, 43, 50 n. 1, 3; 51, 57, 60, 64, 66, 72, 74, 97, 113, 115, 123, 141, 142, 143, 145, 146, 150, 153, 161, 163, 164, 167.
Law-schools, 45.
Legitimation, 127-8.
Leonidas, 134.
Lex Aelia Sentia, 87, 128;
Appuleia, 109;
Aquilia, 34, 98, 116-9;
Cincia, 44;
Cornelia de falsis, 92;
Cornelia de iniuriis, 96;
Cornelia de maiestate, 109;
Cornelia de sicariis et veneficis, 35, 99, 111-2;
Domitia, 24, n. 4;
Gabinia, 113;
Iulia de adulteriis, 35, 89-90, 120-2;
Iulia de ambitu, 106;
Iulia de maiestate, 109;
Iulia municipalis, 24 n. 3, 105;
Iulia peculatus, 106;
Iulia de vi, 90, 111, 113, 115;
Papia Poppaea, 123, 128;
Plaetoria, 131 n. 1;
Plotia de vi, 113, 115;
Rhodia de iactu, 24 n. 2;
Scantinia, 91;
Varia, 109.
Libanius, 4 n. 1, 10 n. 3, 12 n. 2, 15 n. 2, 60 n. 2.
Licinia, 33.
Literary Criticism, 133-148.
Livy, 33 n. 3, 40, 108 n. 1, 111 and n. 9, 113 and n. 5, 124 n. 4, 133, 135, 137, 156, 157-8, 160.
Loci communes, 60-61, 63, 139, 159, 160, 163, 'Longinus,' 42 n. 7, 43, 155.
Lucan, 8 n. 3, 10 n. 2, 36, 77, 141, 145, 165, 167 n. 2.
Lucian, 80, 102 n. 4, 103, 104 n. 6, 156 n. 5.
Lucilius, 139.
Lucretius, 5 n. 6, 7; 138.
Luxury, 36, 42, 58.
Lysias, 89, 96 n. 2, 4; 105 n. 1, 137.

M

MACROBIUS, 21 n. 2, 29 n. 2; 142 and n. 1.
Maecenas, 40, 44 n. 8, 134, 140, 141, 142.
Magic, 25, 80, 82, 112.
Maiestas, 25, 27, 97 n. 4, 98, 108-9, 112.
Manilius, 139.
Manu, code of, 123 n. 4.
Marcellus, 17.
Marcianus, 87 n. 2, 90 and n. 1, 2, 4; 91 and n. 4, 100, 110 n. 2, 3; 111 n. 11.
Marius, 62.
Marriage-laws, 120-4, 128.
Martial, 44 n. 4, 78-9.
Martianus Capella, 8.
Masurius Sabinus, 45.
Matricide, 15, 27, 121-2.
Maximus Lollius, 134.

Mela, 150.
Mela-(Pomponius), 167 n. 2.
Menander, 37.
Messala Corvinus, 40, 64, 133, 140, 141.
Messala (of *Dialogus*), 21, 42, 45 and n. 3, 77.
Metellus, 33 and n. 3.
Military law, 88, 97 n. 3, 103.
Mime, 37 n. 3, 138.
Minucius Felix, 125 n. 9.
Molon, 17, 28.
Moschus, 35, 146.
Musa, 139, 147.
Musonius, 6 n. 5.
Mutilation, 70, 96, 98, 106, 120.

N

NEGLIGENCE, 100.
Nero, 18, 77.
New Comedy, 34 n. 4, 37, 38, 89, 125, 137.
Nicetes, 140.
Nicolaus, 3 n. 2.
Nonius Asprenas, 35, 65, 151.
Norbanus, 14, 109.
Novatus, 150.
Noxal actions, 92.

O

OATHS, 7, 153-4, 164.
Obsecratio, 154.
Occultatio, 154.
Octavius Sagitta, 36, 77 n. 2.
Omens, 56.
Oracles, 75, 80.
Orestes, 15, 23, 24, 27, 121.
Orosius, 93 n. 2.
Ovid, 40, 55 n. 5, 64, 75, 83 n. 4, 133, 134, 143-4, 149-156.

P

PACTS, 114-5, 125.
Pacuvius, 21.
Pansa, 31.
Papinian, 48, 120 n. 7, 129.
Paradox, 55, 147.
Parallelism, 67-9, 159, 160, 166.
Parents, obedience to, 6;
    support of, 7, 83, 95-6;
    injury to, 96-7, 107.
Parody, 66 n. 4, 76.
Paronomasia, 69, 154, 160, 166.
Parrhasius, 34, 98.
Parricide, 25, 27, 37, 101 n. 1, 109.
Passienus, 73.
Pastor Aietius, 40 n. 2.
Pathos, 62-3.
Patrimony, 93, 106, 107, 128-131.
Paul (lawyer), 87 n. 2, 90 and n. 5, 92 n. 2, 93 n. 7, 94 n. 1, 100, 102 n. 7, 104 n. 4, 105 n. 2, 111 n. 2, 11; 113 n. 2, 3; 117 n. 2, 120 n. 3, 4, 7; 125, n. 9.
Peristasis, 75.
Persius, 8 n. 4, 40, 75, 79 n. 1, 82.
Pestilence, 75, 77, 80, 82.
Petronius, 42 n. 7, 56 n. 2, 75-6, 80.
Phidias, 34.
Philip of Macedon, 12.
Philip V of Macedon, 27, 157.
Philodemus, 73 n. 1.
Philosophy, 4-8, 30-31, 61.
Philostratus, 12, 22 n. 1, 38 n. 1, 80, 124 n. 3.
Piracy, 7, 25, 32, 34 and n. 4, 38 and n. 3, 75.
Plagiarism, 144-5.
Plato, 134, *Laws* of, 89, 95, 99, 100 and n. 4, 101 n. 5, 104 n. 2, 122.

Plautus, 19 n. 1, 64, 89 n. 3, 123 n. 1, 137.
Pliny the elder, 77.
Pliny the younger, 44 n. 4, 45, 48, 51 n. 2, 7, 9; 78, 96, 125 n. 8, 126 n. 1, 137, 156 n. 5, 157 n. 4, 167.
Plotius Gallus, 17-18.
Plutarch, 95 n. 3, 108 n. 1, 121 n. 2, 122 n. 5, 130 and n. 3, 134 n. 4.
Poisoning, 35-6, 38, 41, 61, 79, 109, 111-2, 115.
Politics, 39 n. 2, 42-5.
Pollio, 39, 40, 43, 72-3, 133, 134, 136, 145, 146, 156.
Polybius, 156 n. 2, 157 n. 2.
Pompeius Silo, 51 n. 9.
Pompey, 9, 10 n. 2, 18, 34, 62.
Pomponius, 138 n. 1.
Pontius Aufidianus, 37.
Popillius, 27, 33 and n. 3, 50 n. 1.
Popillius Laenas, 108.
Po phyrio, 35 n. 2.
Postumia 33 n. 3.
Praelocutio, 51.
Praetorian legislation, 19, 114, 116 and n. 1, 2; 117, 118, 119, 125.
Prepositions, 67.
Priests and priestesses, 32-3, 103-4, 107.
Proditio, 109.
Prometheus, 34, 98.
Pronuntiatio, 20-1.
Propertius, 36 n. 1.
Prophecy, *locus* on, 61.
Prosopopoeia, 53, 150, 164.
Protagoras, 4.
Proverbs, 55.
Providence, 3, 5, 8; *locus* on, 61.
Publilius Syrus, 55, 138, 165.

Q

Quaestio de maiestate, 109.
Quaestio de veneficiis, 111.
Quaestio (rhet.), 5, 35, 57, 151 (in *status*) 13, 14.
Querela inofficiosi testamenti, 55, 102.
Quintilian, *theses* mentioned by, 3-4;
    on *thesis* and *suasoria*, 8;
    on hist. of decl., 12;
    on *status*, 13, 15, 16;
    on delivery, 20, 21;
    on themes of decl., 25, 80;
    on merits and demerits of decl., 81-2;
    on legal parallels, 48, 52, 81, 93, 94, 102, 131;
    declamatory laws in, 87, 88, 91, 92, 94, 95, 97, 98, 105, 120 and n. 5, 6; 125;
    on *sententiae*, 54;
    on descriptions, 59-60;
    on *loci*, 61;
    on figures, 69, 70, 142, 154;
    on Calvus, 136, 137;
    on Seneca, 62, 74.
    Decl. min. ascribed to, 19, 27 n. 1, 39, 45, 52, 54, 56, 57 and n. 1, 75 and n. 7, 77, 81 and n. 1, 85, 86, 87, 88 and n. 5, 89, 91 and n. 5, 93, 94 and n. 1, 6; 96, 97, 98, 101 n. 8, 103, 104, 111, 112, 113, 116, 119, 122, 125, 133, 157 n. 4.
    Decl. maior. ascribed to, 25 n. 2, 45, 54, 85, 88, 94, 95, 97, 101 n. 8, 116, 117 n. 3, 157 n. 4.
Quintilianus senex, 32 n. 2.
Quintilius Varus, 40 n. 2.

R

RAPE, 25, 33, 36, 37, 41, 77, 89-91, 107.
Ratio (in *status*), 13, 14.
Rationis infirmatio, 13, 14.

Recitations, 39, 134.
Republicanism, 43.
Rewards, 88.
Rhetorica ad Alexandrum, 11 and n. 3, 4; 15, 47.
Rhetorical figures, 66-70, 153-5, 164, 166.
Rhetorical questions, 70, 166.
Rhodes, 17, 24, 28, 112 n. 4.
Roman history, 9, 28, 33 n. 1, 108-9, 156-60.
Roscius, 21 n. 2.

S

Sachsenspiegel, 129.
Sacrilege, 106, 107.
Sallust, 31, 103 and n. 6, 135, 137, 139 n. 2, 156.
Scaevola, 46, 126 n. 5.
Scaurus, 39, 144, 146.
Schema, 65, 66, 67.
Scholae, 30.
Scholastica, 1, 2, 30, 43, 65.
Scholasticus, 43, 72, 78, 142.
Scipio Africanus minor, 23.
Scipionic circle, 16.
Second Sophistic, 38.
Sedition, 113.
Seneca the elder, arrival in Rome of, 31;
 order of composition of works of, 2 and n. 1;
 form of works of, 53, 60;
 memory of, 71, 83, 135;
 evidence of on history of decl., 1-2, 10, 26, 30;
 views of on declamation, 71-2;
 on decline of oratory, 42, 71;
 origins of subjects of, 33-4;
 stock characterisation of subjects of, 37-8;
 subjects of, compared with later collections, 75, 77, 82;
 declamatory laws in, 27, 84-132;
 theses in, 6-8, 10;
 literary passages preserved by, 145;
 value of as a literary critic, 133, 135, 145-8;
 on Calvus, 1, 135, 136, 138.
 on Cicero, 31, 136, 145;
 on Publilius Syrus, 55, 138;
 on Virgil, 140, 141;
 on Ovid, 140, 141, 143-4;
 on *loci*, 61;
 on diction, 63, 64, 72 n. 3;
 on composition, 65, 72 n. 3;
 on figures, 68, 69, 70, 158;
 on style, 137, 147;
 on plagiarism, 145;
 Greek terms in, 65;
 on the declaimers, see s.v. individual names.
Seneca the younger, on style of decl., 42 n. 7, 74-5, 156;
 on 'sing-song,' 22 n. 1;
 decl. influence on prose-style of, 67 n. 2, 157 n. 4, 160;
 decl. influence on *Tragedies* of, 70, 141 n. 4, 160-7;
 theses in, 5 n. 8. 8 n. 5;
 suasoria in, 9;
 loci in, 139 and n. 2;
 on voice-training, 21 n. 3;
 on Haterius, 146 n. 3;
 on Publilius Syrus, 55 n. 1;
 on Leonidas, 134 n. 4;
 on *actio ingrati*, 87;
 on exposure, 125 n. 7;
 Quintilian on, 65, 74.
Seneca Grandio, 32 n. 2, 64, 70.
Sententiae, 42, 54-5, 74-5, 142, 143, 144, 145, 151-3, 157, 158, 159, 160, 161, 164, 165-6.
Servius, 99 n. 4, 143.

Servius Tullius, 62, 139.
Sextus Pompeius, 34.
Shakespeare, 11 n. 1, 69.
Sidonius, 91 n. 5.
Sing-song, 22, 59.
Solon, 89, 95, 96.
Sopater, 103.
Sophocles, 94, 162.
Spain, 31, 32, 165.
Stage, 21.
State offences, 97-8, 108-110.
Statorius Victor, 32 n. 2.
Status-doctrine, 13, 16, 47, 115;
 coniecturalis, 13, 14, 25, 27, 110;
 definitivus (ex definitione), 13, 14, 24;
 generalis (iuridicialis), 13, 14, 25;
 translativus (ex translatione), 13, 24;
 ex scripto et sententia, 14, 24;
 ex ambiguo (ambiguitas), 14, 24, 27, 48;
 ex contrariis legibus, 15, 24, 48, 115;
 collectio, 15, 48;
 ex ratiocinatione, 24;
 legitima, 25.
Stepmothers, 25, 37, 80, 112 115.
Sterility, 122-4.
Stesimbrotus, 34.
Stobaeus, 5 n. 8, 134 n. 4.
Stock characters, 12, 37-8, 62, 162.
Stoics, 2, 5, 7, 8.
Storm and shipwreck, 59, 163.
Stratonice, 37 n. 1.
Suasio, 22.
Suasoria, earliest use of, 22;
 relation of to *thesis*, 8-9;
 early Greek background of, 11-12;
 early Roman exx. of, 22-3, 27;
 distinguished from *prosopopoeia*, 53, 150;
 descriptions in, 60;
 predilection of Ovid for, 143, 151;
 influence of upon Ovid, 150-1;
 influence of upon Seneca, 9, 164.
Suetonius, 10 and n. 3, 6, 11, 16 n. 3, 17 n. 3, 18-20, 25, 29 n. 1, 30 and n. 2, 31 n. 1, 35 n. 1, 37, 41, 44 n. 3, 45 n. 10, 69 n. 6, 77 n. 1, 80 n. 3, 93 n. 2, 97 n. 3, 102 n. 5, 106 n. 2, 113 n. 5, 123 n. 7, 8; 125 n. 8, 126 n. 4, 147 n. 1.
Suicide, 35, 87, 101.
Sulla, 62.
Sulpicius Rufus, 47.
Sulpicius Victor, 23 n. 2, 103, 104, 125, 127, 128.
Swoons, 60.
Syrianus, 27 n. 1, 103, 104.

T

TACITUS, 18 n. 1, 21, 22 n. 1, 26 n. 1, 35, 36, 42, 43 and n. 2, 44 n. 4, 45 and n. 1, 3, 5, 9; 76-7, 92 n. 9, 10; 102 n. 5, 110 n. 7, 142 n. 1, 146 n. 2, 3; 160, 167 n. 2.
Talio, 92, 96-7, 106.
Tarpeian Rock, 33, 92.
Terence, 38, 64, 89 n. 3, 137.
Tetracolon, 65, 139, 161.
Teucer, 23.
Theft, 105, 107.
Thema, 51, 65.
Theodosius, code of, 87 n. 4, 90 n. 7, 9; 112 n. 5, 114 n. 2, 125 n. 9, 126 n. 4, 6; 128.
Theon, 2 and n. 2, 3; 4, 10 n. 3, 5; 11 n. 1, 53 n. 2, 59 n. 1, 135.
Theophrastus, 5, 12.
Theopompus, 156 n. 2.
Thesis, 1-11, 30, 139, 151, 163.
Thucydides, 20 n. 1, 135, 137.

Tiberius, 35, 43 and n. 5, 44, 140.
Timaeus, 156 n. 2.
Torture, 59, 88, 98, 112, 122.
Tractatio, 57.
Treason, 25, 108-110.
Trebatius, 47.
Triarius, 145.
Tricolum, 65, 68, 159.
Tubero, 40.
Turrinus Clodius, 33 n. 2.
Twelve Tables, 25 and n. 1, 92, 99, 100 n. 3, 110 n. 3, 113, 115, 118, 119, 125 n. 7, 130-1.
Tyrannicide, 27-8, 33, 34, 76, 77, 104, 107, 122.
Tyrants, 10, 25, 27, 34, 75, 79, 116, 162.

U

ULPIAN, 87 n. 2, 3, 90 n. 3, 93 n. 5, 94 n. 1, 106 n. 6, 107 n. 1, 113 n. 8, 114 and n. 4, 5; 115, 116 n. 1, 117 n. 3, 5; 118 n. 6, 119 n. 2, 3; 124 n. 2, 125.
Ulysses, 15, 23, 25, 27, 151, 162.
Unwritten law, 86.

V

VACCA, 36, 77 n. 2.
Vagellius, 79.
Valerius Antias, 33 n. 3, 108 n. 1.
Valerius Licinianus, 78.

V

Valerius Maximus, 37, 52 n. 4, 87, 97 n. 3, 101 n. 2, 5; 102 n. 5, 108, n. 1, 109 n. 2, 122 and n. 5, 134 n. 4, 139 n. 2, 160 and n. 1, 167 n. 2.
Vallius Syriacus, 151.
Varro of Atax, 74, 141.
Vatinius, 138.
Velleius Paterculus, 42 and n. 5, 135, 136, 139 n. 2, 150, 158-160.
Veneficium, see s.v. Poisoning.
Vestals, 33 and n. 3, 93, 104, 107.
Vibius Gallus, 59.
Vinicius, 74, 144.
Violation of sepulchre, 119.
Violence, 114, 115.
Virgil, 60, 133, 140-1, 144, 154, 163.
Virginia, 62, 91.
Vitruvius, 95 n. 3, 167 n. 2.
Voice-training, 20-21.
Voluntas, 47-8, 81.
Votienus Montanus, 41, 72, 73-4, 83, 108, 144.

X

XENOPHON, 87, 98 n. 1.

Y

ZEUGMA, 63, 154.

DATE DUE			
JE 4 '64			
JE 3 '66			
JA 3 '68			
MR 1 '69			
GAYLORD			PRINTED IN U.S.A.

875.09
B64